Organisational Performance Management in Sport

Effective performance management systems are essential in any successful organisation. In both commercial sport business and not-for-profit sport organisations, the pressure to follow international best practice in performance management has grown significantly in recent years. *Organisational Performance Management in Sport* is the first book to show how performance management concepts, tools and principles can be applied in the modern sport environment.

Linking theory and practice throughout, the book defines fundamental performance parameters impacting on sport organisations, and introduces key issues such as individual performance management through to board-level governance structures, presenting extended real-world case studies and practitioner perspectives. As such, it offers the most clear and complete outline of performance management in sport organisations available.

With case studies, insight boxes and industry examples integrated throughout the text, *Organisational Performance Management in Sport* offers accessible and vital reading for all sport management students, researchers and professionals with an interest in this important area of sport management research and practice.

Ian O'Boyle is a lecturer in sport and recreation management in the UniSA Business School, Australia. He is also a member of the Centre for Tourism and Leisure Management (CTLM) based within UniSA's School of Management. Dr O'Boyle is a leading researcher in the area of organisational performance management, sport governance, leadership and other associated disciplines within the field of sport management. He has previously been affiliated with Ulster University in the UK and Massey University in New Zealand. Through his strong links with industry he has most recently been involved in a number of research projects analysing issues such as performance management and governance at the National Sport Organisation level and has been successful in obtaining numerous research grants to carry out this work. His work appears in leading sport management journals including *Journal of Sport Management*, *European Sport Management Quarterly*, *International Journal of Sport Management* and *Sport Management Review*, and also within traditional management-based journals such as *Journal of Career Development* and *Organization Development Journal*.

Routledge Research in Sport Business and Management

Organisational Performance Management in Sport

Ian O'Boyle

Routledge
Taylor & Francis Group

LONDON AND NEW YORK

First published 2016
by Routledge

2 Park Square, Milton Park, Abingdon, Oxon OX14 4RN
711 Third Avenue, New York, NY 10017, USA

Routledge is an imprint of the Taylor & Francis Group, an informa business

First issued in paperback 2017

British Library Cataloguing-in-Publication Data
A catalogue record for this book is available from the British Library

Library of Congress Cataloging in Publication Data
Names: O'Boyle, Ian, author.
Title: Organisational performance management in sport / Ian O'Boyle.
Description: New York : Routledge, 2016. | Series: Routledge Research in
Sport Business and Management ; 4 | Includes bibliographical references
and index.
Identifiers: LCCN 2015024462| ISBN 9781138941328 (Hardback) |
ISBN 9781315673783 (eBook)
Subjects: LCSH: Sports administration. | Sports–Societies, etc. |
Performance–Management.
Classification: LCC GV713 .O36 2016 | DDC 796.06/9–dc23
LC record available at http://lccn.loc.gov/2015024462

ISBN: 978-1-138-94132-8 (hbk)
ISBN: 978-1-138-08796-5 (pbk)

Typeset in Times New Roman
by Wearset Ltd, Boldon, Tyne and Wear

Contents

Figures

Tables

Preface

The economic and social benefits synonymous with the sport industry have been well documented (Dalziel, 2011; Shilbury, Deane & Kellet, 2006). However, it has become apparent that many of the organisations responsible for the delivery and development of sport within many countries have grossly underperformed and continue to do so. This book identifies and focuses upon fundamental performance dimensions that impact upon Non-Profit Sport Organisations (NPSOs), and explores ways in which these entities can manage and overcome specific performance challenges to facilitate their success as key social institutions within society. The emphasis on NPSOs is justified in the first instance as it is they that represent the primary means of offering sporting opportunities and competition for citizens of a state.

Thus state sport agencies and National Governing Bodies (NGBs) represent the principle foci of this book, while a comparative analysis is utilised to analyse performance within selected organisations. The organisations that are afforded most attention emerge from Ireland and New Zealand; however, secondary case study organisations from other selected countries are also examined and key lessons from their governance and function drawn upon.

Following a thorough review of performance management in the traditional business and sport management environments, the general tools, systems and processes that are available for use when managing organisational and individual performances within NPSOs are identified. This is followed by a more detailed examination of the literature around issues of governance, finance and industry participation. The case study organisations, referred to above, are then analysed to assess their use of traditional performance management practices and the management of selected performance dimensions, and to identify any root causes explaining possible underperformance of entities within this unique sector.

This text discusses how it is apparent that NPSOs have not yet fully engaged with performance management practices and in some cases there is a complete absence of any form of systematic and/or identified organisational performance appraisal in place. Furthermore, the manner in which individual performance (including the performance of volunteers), finance and participation (i.e. by the end users) are managed appears to remain largely inadequate in relation to those organisations performing at the highest possible level. Outdated and flawed governance structures are identified as the primary explanation for the often spectacular underperformance of some organisations with little prospect of immediate recovery for most. This has created a percolating effect within all levels of these organisations, with performance failures being identified along several key organisational and performance dimensions. Consequently, the final section of this text largely focuses on the evaluation and restructuring of current governance practices to combat performance issues within NPSO bodies, specifically within the countries highlighted within this book.

Abbreviations

AFL	Australian Football League
BI	Basketball Ireland
CEO	Chief Executive Officer
DIF	The National Olympic Committee and Sports Confederation of Denmark
ESRI	Economic and Social Research Institute
FAI	Football Association of Ireland
GAA	Gaelic Athletic Association
GDP	Gross Domestic Product
ICC	International Cricket Council
IIS	Irish Institute of Sport
ISC	Irish Sports Council
KPI	Key Performance Indicator
LSP	Local Sport Partnership
MIS	Management Information System
NGB	National Governing Body
NPSO	Non-Profit Sport Organisations
NRL	National Rugby League
NZC	New Zealand Cricket
NZRU	New Zealand Rugby Union
OD	Organisational Development
ODT	Organisational Development Tool
OPMS	Organisational Performance Management System
PDRS	Performance Development Review System
RST	Regional Sport Trust
RTE	Radió Telefís Éireann
SANGBS	Self-Assessment for Non-Profit Boards Scale
SMART	Specific, measurable, achievable, relevant, timely
Sport NZ	Sport New Zealand
TQM	Total Quality Management
UKA	UK Athletics
WADA	World Anti-Doping Agency

1 Introduction

Managing organisational performance is a fundamental requirement for any successful Non-Profit Sport Organisation (NPSO). It is an integral component of an NPSO's ability to deliver a quality service to stakeholders existing within all areas of its sporting reach, including those at club, regional, national and international levels. However, it has become clear over time that many of these organisations have failed to manage their performance in anything resembling a robust fashion, with many operating simply on an ad-hoc basis, and instead serious flaws now exist within such organisations giving rise to the endemic underperformance of many of these entities. In the past, the mismanagement and underperformance of certain National Governing Bodies (NGBs) led to calls for an evaluation of these organisation's policies and practices in relation to their overall performance, yet it would appear little progress has been made in this regard with continuous reporting of widespread management failures within the NPSO sector.

Given such systemic management failures and the continued underperformance of some NPSOs, it quickly becomes clear that many of these entities have failed to properly engage with traditional performance management practices that have proven to be successful within the wider corporate world. Furthermore, it can be assumed that one of the root causes of this mismanagement lies within the governance structures of these organisations, which has proven to be a fundamental aspect in establishing the overall performance of an NPSO (Hoye & Doherty, 2011). Recent work that has also focused specifically upon corporate governance within NPSOs has arrived at similar conclusions, with several authors – notably Hoye and Cuskelly (2007), Yeh and Taylor (2008), and Hoye and Doherty (2011) – in agreement that governance remains a fundamental performance dimension within any NPSO.

Notwithstanding the importance of ameliorating poor governance structures, the extent of underperformance and mismanagement of NPSOs has only typically become apparent upon their complete financial collapse. It would appear that the inability of these organisations to ensure their financial propriety and sustainability has its genesis amid their ineffective governance and an absence of traditional performance management practices, creating a culture of underperformance within these and other NPSOs. Moreover, this trickle-down effect contaminates and ultimately impacts upon actual levels of participation in the sport in question. As growing and sustaining participation levels is the key raison d'être for almost all NPSOs, when there is an absence of appropriate performance management, governance, and financial systems and processes, these entities rarely perform well when compared to any reasonable performance criteria.

The underperformance and mismanagement of sport have ultimately raised questions about those who have been charged with leading sport within different national settings. The need to question the individual capacity and skillset of such key players is justified given the sizeable amount of public funding channelled into mass participation sport and the predominantly volunteer-led approach to which many NPSOs still owe their existence. Furthermore, previous involvement at a high level in a specific sport can no longer exist as justification for assuming a position of leadership within an NPSO as these organisations now require specific expertise and knowledge to compete and thrive within in an ever-more modern, commercially driven and professional environment (Kikulis, Slack & Hinings, 1995; Cuskelly, Taylor, Hoye & Darcy, 2006). The question remains, however, as to how exactly NPSOs can manage their performance more effectively, and how do these fundamental dimensions determine success or failure of overall performance within such entities.

Crucial to addressing this central theme is the requirement to establish a clear and common acceptance of what performance management in general is, and specifically performance management within certain NPSOs. There is no single definition for 'performance management' within the literature, with the term encompassing various elements of organisational, departmental and individual management of performance. It can also be used to describe practices and process that exist within organisations, such as the use of specific tools to measure and manage on-going organisational performance. This book adopts a broad view of the term 'performance management' through acknowledging its role in managing organisational and individual performance, but also examines the issue within the specific context of sport management and the unique performance dimensions that affect these organisations. Therefore, performance management within NPSOs will be explored at the organisational and individual levels, but also within fundamental performance dimensions affecting these entities such as governance, finance and participation.

The significance and impact of sport

Sport has been shown to have major social and economic benefits to society as confirmed in the publication of various reports at both national and transnational levels (Irish Sports Council, 2010; Dalziel, 2011). Sport is not only important in terms of establishing international reputation and respect through national sporting prowess, but also has significant benefits for domestic economies and, in addition, often carries considerable political influence. The important impact that sport has upon individual countries, in terms of economic and other associated benefits, has been a constant theme of work undertaken by academics over recent years (Auld, 1997; Dalziel, 2011; Shilbury *et al.*, 2006).

Taking Ireland as a brief example, the most recent figures from the Irish Sports Council in relation to sport-induced economic activity suggest that:

- The sport industry accounts for 1.4 per cent of Gross Domestic Product (GDP).
- Central government investment in Irish sport exceeds €618.3 million annually.
- The Irish sport sector employees 38,000 individuals, which accounts for 2 per cent of the overall workforce.

The results of creating and adopting suitable performance management practices and systems within NPSOs could have potentially significant positive impacts on the enhancement and protection of sport, most notably through the efficient provision of opportunities and development within sport. Moreover, these organisational practices could lead to greater performance of athletes and teams on the national and international stage, and facilitate increased general participation in line with the individual targets established by NPSOs. These issues are integral precursors to the economic activity that sport contributes to a nation, and in turn to the prospering of communities and society in general.

The core issues

By examining core issues that enable NPSOs to manage their performance effectively, this book offers an empirical basis for NPSOs to ensure better management of their organisations in the future. It will also make a novel contribution to the mainstream literature in the areas of both sport management and performance management as an important addition to this field of emerging research.

The primary foci of this book are therefore to explore performance management within NPSOs, including an examination of fundamental performance dimensions affecting these entities. The overarching theme therefore surrounds how NPSOs manage key performance dimensions within their organisations, which in turn gives way to a number of more discrete foci including:

- What traditional business performance management tools are being used by NPSOs?
- How do NPSOs manage individuals' performances within their organisations?
- Are the governance structures within NPSOs appropriate (i.e. 'fit for purpose') to facilitate consistently high levels of performance?
- How do NPSOs generate income and manage the crucial revenue aspect of their organisations?
- How do NPSOs measure their success in facilitating increases in participation (including volunteers) in the sport(s) they promote?

Book structure

This introduction precedes a thorough review of the literature that creates the theoretical grounding for the following chapters. Chapter 2 examines the literature relating to performance management within the traditional business environment to uncover common practice in the field, while theories related to performance management are also explored within this section. Chapter 3 analyses studies relating to performance management, specifically in sport, which have been previously undertaken. This chapter also analyses the impact that government policy has on organisational performance in NPSOs. Chapter 4 explores the literature relating to the role of the individual in determining overall organisational success and how organisations manage this aspect of their performance. Chapter 5 focuses on the unique performance dimensions affecting NPSOs, while the literature that is relevant to each of these dimensions is examined in depth to uncover what is considered to be a best-practice approach to managing each dimension. A large portion of this chapter focuses on the sport governance literature, given its crucial relationship with organisational performance as argued above. Chapters 6 to 9 form the empirical research element of the book, with Chapter 6 largely focusing on offering background information and context for the primary case study organisations. Chapters 7 to 9 focus on a discussion of interview results undertaken with various participants from the case study organisations, coinciding with a discussion relevant to the various themes that emerge from these empirical results. These chapters are designed to provide a more holistic account of performance management in the non-profit sport sector. Finally, Chapter 10 provides the theoretical outcomes of the book, implications for practice and areas that future research should, in the opinion of the author, seek to address.

Parameters

The author acknowledges that sport organisations consist of public sector and private sector entities. However, this particular book focuses on those sport organisations that operate within the not-for-profit environment. More specifically, the research centres on NPSOs which are either the major state agency for sport in a given nation or a NGB for a particular (typically dominant) sport within a pre-selected country. Of the nine organisations that are analysed within this book, three are state sport agencies and the remaining are NGBs representing a variety of sports. Therefore, any conclusions offered within this study can only be generalised to those NPSOs that share similar characteristics to the chosen primary and secondary case study organisations within this research.

Conceptually, the book relates to the performance of state sport agencies and NGBs, essentially addressing how NPSOs manage on-going fundamental performance issues within their organisations. In addition, this book refers to the work of senior management and often that of the Chief Executive Officer (CEO) within these organisations, especially their ability to facilitate the adoption of performance management practices within the selected NPSOs. The significant impact that regional bodies affiliated to these NPSOs can have on overall organisational performance is also acknowledged within the content of this book.

In summary, the parameters of this book are:

1   State sport agencies and NGBs from Ireland and New Zealand are the primary case study organisations used within the book.
2   A state sport agency from Denmark and NGBs from Australia and the UK are the secondary case study organisations used within the book.

Chapter summary

This introduction discussed the basis for the book in relation to both practice and theory. The impact and significance of sport in general was discussed in relation to its economic and social value, before explicitly relating both theory and practice within sport management to the focus of the book: performance management within NPSOs. Further specifying the topic, the major research questions were identified, addressing the fundamental performance dimensions to be examined within the selected NPSOs. Through the use of case study methodology, this book investigates performance management within the selected organisations. As a consequence, this book may be used to provide a platform for improvement within sport management practice in general.

2 What is performance management?

Introduction

Several areas of research are relevant to a book that examines performance management within NPSOs. The first component that it is necessary to examine is extant literature and current practice in relation to performance management concepts, systems, processes and theories within various organisations – not just NPSOs. This chapter introduces the concept of a performance management culture and the value it may create for organisational results. The various theories that are grounded within this concept are also examined and the evolution of the tools used by contemporary organisations to manage performance are explored, including a short case study to illustrate one of these tools within a practical (non-sport) setting.

The performance management culture

In management literature, the term 'performance management' was first introduced by Dr Aubrey C. Daniels in the late 1970s to describe a method of managing organisational behaviour and ensuring results, considered to be the two most important components of what is referred to as organisational 'performance' (Daniels, 2004). The term covers a range of otherwise diverse, if ultimately inter-related, factors, including the performance of employees, project performance and overall organisational performance (Bourne, Franco & Wilkes, 2003). For instance, organisational performance management constitutes a particular management system which assists management in making the most efficient use of the resources available to them, such as human, financial and material resources. This can be contrasted with operational performance management, which focuses on applying standardised methods of improving business performance or results across all aspects of an organisation. Whereas individual performance management is concerned with assessing and improving the contribution of individual employees to achieve organisational goals in a more efficient manner, operational performance management utilises a more holistic approach.

We live in a world of continual change and rising expectations (McCracken, 2012). For organisations, these expectations derive from many different perspectives including customers, suppliers, organisational membership and the local community. The implementation of an Organisational Performance Management System (OPMS) and the establishment of an overall performance management culture are essential in meeting stakeholder expectations (Lopez, Peon & Ordas, 2004). A culture of organisational performance management is the on-going process of quantifying and monitoring organisational performance and aligning this performance to the needs of the many stakeholders of the organisation. A culture of performance management must be based on simple concepts for the creation of a holistic and quantifiable view of organisational performance. A culture such as this can be applied to whole organisations and is inclusive of for-profit and non-profit organisations, but, as culture relates to all aspects of an organisation, performance management cannot simply be applied to standalone aspects of an organisation (Deming, 1986).

Culture can be described as the sum total of an organisation's methods of operating and working together (Fuller & Vassie, 2002). Culture can exert influence on an organisation in many ways through the manner in which people interact with each other and their willingness to adopt new ideas and initiatives. Therefore, culture also has a powerful influence on the effectiveness of any performance management system operating within an organisation. Some of the direct financial benefits of establishing a performance management culture can include an increase in sales, a reduction in overall operation costs and a potential decrease in any project overruns that may have otherwise occurred (Bititci, Mendibil, Nudurupati, Turner & Garengo, 2004). Other major benefits for organisations that employ performance management practices include an improvement in managerial control, the alignment of all aspects of the organisation with the goals set out by the CEO, and a decrease in the length of time it can take to implement new strategic or operational changes through improved communications networks now operating within the organisation.

Performance management is often an end result of an efficient and effective management approach. This management technique plays an integral role in establishing suitable conditions for the success of the organisation and every department within it (Bititci *et al.*, 2004). It requires that performance management is implemented within all aspects of the organisation to allow employees to conduct their work successfully and to establish a motivational workforce wholly committed to the success of the organisation, and across all types of drivers of business success (Lopez *et al.*, 2004). Aspects of the organisation include mergers and acquisitions, managing culture changes within an organisation, implementing new strategic plans, developing safe and effective working conditions and ensuring all corporate objectives are being met. Performance management can inform senior management of performance issues as it drives a process or organisation towards its stated objectives, and encourages the implementation of positive daily behaviour patterns across all departments and employees within an organisation (Fuller & Vassie, 2002).

For an effective performance management culture to be established within an organisation, all stakeholders must feel a sense of ownership and responsibility concerning any new practices to be introduced. They must trust in these systems and have a clear idea of what needs to be achieved and why this is the approach to be adopted. Innovation is crucial to the overall success of this process, and employees must be empowered to contribute to the improvement of the organisation. Clear direction must be conveyed through senior management, but opportunities should also be in place for employees to contribute to this 'direction of travel' and also within the review process.

It may often become apparent that the culture within an organisation is not suitable for the implementation of new performance management initiatives. Cultures such as these find it difficult to create conditions that can improve performance. Issues that contribute to this scenario typically constitute a resistance to change, a lack of creative and innovative thinking within the organisation, and a high staff turnover as a result of low employee morale and motivation (Essers, Bohm & Contu, 2009). In a culture where performance management processes are easily adopted, employees feel comfortable discussing overall performance with co-workers and management; individuals understand how their own contribution directly affects the organisational objectives, and they work together successfully in teams to solve any problems that may arise. To be successful at continually improving performance, all members of an organisation must be engaged in performance management (McAfee & Champagne, 1993). Performance management can even extend beyond the boundaries of the organisation to include suppliers, consumers and the community. To ensure that performance reflects all stakeholders' perspectives and interests, regular interactions with stakeholders concerning management and the organisation's performance are essential (Simmons, 2008).

Performance management systems can be in place permanently or for a specific period of time, from months to years, depending upon the individual needs of the organisation. During the course of this implementation, it is important for management to review progress and establish continual goals that show visible progress and performance improvement (McAfee & Champagne, 1993). If this does not occur, employees can often lose sight of the true objectives of the organisation as established in the strategic plan, and view these performance management processes as a largely pointless exercise and one of collecting meaningless data. To ensure competitiveness and relevancy, measures of performance must be constantly reviewed and assessed as the operating and economic environments evolve and redefine themselves (Lam, 1997; Rummler & Brache, 1995).

Performance measurement

An integral component of performance management is an organisation deciding what to measure and how to measure it. Regardless of what process concerning performance management is being driven, appropriate and clearly established measures need to be in place to effectively define the desired outcome and preferred goals of an organisation (Town, 2000). Performance management systems often fall short in achieving the stated goals of the organisation due to goal measurement being too vague or wrongly implemented. From a traditional business perspective, the most common approach is the creation of 'SMART' goals – those which are specific, measurable, achievable, relevant and timely.

Neely, Adams and Kennerley (2002) suggest that measuring performance is a process to establish the boundaries where systems and practices, acquisitions and investments are achieving the results required by management. Measurements will largely depend on the industry within which the organisation operates: educational institutions assess students to determine academic ability; in a sporting context, an athlete's time is gauged in order to assess their athletic ability; and in sport organisations, domestic and international results play a large role in how they are deemed to be performing their duties. Similarly, in teams and other organisations, many different processes and measurements exist to help with the evaluation of organisational performance (Gamble, Strickland & Thompson, 2007).

The task of measuring performance for organisations within various countries and establishments, identifying top performers, and examining their drivers of success was not conducted until Peters and Waterman began researching and writing their ground breaking performance measurement book, *In search of excellence* (1982). This research was the first to ask questions of organisational management actions and attitudes, and inspired further research to investigate issues surrounding high performance, an integral component of management within all organisations (Peters & Waterman, 1982). Measuring performance becomes increasingly difficult as organisations continued to evolve and diversify into various industries and subsidiaries. This issue must be considered in any comparative analysis of organisations within the for-profit and non-profit environments, such as NPSOs.

The original control-based performance measurement systems present within the industrial setting, such as Total Quality Management (TQM), experience difficulty in adapting to the ways in which businesses' and organisations' activities are conducted in the present, technology-led era. Organisations are now being reshaped into flatter, more multifunctional hierarchies. Town (2000) suggests that globalisation, and the increasing complexity of an organisation's business models, role of teams and responsibilities, will mean that performance measurement will become more difficult to undertake. The diverse nature of many organisations is now posing a huge problem for the ways in which performance measurement practices can be facilitated. Not only have traditional organisations become more diverse but new industries have also developed, creating many different types of organisation. Government, educational, manufacturing, financial services, retail and sport organisations all are required to adopt systems of performance measurement that have the ability to cater for their own individual needs. It is becoming a struggle for all large organisations to maintain a performance measurement system that can be applicable to all aspects and sectors of its operations, while simultaneously ensuring alignment of the organisation's mission and goals to that performance management system.

The measurement of non-financial and intangible aspects of an organisation is another problematic issue that faces many organisations. Traditionally, the accounting department has played a large role in the process of measuring the success of an organisation. As a result of this, management have often not developed the foresight to establish strong capabilities required for future growth, such as intangible assets that are accounted for in an effective performance measurement system. Measurements that are non-financial are required to align an organisation's long-term strategic plan with short-term objectives. In contrast to financial measurements, which can be conveyed clearly to all stakeholders, non-financial measurements are also more susceptible to misinterpretation and sometimes manipulation for the purposes of individual gain (Hussain & Islam, 2003). Therefore, it is essential that these measurements must be portrayed honestly and free of manipulation if they are to prove useful to the organisation.

Consistent with all organisational change management programmes, the implementation of any performance measurement process may experience a degree of resistance, particularly in large bureaucratic organisations. Initially, employees' natural resistance to being measured will inevitably cause an obstacle (Saka, 2003). Furthermore, Fitzgerald and Van Eijnatten (2002) claim that within large global organisations the consistent implementation of the performance management process across all sections of an organisation may be difficult if adequate communication mechanisms are not in place. Finally, managers who are lacking in experience may collect data that is irrelevant to the overall process and these statistics may ultimately prove useless. This can cause unnecessary effort and frustration amongst employees at the 'base' level in preparing vast amounts of reports and data that end up serving little purpose.

The measurements that are collected must be displayed in a clear and concise report. Moreover, they should convey the most important aspects of the organisation and be relevant to strategic imperatives. If too much data is collected and is not relevant to the performance measurements required, this can lead to further frustration and lack of efficiency on the part of the staff involved in collecting this data (Neely *et al.*, 2002). A well-manufactured performance measurement system should develop into a mechanism for carrying out daily operations within an organisation. Neely *et al.* (2002) argue it should allow employees to track their progress relating to performance and see how they are aligning their own performance with the strategic goals and objectives of the organisation, giving different departments the ability to communicate with each other about various issues using the same consistent language.

A well-designed performance measurement system must also show relevance to all visions of the organisation and act as a means of developing new strategic directions for the organisation (Kaplan & Norton, 1996a). It should briefly analyse past results then focus on the future objectives of the organisation and the performance it will require in order to achieve strategic goals. It is important for all employees not to lose focus, become frustrated with the system or just focus on short-term goals, as the long-term results will have a greater benefit for the organisation (Fariborz, 2001). For objectives that may not be achieved for a number of years, such as many initiatives within NPSOs, meaningful results-focused benchmarks leading to the achievement of longer-term outcomes should be in place. Town (2000) suggests performance measurement must not sacrifice one aspect of the organisation just to improve performance in another. He adds that all performance measurement systems should incorporate a wide scope of data which must include both tangible and intangible measurements. These measures must be agreed upon by management and staff, be challenging and ambitious, but also be realistic and attainable. If little emphasis is placed on an effective measurement system, staff can often become complacent. However, Booth (2006) claims that if too much emphasis is placed on this system then employees can often become frustrated and rebel against management, which ultimately will lead to a drop in performance level. A careful balance must be established in this situation and it is management's responsibility to make decisions where disagreements may arise.

Before any performance measurement system can be applied within an organisation, senior management must fully adopt principles that are based on performance improvement (Bond, 1999). In line with the literature related to 'culture', management must be seen to endorse the new system at all levels within the organisation while maintaining a consistent relationship with other pre-existing initiatives. Lyons (2006) claims an organisation must focus on its strategies and vision as opposed to the daily internal operations of the organisation. Strategic objectives must be directed by management to ensure that all employees are aware of how their own responsibilities fit in with the strategies and goals of the organisation. Lyons (2006) goes on to claim that individuals and organisational teams should be the owners of the measurement system and be accountable for all aspects of the measurement system. Management should allow individuals and teams to dictate which measures will assist them in the implementation of their roles most effectively. Management must not assume that they are aware of what is best for the individuals or teams as this means they will have removed employee ownership of the system and returned to a 'command and control' style of management, leaving employees powerless (Lyons, 2006; Moffat, 2000).

An integral part of many performance measurement systems is to set various targets. Performance targeting (Walsh, 2000) has the ability to make positive contributions to any measurement system. It is important that organisations make proper use of performance targets as this technique has a number of limitations and, if not implemented properly, can have adverse effects on the performance measurement system. Hood (2003) claims that, if targeting processes are not carefully designed and implemented, employees can become solely focused on the targets themselves and lose sight of the long-term objectives and aims of the organisation. This issue has proven to be one of the major pitfalls when establishing performance targets. In NPSOs and many other public-sector entities, performance pitfalls can be viewed as being of critical importance due to issues of responsibility and accountability in the public sector that may not be as imperative in the private (Schacter, 2002).

In addition, Walsh (2000) suggests that performance targets are created in order to place attention on particular processes and outcomes relating to a given organisation, and also to align the behaviour and actions of individuals (Daniels, 2004) to the overall goals and objectives of the organisation, along with the expectations of stakeholders. The case often arises where unintended consequences related to performance targets become adverse to the overall performance of the organisation, requiring constant monitoring and review of this process (Van Dooren & Van De Walle, 2008). The most prominent example of this, as stated above, occurs when individuals become solely focused on the targets that are set out for them and place less emphasis on producing quality products, services or benefits to the consumer which, along with earning a profit, is ultimately the main objective of many organisations. Maleyeff (2003) claims that, if targets are not properly monitored and used in the most appropriate ways, they can often cause individuals to lose sight of the organisation's main goals and objectives, and therefore prove to be immensely counterproductive.

Performance management theories

Stakeholder theory

The stakeholder theory of management relates to morals and ethics involved in the management of an organisation. Freeman (1984) was one of the first authors to begin writing about this theory and in his book *Strategic management: A stakeholder approach* (1984) he identifies the various entities that make up the stakeholders of an organisation. He argues that stakeholder theory is concerned with satisfying the wants and needs of these entities while maintaining the success of the organisation in a sustainable manner.

The traditional view of many organisations has been to simply satisfy the needs of the shareholders of that organisation, as these individuals were essentially the owners of the organisation and as such their needs should be of the foremost importance. Another traditional view of an organisation relates to an 'input–output model' first described by Leontief (1986) where the organisation converts the inputs of the shareholders, employees and the suppliers to either manufacture products or to supply a service to the consumer, and as a result return an amount of capital benefit back into the organisation. The issues arising with these traditional views on shareholders are that they do not take into account the other stakeholders of an organisation that are affected by the operating environment of that organisation, such as trade unions, government agencies, pressure groups, other associated organisations and the general public. Occasionally, in certain situations even competitors can be considered stakeholders of an organisation.

In modern traditional business environments, stakeholder theory has developed into an important theory of the organisational management process, integrating resource-based, market-based and socio-political aspects with the more traditional approaches. This trend now outlines the various and sometimes vast number of stakeholders that an organisation may have (Donaldson & Preston, 1995) and also identifies the ways in which an organisation should interact with these entities (Mitchell, Agle & Wood 1997). Stakeholder theory in modern business consists of these two interlinked elements of organisational (stakeholder) management.

Given the growth of stakeholder management in the practical setting, it is unsurprising to note that theory in relation to this issue has also been explored in greater depth. Stakeholder theory has also been explored by Rossouw, du Plessis, Prinsloo and Prozesky (2009) in *Ethics for accountants and auditors* and by Mintz and Morris (2008) in *Ethical obligations and decision making in accounting* in relation to financial decision making. However, Donaldson and Preston (1995) are the foremost authors on this issue and they suggest that the "identification of moral or philosophical guidelines for the operation and management of the corporation" (p. 71) is the central core of this theory. In comparison, Mitchell, Agle and Wood (1997) develop a common perspective on stakeholders, focused on attributes of power, legitimacy and urgency. Power refers to the extent of influence the stakeholder exerts over the organisation. Legitimacy relates to the culturally accepted and structure of behaviour of the stakeholder. Urgency refers to time sensitivity or how critical a particular stakeholder may be to an organisation. From an analysis of these attributes it is possible to generate a potential list of the various stakeholders that an organisation may be forced to interact with. These can include but are not limited to: investors, employees, suppliers, consumers, government agencies, political groups, trade unions, trade associations, communities, and associated organisations.

Stakeholder theory becomes increasingly important as we begin to analyse models such as the Balanced Scorecard or the Performance Prism. When implemented correctly, such performance management tools can help to satisfy the needs of stakeholders, providing the organisation has chosen appropriate measures within these models. Stakeholder theory has been developed and justified in the management literature on the basis of its descriptive accuracy, instrumental power and normative validity (Donaldson & Preston, 1995; Berman, Wicks, Kotha & Jones, 1999). However, little empirical work has been carried out on the effect that stakeholder theory has on organisational performance and it is imperative that this issue is analysed when examining the performance management models that relate to this theory.

Achievement goal theory

A goal or an objective can be described as the object of an action, or what an individual seeks to accomplish from a given task. Goal theory is important in terms of individual performance management as it relates to the ways in which individual employees view the goals that are set for them by management and provides a direct correlation between the difficulty of the objective and the performance of the employee in achieving that objective (Emsley, 2003). Goal theory can have a significant impact on the performance of all employees operating within an organisation and can affect the efficiency and effectiveness (performance) of individual workers. Emsley suggests that an effective goal-setting system can help individual employees achieve goals that can lead to an increase in organisational performance. Locke (1968) was one of the first authors to propose the theory of goal setting, and his initial work focused on the acceptance that goal setting is a cognitive behavioural process based on the use of a practical utility. He proposed that an employee's behaviour and performance can be directly associated with the manner in which goals and objectives are set and how difficult or simplistic it may be to achieve these goals. Achievement goal theory, as described by Locke, places important emphasis on reinforced goals playing a large role in the motivation and levels of high morale experienced by employees in the workplace. Greenhaus, Callanan and Kaplan (1995) add that the four integral components of goals that must be adhered to within any goal-setting practice are: the specificity of the objectives; the complexity of the goals; the intensity of the aims that are set to be achieved; and the acceptance of the goals as belonging to the individual or team operating within the organisation.

Another crucial element of a goal-setting system is that individual employees are allowed to participate in the goal-setting design and implementation process. Research suggests that the commitment and performance relating to the achievement of goals will not be affected regardless of whether or not these objectives have been assigned by management or have been agreed upon after prior consultation with individual employees (Greenhaus *et al.*, 1995). However, De Jong and Den Hartog (2007) suggest that employee involvement in the goal-setting process is a crucial element if objectives are to be achieved in a timely and efficient manner. Their research also suggests that if individual employees are not involved in the process, little or no commitment will be associated with the objectives assigned by management. Further research has shown that as individual involvement in the goal setting process increased, performance, commitment and productivity increased proportionately in the completion of these goals (Locke & Latham, 2002). Furthermore, Emsley (2003) adds that individual differences often exist when judging the effectiveness and efficiency of goal setting as a source of motivation within an organisation.

Employees' individual personalities and position in the organisation are two of the variables that can have an impact on their commitment to the goal-setting process and implementation. Baker (2001) suggests employees who already experience high levels of motivation within an organisation, due to personality traits, are often more enthusiastic about the goal-setting process and view goals as an adequate benchmark with which they can measure their own individual performance. As the literature has already suggested, there is a direct relationship between the setting of goals and the performance of an organisation, both at the individual and organisational level (performance targets). From the above, it is apparent that there are three distinct ways in which goals can affect performance:

1   Goals can force employees to focus on the achievement of the objective by setting a clear and precise timeline within which the goal should be achieved.

2 The setting of goals can lead to increased effort of individual workers. If management and employees agree to increase productivity to a certain level, it can inspire individuals to adopt a greater level of intensity relating to their tasks within the organisation.
3 Goals can help employees overcome adversity that may arise within the achievement process of the objectives and develop a strong sense of persistence relating to the successful achievement of the agreed-upon goal.

The final part of an effective goal-setting process is that the individual receives adequate feedback from management on their progress in relation to the achievement of the required objectives. In a case where no feedback is provided by management, the goal-setting process will be flawed and the desired results will ultimately not be achieved as employees lose focus and have no method of measuring their progress in relation to the set goals. Individuals must be aware of the position they occupy in relation to the achievement of their goals in order to assess if methods of achievement must be changed and/or satisfactory progress is being made (Baker, 2001). The advancement of technology operating within many organisations has made the process of feedback relating to goal setting far more effective. Software systems have been designed and adopted by organisations in order to track and monitor the process of goal achievement. These software applications may only manage an individual's goals and deadline for achievement, but are useful as they provide a constant means of evaluation and reinforce the importance of the identified objectives in the execution of the organisation's overarching objectives.

In line with many theories and processes operating within organisations, goal setting is by no means devoid of limitations. A critical component of performance management is to ensure that the systems in place help individual managers and other employees recognise how their individual performance relates to the overall objectives and aims of the organisation. It may not always be possible to set goals at an individual level that are in direct alignment with overall objectives within the organisation; however, management should try to facilitate this situation as best as possible. Furthermore, for tasks that carry a high degree of complexity, the goal-setting process may also have negative effects on performance as individual employees become solely involved in the achievement of their goals rather than the 'performance' of the task.

Path–goal theory

The path–goal theory is grounded in the concept of organisational psychology and relates to the effectiveness of a manager in relation to the levels of morale and motivation of their subordinates (House, 1971; 1996). It describes how an individual manager's behaviour and actions are associated with how satisfied and committed their employees are within the organisational setting, and ultimately how well they execute their roles. The theory also suggests that the individual manager's actions have the ability to complement the ability of their subordinates and compensate for any deficiencies that may be present. It is known as 'path–goal theory' as the leader influences the individual's goals and the paths that exist within the achievement of those goals. The foundations of path–goal theory began with studies by Vroom (1964) and Evans (1970), who proposed expectancy theory which relates to motivation within an organisation.

Silverthorne (2001) suggests that the function of a leader within an organisation is to guide individuals and teams in the achievement of certain tasks and goals that have been set for them by management. Leaders should be a source of constant feedback and knowledge when it comes to dealing with adversity and other issues that may hinder the progress of the individual employees in achieving a defined objective. He adds that the behaviour and actions of a leader will also be dependent upon the unique circumstances within the organisation, such as the personality traits of employees and the various operating environment pressures that workers must cope with while undertaking their roles. In addition, House (1996) claims that employees with higher capabilities in terms of achieving goals may be more resistant to coaching from their manager or leader. When objectives and the 'paths' in place to facilitate achievement are clear, any attempt by management to impose restrictions can result in a lack of cohesiveness in the project. Furthermore, House suggests that employees will continue to resist compliance with the defined goals if management continue to enforce organisational procedures and rules associated with the achievement of the objectives.

Path–goal theory suggests that a leader must engage in various leadership styles given the diverse range of organisational circumstances they may face, which is further complicated by the nature and demands of the goals that are to be achieved. House (1971) argues that the behaviour of a leader in an organisational setting must facilitate, coach and reward effective performance. House and Mitchell (1974) and House (1996) suggest path–goal theory contains four different styles of leadership that must be present in all effective leadership regimes:

1   The directive leader – informs subordinates of acceptable behaviour and clearly identifies what is required of them in order to fulfil their roles within the organisation. Path–goal theory claims that this style of leadership is most effective when employees' tasks and goals are ambiguous and fundamentally rewarding (House & Mitchell, 1974).
2   The achievement-orientated leader – displays supreme confidence in their subordinates and sets goals that are challenging and often involving a high level of complexity, expecting his/her staff to operate at an optimum level of performance. This leadership style is often displayed where tasks and roles are related to technical ability, such as architecture, engineering and entrepreneurship (House, 1996).
3   The participative leader – constantly consults with his/her subordinates on the vast majority of issues and particularly when it comes to the area of goal setting. This leadership style is often displayed when employees have a strong personal interest in their tasks and roles within an organisation (House, 1996).

4 The supportive leader – shows concern and interest in ensuring employees' needs and levels of satisfaction are constantly being met. The psychological well-being of their subordinates is high on the agenda within this style of leadership (House & Mitchell, 1974). The supportive leader is required in situations when employee roles can be mentally or physically demanding (House, 1996).

The major limitation of path–goal theory is that it automatically draws the assumption that leaders have the ability and flexibility to display these various styles of leadership as the circumstances within the organisation require. Furthermore, the theory does not adequately explain the relationship between leadership actions and employee motivation levels, and fails to accept that two-way relationships exist within organisations where leaders can also be affected by the actions and behaviours of subordinates.

Performance management tools

The Balanced Scorecard

Kaplan and Norton (1992) developed the Balanced Scorecard performance management model, which has been used as an effective strategic planning and management tool by many organisations and across a vast number of industries. It has provided senior management with an effective way of monitoring actions and processes undertaken by employees, and allowed them to keep a record of these actions and consequences in an efficient and defined manner. The Balanced Scorecard is perceived to be the most widely used of the various performance management tools that have become available and, although initially only adopted in mostly western countries, it has now spread throughout the global business environment. Since 2000, use of the Balanced Scorecard and its derivatives, such as the Performance Prism (Neely *et al.*, 2002) and other similar approaches to performance management, including Results Based Management, has become commonplace in organisations throughout the world. Kurtzman (1997) claims that almost 70 per cent of companies responding to a questionnaire were measuring organisational performance in a way that was extremely similar to that of the Balanced Scorecard. This method of performance management has been implemented by government institutions, small businesses and corporations, but as yet there is no evidence to suggest that it has been adopted by NPSOs.

Standardised Balanced Scorecards are easily accessible for organisations and can have a potentially positive impact on many of them. However, using one organisation's Balanced Scorecard and attempting to apply it to another organisation can prove very difficult, and research has suggested that one of the major benefits of the Scorecard lies within the design process itself (Kurtzman, 1997). Early designs, during the initial stages of its adoption, often experienced problems because of this issue as they were designed by external consultants who may not have had specific knowledge of operations within the organisation. As a result of this, management became wary and failed to engage with the process due to the system being created by individuals who were lacking knowledge of the organisation and the specific responsibilities of management.

The unique aspect of the Balanced Scorecard, which was a new development in the measurement initiatives adopted by organisations, was that it combined financial and non-financial aspects of organisations to give a more detailed view of how the organisation was actually performing within its operating environment. In addition, its utility and clarity were enhanced as Kaplan and Norton suggested that measures within an organisation should be condensed and grouped together so they could be easily displayed within a simple four-box model (Kaplan & Norton, 1992; 1993). Aside from this new approach to measurement within an organisation, the original definitions of the Balanced Scorecard model were sparse. From its initial inception, however, it became clear that selection of measures, relating to both the filtering and clustering process, would prove to be the integral activities that management must address in the implementation of this system. The measures that were to be selected, according to Kaplan and Norton, should be synonymous with issues and initiatives that were relevant within the organisation's strategic plan, and a simple process of requiring information concerning attitudinal issues would determine which measures should be associated with each perspective (Kaplan & Norton, 1992).

A major criticism that became apparent after the publication of Kaplan and Norton's book *The Balanced Scorecard: Translating strategy into action* (1996b) was that the model did not address the managerial issue of the development of long-term sustainable strategies. Following on from this publication, a subsequent book, *The strategy-focused organization* (Kaplan & Norton, 2001), echoed research previously conducted in this area (Olve, Roy & Wetter, 1999) relating to the visual documentation of the links associated with measurement and the development of the 'strategy map' (Kaplan & Norton, 2004). This important development within the model inspired a number of very similar variants, improved the model's utility, and propelled it into mainstream industries that saw the value in adopting such a performance management technique. Modern versions of the Balanced Scorecard can be closely associated with this type of concept and the initial samples of the model have become mostly redundant. Modern Balanced Scorecards have also evolved to be more flexible and 'user friendly', and in theory can be applied to almost every type of organisation both in for-profit and non-profit sectors.

As hinted at, Kaplan and Norton's (1992) initial design was laid out as a simple 'four box' model that could help organisations ensure they were getting the best results out of all the resources available to them. The model suggested that financial measures should not be the only perspective to be analysed. They proposed three other perspectives along with the traditional financial one: 'internal business process', 'learning and growth' and 'the customer' were also selected to form the major concerns within an organisation (see Figure 2.1). Research surrounding Balanced Scorecards is vast and some authors have suggested renaming these perspectives along with the addition of further perspectives within the model. These arguments have become apparent as a result of recognition that dissimilar but equivalent perspectives would potentially give rise to a different set of measures. A crucial element of the adoption of this model is that users have confidence around the aspects chosen to be measured and that they are relevant, otherwise results achieved may be regarded as being insignificant. Indeed, this has been the predominant factor in first-generation Balanced Scorecards becoming redundant (Olve *et al.*, 1999, Kaplan & Norton, 2001, Niven, 2006).

Despite its popularity as a concept, literature relating to the design of first-generation Balanced Scorecards is comparatively absent. Literature that does concentrate on the application of the first-generation Balanced Scorecards (Butler, Letza & Neale, 1997) and related organisational experiences (Ahn, 2001) generally support the model but also detail the weaknesses in the initial design phase of the approach, and suggest improvements that eventually do become incorporated into future Balanced Scorecard designs (Epstein & Manzoni, 1997; Eagleson & Waldersee, 2000; Kennerley & Neely, 2002).

Since its initial inception in the early 1990s, many variants, derivatives and alternatives of the Balanced Scorecard's 'four box' approach have emerged throughout the performance management literature. Bourne *et al.* (2003) suggest that many of these variants serve little purpose and indeed have little utility. They argue that they are largely created by private consultants who develop similar models in order to increase profits from book sales or conference appearances. Many of these related models are unquestionably similar, and research (Cobbold & Lawrie, 2002) has attempted to establish a pattern in these similarities, noting three distinct types of variations. These models can be grouped into 'generations' as part of the evolving process of this performance management model (Cobbold & Lawrie, 2002). The original Kaplan & Norton (1992) design,

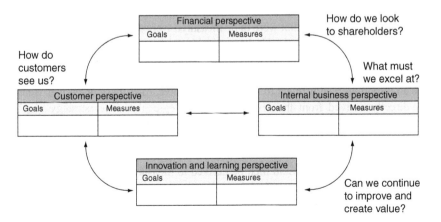

Figure 2.1 First-generation Balanced Scorecard (adapted from Cobbold & Lawrie, 2002).

along with other models that propose the simplistic 'four box' approach, are often classed as the first-generation of Balanced Scorecards. The emergence of the 'strategy map', such as the Performance Prism (Neely *et al.*, 2002) and the Performance Driver model (Olve *et al.*, 1999), coincided with this original design and constitute second-generation Balanced Scorecards. And more modern designs, which incorporate a narrative relating to the long-term vision of the organisation called 'destination statements', have now become known as third-generation Balanced Scorecard models (Cobbold & Lawrie, 2002).

Second-generation Balanced Scorecards

One of the major criticisms of the first-generation Balanced Scorecards was that, while it was perceived to be a good idea in theory, when put to the test through practice a number of difficulties arose, resulting in many practitioners scrapping the model due to its lack of utility and vagueness (Cobbold & Lawrie, 2002). Throughout the 1990s, new design methods began to emerge, some from Kaplan and Norton themselves and others from independent consultants with similar theories and thought processes. These new designs incorporated the 'strategy map' which consisted of a set of objectives strategically placed within the model in order to further assist the organisation in maintaining focus on its long-term visions. Under this new design method, Balanced Scorecards began to associate strategic aims alongside the pre-existing four perspectives, and as a result were able to 'connect the dots' by visual means of the objectives and the aspects of the organisation that were to be measured as part of this new initiative.

Kaplan and Norton (1992) argued that for an organisation to be successful in the financial sense it must analyse the ways in which it appears to its stakeholders. Strangely, second-generation scorecards did not adopt this synopsis, and instead created a process of associating a limited number of performance measures to be placed alongside each perspective within the model. Strategic objectives now became a key priority of the concept and were used in order to convey the core of the entity's strategic operations associated with each performance aspect. The aspects of the organisation that were to be measured were then carefully selected in order to ensure they coincided with these prioritised strategic objectives (Kaplan & Norton, 1993). Cobbold and Lawrie (2002) suggest that, although initially not considered as a major redesign of the pre-existing model, strategic objectives proved to be an important readjustment to the Balanced Scorecard as these objectives were now directly derived from the organisation's strategic plan. The 'strategy map' element of the revised model comes about as management select the aspects of the organisation they feel to be most important to measure, and then the 'cause–effect' relationship between these aims can be defined through the establishment of links between them. The model could then be derived to measure the strategic performance of an organisation by analysing strategic objectives and the selected measures with the visual assistance of the 'strategy map'. This innovation within the Balanced Scorecard model allows management greater ease of use and provides justification for choosing the selected measures.

The changes of design and evolution of the tool were recorded in Kaplan and Norton's (2001) book *The strategy-focused organization*. They claimed that by this point the Balanced Scorecard model had evolved from a simple performance management tool into a core aspect that should be applied within all organisations (Kaplan & Norton, 2001). Coinciding with their belief that the Balanced Scorecard can help an organisation with the achievement of strategic objectives, Kaplan and Norton argued that this model should be at the core of all strategic management activities within an organisation. From 1996 onwards, second-generation Balanced Scorecards became popular throughout all sectors and industries, and were established as the leading performance measurement tool available to an organisation. A number of criticisms are still apparent with such second-generation Balanced Scorecards but they have proved through practical application that they are still more successful when compared with the original Kaplan and Norton models.

Third-generation Balanced Scorecards

In the late 1990s, evolution of the Balanced Scorecard began to take place once again. This further development was required in order to address the deficiencies evident within the second-generation scorecards, designs which failed to acknowledge that opportunities to intervene in the strategic process must be made available in order to anchor objectives in any 'present', real and current management activities. Cobbold and Lawrie (2002) suggested another major weakness of the second-generation designs was that they ignored the need to 'roll forward' and assess the impact that strategic objectives would have on the organisation in the time ahead. As a result, a further element was added into the mix within the Balanced Scorecard design known as the 'destination statement'. This instrument consisted of little more than a brief paragraph of what the 'strategic success' or 'end date' of the strategic plans would typically be. Initial destination statements were constructed with a particular timeline associated with them, detailing which objectives needed to be achieved in a certain timeframe. Through the application of this new instrument, organisations could now assess how targets were being met on an annual basis and whether the strategic vision of the organisation was on its way to being achieved. Management quickly began to understand that if a destination statement was to be incorporated within a Balanced Scorecard model, the selection and measurement of strategic objectives would become an easier exercise for the organisation through the allocation of targets and measures that could be readily interpreted and show progress towards strategic objectives.

Organisations quickly began to realise that through the implementation of a destination statement senior management and individuals within the workplace were now able to relate their roles directly to the destination statement without having to constantly make reference to strategic goals set out by the organisation. As a result of this revelation, the design approach of the model was 'reversed' with destination statements attracting the initial attention of the designers as opposed to being the final element of the design phase. It was further uncovered through practical application that establishing a destination statement first made the selection of strategic objectives within the organisation more efficient. For an organisation to have the ability to make rational decisions relating to its operations and to set performance targets for strategic objectives, it must be able to articulate exactly what the entity is aiming to attain (Kotter, 1996; Senge, 1994). Through the application of a destination statement, an organisation can detail how exactly it will look within an agreed-upon time period (Olve *et al.*, 1999; Shulver, Lawrie & Anderson, 2000). The Balanced Scorecard may build upon some existing strategic plan or documents, but its ability to offer the certainty and clarity needed in order to assist an organisation in the performance of its strategic objectives appears to be unrivalled.

Criticisms of the Balanced Scorecard

The Balanced Scorecard and its many variants have attracted criticisms, from its initial inception to the present day. The majority of these criticisms have surfaced within academic circles, as the empirical nature of the model has been a major source of debate relating to the validity of the practical applications of the model. Kaplan and Norton (1992) did not cite previous models and academic work when establishing their own performance management model, therefore supporting the argument made by a number of academics that the framework lacked substance and legitimacy (Norreklit, 2000). Defenders of the Balanced Scorecard argue that this criticism carried little weight as most critics assess the design of the model based on Kaplan and Norton's original framework. Supporters argue weaknesses and areas for improvement have been addressed through later Balanced Scorecard models. A large proportion of the critics focus on the design flaws within the various models and as a result have indirectly contributed to the evolution of the Balanced Scorecard through the redesigning and 'generations' concept of the framework, as described by Cobbold and Lawrie (2002).

Although an abundance of literature is available relating to the practical utility of the Balanced Scorecard, there is a general lack of empirical research relating to the use of a model such as this when contributing to an organisation's improved financial performance or better decision-making processes. Case study research that does analyse single organisations suffers from a lack of control in justifying results, as it is almost impossible to predict how the organisation may have performed if a model such as the Balanced Scorecard had not been introduced. However, the studies that have been conducted within this area generally do endorse the Balanced Scorecard as a useful tool for management to avail of and implement (Mooraj, Oton & Hostettler, 1999; Malina & Selto, 2001).

The future of the Balanced Scorecard

Throughout the immediate future, it can be anticipated that the Balanced Scorecard will continue to be a model synonymous with the process of performance management in organisations, but inevitably further evolution will take place in the future. Strategy maps have been proven to be successful in practical applications and these instruments, along with destination statements, will continue to be used through the adoption of the Balanced Scorecard model. Organisations have begun to use the Balanced Scorecard in order to guide and monitor the performance of their strategies and assist organisations' boards in strategic decision making. The measurement of data required in order to satisfy the demands of the model will become more efficient, and annual reports will begin to focus on the results that the Balanced Scorecard reflects. It can be assumed that information technology and Balanced Scorecard software will continue to play a key role in the operations of organisations, and the issue of adopting and implementing a performance management culture will continue to be reinforced throughout all industries as its importance begins to be fully realised.

The theories relating to management control and the practical applications of the Balanced Scorecard have begun to align along a similar path. This is a positive indicator that can support the argument that latter-day Balanced Scorecard designs are indeed more useful compared with the initial model proposed by Kaplan and Norton (1992), creating a more positive impact upon the organisation. Although modern Balanced Scorecard models have shown significant improvements and offer greater scope for utility, the evolution process is far from complete. The model can become far more attractive if financial values for pre- and post-case scenarios can be incorporated within the framework. Another important condition for the successful implementation of the scorecard in organisations is the capacity to provide further added value through its implementation. Many authors and academics (Mooraj *et al.*, 1999; Malina & Selto, 2001; Olve *et al.*, 1999; Shulver *et al.*, 2000) suggest that there are unquestionable benefits for the organisation that decides to implement the model; however, there is an alarming scarcity of concrete examples that support this claim in relation to both public and private sector organisations. When an organisation does adopt the Balanced Scorecard model, it is clear that it can be implemented throughout each department and utilised as a strategic planning and performance management tool (Shulver *et al.*, 2000), although the model's flexibility and effectiveness require further analysis.

The Performance Prism

The Performance Prism performance management model is a design that has been developed by Neely, Adams and Kennerley (2002) to further aid organisations in measuring the overall performance of their activities. The model has received a fraction of scholarly analysis in comparison with the Balanced Scorecard, but nonetheless appears to be an alternative approach implemented in practice. In line with stakeholder theory, the creators of this model suggest that for organisations operating within any industry the most important aspect of management is to deliver on the expectations of their stakeholders. Therefore, the Performance Prism is primarily designed to help with the complex relationships that organisations have with their often vast array of stakeholders. Furthermore, the authors propose that the model helps management analyse the on-going performance of systems and processes already in operation within the organisation, and provides a new and self-sustainable performance management initiative that has the ability to transform the performance problems that face an organisation.

This model attempts to distinguish itself from other similar models, such as the Balanced Scorecard, by offering a unique perspective on a measuring system that can ultimately be adopted as a way of operating within an industry, rather than just measuring the performance of an organisation. The Balanced Scorecard (Kaplan & Norton, 1992) only outlines four different aspects of an organisation to be measured: finance, customers, internal processes, and innovation and learning. As a result, Neely *et al.* (2002) suggest it ignores the crucial role that the various stakeholders of an organisation have in determining the success or failure of its strategic objectives. Other models, such as the Business Excellence model (EFQM, 2005), combine outcomes that can be easily measured with business enablers. Similarly, models such as Shareholder Value Frameworks (Srivastava, Shervani & Fahey, 1998) incorporate the overall cost of capital into their models but still fail to acknowledge performance issues relating to stakeholders. In addition, Kaplan and Bruns' (1987) model relating to 'activity-based costing' and Feigenbaum's (1991) 'cost of quality' model focus on aspects that do not necessarily add value to the organisation. Furthermore, the major limitation of these models is that they do not analyse the importance of stakeholders to an organisation in relation to performance. The other extreme of this issue can be seen in benchmarking (Camp, 1989), which takes an almost exclusively external perspective by analysing the performance of other organisations within the industry. The major limitation of this process is that it cannot be used as a long-term system of performance management and is more suited to a one-off exercise for the generation of short-term performance-improvement initiatives.

The abundance of performance management systems/tools/processes available would suggest that no model has been completely successful in satisfying the needs of all organisations. Each may to a certain degree provide management with a method of measuring and assessing components of the organisation relating to performance. However, an organisation must acknowledge that there may not be a 'holy grail' of performance management models or best method to analyse organisational performance. Through the Performance Prism, Neely *et al.*, (2002) suggest this situation is addressed as a result of performance management itself being a multi-faceted concern facing an organisation.

The designers of this model use the word 'prism' in its title to establish a connection between performance management and the fact that a prism is a device that refracts light. A prism can reveal the "hidden elements behind something as apparently simple as white light" (Neely *et al.*, 2002, p. 4). This is relevant to the thinking behind Neely *et al.*'s model of the Performance Prism. It illustrates the hidden complexities behind the issues of performance management that can affect an organisation. The authors argue that previous performance management models have failed to address all areas of performance within an organisation.

They further argue that while each of these frameworks has given a unique perspective on performance, they do not analyse the organisation from a performance perspective as an entire entity. In contrast, they suggest that the Performance Prism attempts to establish five different fundamental organisational questions for management to draw upon in order to assess the true scope of the organisation's performance management issues (see Figure 2.2):

1   Stakeholder satisfaction – what are the wants and needs of our stakeholders?
2   Stakeholder contribution – what can our stakeholders provide to us?
3   Strategies – which strategies are best to implement in order to satisfy stakeholder demands?
4   Processes – which processes should be adopted to satisfy stakeholder demands?
5   Capabilities – what practices, people, technology and infrastructure is required so processes and strategies can be fully implemented?

(Neely *et al.*, 2002)

Neely *et al.* (2002) claim that these five different perspectives on organisational performance have the ability to establish a complete and coherent system for managing performance and, by answering these five key criteria, a successful and effective performance management model can be created. To understand this concept better, it is necessary to explore these perspectives, as suggested by Neely *et al.*, in greater depth.

Stakeholder satisfaction: organisations exist primarily to provide either a product or service, and to deliver 'value' to their key stakeholders. The term 'stakeholder' can be used to describe a broad range of entities including investors, customers, employees, suppliers, regulators and pressure groups. Freeman (1984) defines a stakeholder as "any group or individual who can affect or is

The five facets of the Performance Prism

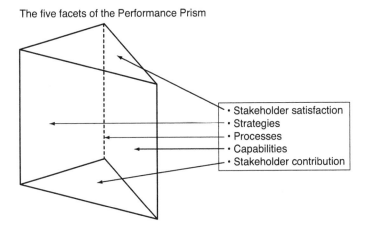

• Stakeholder satisfaction
• Strategies
• Processes
• Capabilities
• Stakeholder contribution

Figure 2.2 Facets of the Performance Prism (adapted from Neely *et al.*, 2002).

affected by the achievement of the organisation's objectives" (p. 53). The term 'value' can be assessed in different ways for various stakeholders, depending upon their interest in the organisation: consumers will demand high-quality products and services that are fit for purpose and are good value for money; employees will require fair compensation for their hard work within the organisation, development and learning opportunities, and clear pathways for promotion; and shareholders will view the term 'value' through analysis of their return on their investment and the potential for growth and expansion in comparison with other entities within the industry.

Stakeholder contribution: "Organisations and their stakeholders have to recognise that their relationships are reciprocal" (Neely *et al.*, 2002, p. 6). An important issue that must not be ignored by stakeholders is that the organisation will attempt to satisfy their needs but will also expect stakeholders to fulfil their roles relating to the organisation. This can often be a subtle if dynamic relationship which exists between the two parties. From a consumer's perspective, they expect quality products, speedy delivery and competitive prices. In return, the organisation expects the consumer to be willing to pay a fair price for a quality service or product, to remain loyal to the organisation, and to offer relevant and critical feedback when asked. From an employee's perspective, they expect roles that allow them to contribute to the overall success of the organisation and to gain knowledge through adequate learning and development initiatives. In return, the organisation may ask for loyalty, commitment, honesty, productivity, and to use innovation and creativity to contribute to the organisation's purpose.

Strategies: when each stakeholder's wants and needs have been firmly established, the organisation must come to an agreement relating to the extent that they will prioritise these, ensuring they are achieving an adequate return on their investment and not putting other aspects of the organisation in jeopardy. For instance, in a traditional business organisation creating shareholder value may be conveyed as the long-term 'destination', and the ways in which the organisation can reach that 'destination' can be illustrated through the processes and strategies that must be put in place.

Processes: whatever strategies are implemented within the organisation, they must be supported by adequate processes and systems that can help the organisation achieve its potential. Effective systems and processes are integral for the successful operation of an organisation and are the mechanisms for it to achieve its goals and objectives (Neely *et al.*, 2002). These processes and systems are essentially cross-functional and are the cornerstones of what results occur within the workplace and how they were achieved. Each of these processes is often underpinned by various assortments of sub-processes, created to help the organisation function at an optimum level of efficiency and effectiveness (performance).

Capabilities (individual performance management): processes cannot merely function without any input from individuals within the organisation, and they require employees that have gained a particular set of skills. In addition, effective procedures and policies relating to operations management must be in place, along with adequate facilities, infrastructure and appropriate technology implementations to enhance and enable processes. Capabilities such as these can be viewed as a collective system of the organisation's resources which when combined define an entity's capacity to create value for the satisfaction of stakeholders through effective strategies and processes.

The Performance Prism case study – DHL

Ryan (2012) suggests that one of the criticisms of the Performance Prism model of performance management is that there has not been enough adoption of the model within real-life organisations to prove its value. However, there are a number of organisations that have adopted the model and in 2000 the UK division of DHL, one of the leaders in the international express delivery industry, opted to employ this method of performance management. The following case study, adapted from Neely, Adams and Crowe (2001), details the success of this decision.

DHL and performance management

DHL implemented the Performance Prism in order to obtain the data and results it sought, which previous initiatives had failed to deliver. Neely *et al.* (2001) claim that data being collected was not being acted upon and that the organisation was slowly beginning to lose sight of its aims and objectives. As a consequence, the organisation decided that a model such as the Performance Prism would be the best way of reorganising their operations, to focus on the two-way relationship between the organisation and its stakeholders.

According to Neely *et al.* (2001), senior management restructured the performance management system in four major steps that underpin the adoption and implementation of the performance management system:

1 Design – the contribution of the stakeholders and their wants and needs in return for their investment was initially identified. Capabilities, processes and strategies were also identified in order to assess how the wants and needs of the stakeholders could be met. The types of questions that are raised at performance-evaluation meetings were considered in relation to this new model that had been implemented throughout the organisation. The aspects of the organisation that were to be measured became apparent once the answer to the identified questions had been conceived. The final step in the design process was to consider what measures were required, and how data could be collected and analysed in order to provide answers to these questions. The resulting scenario produced measurements directly related to the specific questions that had been identified by management.

2 Plan and build process – this process involved communicating and reinforcing the most important elements of the Performance Prism model. The focus began to shift primarily to the organisation's relationship with its

stakeholders; the alignment of strategies with objectives; effective implementation of capabilities and processes; and ensuring data collected was
used to answer questions, not simply as a management exercise that adds
little value to the organisation. A process manager was also put in place to
oversee the entire performance management system. The organisation also
developed learning and development programmes for individuals who
would be performing tasks relating to this new process and in particular
those who would be briefing senior executives prior to any performance
review meetings, along with providing documentation that would support
issues which needed to be raised regarding performance. These individuals
were also expected to share opinions and experiences, therefore supporting
cross-functional understanding and fluidity.

3   Implement and operate process – the critical change that was required within
DHL was to approach the organisation's quarterly reviews from a new perspective. Issues that were to be raised within the agenda would now be
reflective of questions that shareholders wanted answers to and other key
issues that senior management decided were of critical importance.

4   Refresh process – as a result of adopting the Performance Prism model,
Neely *et al.* (2001) claim that reviews and processes have continued to
evolve within DHL, along with providing a foundation for future development to continue within the organisation.

Neely *et al.* (2001) conclude by suggesting the process requires constant monitoring and intermittent changes to prove of maximum benefit. They add that the
organisation was able to reshape all issues relating to performance management
due to their decision to implement the Performance Prism, and as a consequence
provided management with a structured and coherent framework to achieve strategic objectives.

The Performance Prism conclusions

This strategic performance management framework suggests that, in order for
organisations to fully benefit from all their systems and processes, there are two
major issues that management must address:

1   Understand the complex relationship that exists between stakeholders and
the organisation, and strive to establish a common ground of compromise
where both parties can be satisfied with each other's contribution.

2   The alignment and linking of strategies, capabilities and processes is an
integral component in ensuring the wants and needs of various stakeholders
can be satisfied appropriately without compromising the overall success of
the organisation.

This model has attempted to distinguish itself from other models, such as the
Balanced Scorecard, by providing a unique approach to the performance

management issue. It has proven to be successful for some organisations, but not enough evidence exists in support of this model being either superior or inferior to other such processes (Ryan, 2012). 'Success mapping', which Neely *et al.* (2002) describe as the identification of critical links between stakeholders and strategies, processes and capabilities (p. 7), is one area in which this model has somewhat distinguished itself from the others and epitomises the essence of the Performance Prism. Therefore, in theory, it is argued that when the Performance Prism is applied correctly the crucial links between the wants and needs of stakeholders and the needs of the organisation can be identified through alignment of these strategies, processes and capabilities.

3 Performance management in sport

Chapter introduction

This chapter initiates the focus of analysing performance management within NPSOs. It provides a robust analysis of the significance and impact of sport in general, as alluded to in the opening chapter, including a discussion identifying the uniqueness of managing these entities when compared with their traditional business counterparts. Following on from this analysis, the extant literature specifically focusing on performance within NPSOs is examined. Given the clear significance and impact of sport and the potential consequences of mismanagement within this sector, it is surprising to find that this area of research within the sport management literature is relatively sparse, highlighting the critical importance of this current book. Moreover, as all the selected NPSOs within this book are solely or partially government-funded entities, it is also imperative to examine the area of governmental sports policy and its relationship with organisational performance, which is addressed towards the end of this chapter.

Performance management in NPSOs

The principles of performance management are required whenever any organisation, irrespective of its particular type, interacts with their environment to produce desired results. Yet performance management in NPSOs in many nations is a new phenomenon. Few studies have been carried out to analyse how NPSOs view the issue of performance management and whether they use models such as the Balanced Scorecard (Kaplan & Norton, 1992), the Performance Prism (Neely *et al.*, 2002) or the European Foundation for Quality Management (EFQM) model (Wongrassamee, Simmons & Gardiner, 2003) in order to assist them in achieving their strategic goals and to manage performance effectively. These models have been proven to be successful in the traditional business environment and, given that many NPSOs now share much common ground with the traditional business industry, it is imperative that research is conducted to critically examine this issue in greater detail.

NPSOs have members and stakeholders, much like traditional businesses have customers and clients. Given that they belong to the world of non-profit organisations, NPSOs' main aspiration is not financial return, rather the performance of their mission (Chappelet & Bayle, 2005). This illustrates why performance management is an important area for such entities, perhaps even more so than organisations operating within the traditional business environment.

Chappelet and Bayle (2005) suggest that sport is playing an increasingly important role in a rapidly changing economic, political, cultural and social world. A new context for all levels of sport is developing around the globe, providing an extraordinary opportunity to discover and develop new areas of sport management in amateur and professional contexts. Many commentators on sport as a business (Mahony & Howard, 2001; Miller, 1997) suggest that the managers and governors involved in the sport industry are limited by their ability to transfer knowledge of conceptual business practices to the sports business environment. However, Chelladurai (2005) insists that NPSOs are in desperate need of managers/governors from within their own ranks who have the capabilities of managing the performance of their organisation and developing their strategic goals. Regardless of where they are sourced, one of the greatest challenges for NPSOs is to ensure that their current and future managers/governors have the necessary skills to lead in the twenty-first century's sport industry (Chappelet & Bayle, 2005). It is imperative that individuals within these organisations familiarise themselves with performance management techniques and have the ability to adapt them to this unique sector.

It is clear that the modern NPSO's administration and daily operation requires increasingly specific industrial knowledge. To sustain the development of sport, managers and governors must be equipped with the necessary skills to lead these organisations into the future and a more professional approach must be adopted, particularly at executive and board levels. Managers and governors must familiarise themselves with the various management techniques required to perform well within the modern sporting environment, which often requires adaptation of existing techniques applied in traditional businesses practices. Sport has evolved to encompass a role in education, healthcare, economic development, the labour market and various social issues. The way in which these organisations are managed is therefore required to differ from traditional organisational management. The principles, methods and conditions that exist within NPSOs must be analysed before senior management decide on the best style and form of management that suits their organisation. Management must ultimately address two key issues when establishing principles and practices: the nature of the performance that the organisation seeks to achieve, and how this performance is going to be realised. These organisations are being confronted with an operating environment that has seen substantial change relating to competitiveness and professionalisation. As a result, there is a need for these organisations to progress from simply an administrative function to being held accountable through a performance-based approach.

The issue of performance for an NPSO contains many different layers. Performance for these organisations can be measured in economic terms (for example the growth of the organisation), in financial terms (how profitable the organisation has become) and also in social terms (by evaluating its impact on communities and the environment it serves). It is also clear from the literature that any evaluation of performance relating to NPSOs requires a multi-criteria approach (Bayle & Madella, 2002; Madella, Bayle & Tome, 2005). NPSOs often combine a mixed and paradoxical approach when it comes to the issue of evaluating performance. Chappelet and Bayle (2005) argue two main issues are most commonly analysed: public service logic, often applied in countries where a ministry of sport exits (such as the Republic of Ireland and New Zealand), and commercial logic (the organisation's business-like ethos).

In relation to public service logic, local, regional and state authorities are now playing a significant role in the way many NPSOs operate within their environment and are having an impact on the decision-making process of these entities. Although they are often a primary stakeholder as a result of providing crucial financial resources to these organisations, they also position themselves more and more as a partner and regulator within the sporting environment, depending upon various political pressures. NPSOs are forced to operate in an environment that is constantly becoming more professional and competitive because of pressure brought to bear by these entities and others, such as event organisers, sport consumers, sport manufacturers and the media.

Commercial logic in the context of an NPSO can be defined by several factors. First, the increase in the professionalism and intensity of financial issues at stake within elite sport, competitions and in the industry in general could lead to many NPSOs being taken over by privately run entities that have acknowledged its potential and are seeking to take advantage. Second, the way sport is now being consumed is having a major impact on many organisations (Hoye & Cuskelly, 2003). In countries where strong sporting infrastructure and culture have been developed, there exists a growing demand for the availability of sporting outlets, various forms of sport competitions, a growth in the number of newly adopted or emerging sports, and the appearance of alternative forms of practice that form the basis of a new sporting culture. An increasingly heterogeneous and uncertain internal situation is developing within the system of many NPSOs and within the sport movement in general. The non-profit status of these organisations adds to the complexity facing the modern NPSO. Their challenge is to establish a system that can meet the varying needs and expectations of their stakeholders, both commercial and public, while maintaining adequate service and value to their association.

The need for performance management in sport

The need for a performance-based approach within NPSOs can be illustrated through the economic and social value that sport carries and the high level of government subsidy these organisations receive. The Irish Sports Council's 2010 report estimates that in 2008 Irish households spent €1.8 billion on sport or sport-related products, which equates to 1.4 per cent of national GDP. The total government investment in Irish sport in 2008 was €618.3 million which provided a tax return of €922.7 million in government income from the sport sector – 1.5 times the investment. Furthermore, the Irish sport sector employs 38,000 individuals, which accounts for 2 per cent of the overall workforce. When a value is placed on the contribution of the 270,000 volunteers within the Irish sport sector, their monetary value is estimated to be between €322 and €582 million annually (Irish Sports Council, 2010, p. 15).

Similar reports on the economic and social value of sport have been conducted in New Zealand. Dalziel's 2011 report (commissioned by Sport NZ) is one such study. The report estimates that the contribution of the sport and recreation sector to the New Zealand economy in 2008–2009 was NZ$5.2 billion or 2.8 per cent of GDP. Dalziel (2011) illustrates the significance of this figure by comparing it to the contribution of the dairy sector which is seen as a "mainstay of the national economy" (p. 23). Furthermore, the report claims that the sector contributes NZ$1.3 billion in tax revenue for the New Zealand government. In 2008–2009 the New Zealand government spent NZ$483.1 million on the sport and recreation sector, and therefore the tax revenue is more than double the expenditure from central government. In addition, the report suggests that 750,000 individuals volunteered within the sport sector in 2007–2008, which equates to NZ$728 million in monetary terms.

Aside from the clear direct economic benefits that sport carries, there are also a number of wider socio-economic benefits associated with this unique industry. The Irish Sports Council (2012) states:

> Participation in sport brings many benefits in terms of health and wellbeing which in turn produces an economic dividend through reducing costs to the health service. Further, the immense contribution of sport in generating social capital, particularly through voluntarism, is a vital national resource which must be protected.

The Irish Sports Council's 2010 report identifies a number of these important socio-economic benefits associated with the sport industry. The report suggests that pressures placed on the country's healthcare system can be reduced through the direct physical benefits that are associated with participation and involvement in sport, including volunteerism (Irish Sports Council, 2010). It also suggests that productivity within the workforce has a positive correlation with regular participation in sport activity. An area that has received much scholarly attention (Putnam, 2000; Coalter, 2005; Delaney & Fahey, 2005) that is also addressed in this report is the positive impact that sport can have on social capital and cohesion within nations. Finally, it is suggested that investment in elite sport is associated with community benefits through provision of sporting infrastructure which (when used by the general public) contributes to increased academic performance, a reduction in crime and increased potential for facilitating further participation in sport (Irish Sports Council, 2010).

In a New Zealand context, similar studies have been conducted analysing the socio-economic benefits that sport carries and they have produced almost identical results to the Irish Sports Council's 2010 report. Dalziel (2011) concurs that regular participation in sport results in increased productivity in the workplace and possesses a number of associated health benefits. Dalziel goes as far as to place an economic value of the increased work productivity and associated benefits through involvement in sport, suggesting their economic contribution to be NZ$281 and NZ$3,947 million respectively, based on 2009 figures. However, the author also correctly points out that, in the same year, the associated costs of participation in sport in terms of accidental deaths and serious injuries equated to NZ$3,190 million, leaving a monetary surplus of NZ$1,038 million to the New Zealand economy.

Although there appear to be clear economic and social benefits associated with participation and investment in sport, it is also important to acknowledge a number of weaknesses that are present in the literature relating to this area of research. Referring to the conceptual weakness of such research, Coalter (2007) suggests studies relating to sport offer an extremely vague description of 'sport', the nature, extent and duration of participation, and the effect of sport on participants in relation to behavioural or social change. He argues that these issues, combined with a lack of precise evidence, give rise to a lack of validity and comparability. There is also a clear methodological weakness present in the literature surrounding this area of research in terms of a substantial lack of systematic and robust studies of a high degree of programmes. This can be attributed to the perceived "mythopoeic status" (Coalter, 2007, p. 1) of sport in assuming that all outcomes for sport are inherently positive (with exception of Dalziel, 2011), with little need for monitoring and evaluation of programmes and initiatives (performance management). From the existing literature relating to studies of sport participation and development, it is alarming to notice how much of this research concludes by outlining the many limitations of the selected methodology. As a result of this, issues of reliability are constantly being raised with appropriate causation.

The sufficient conditions necessary for individuals to receive the associated benefits of participation in sport is also absent in the literature. There is a clear lack of evidence outlining the various ways in which people participate and interact with sport, and no evidence of what type of sport produces a certain outcome for certain participants under certain circumstances. These middle-range mechanisms (Pawson, 2006) are a major criticism of the literature available. Finally, Coalter (2007) suggests that the criticisms of the sport participation and development literature pose many questions that remain unanswered about sport and its associated benefits. He claims the four major questions relating to a lack of evidence-based literature within this field are:

1   What is the nature of the evidence that participation in sport produces various intermediate impacts (e.g. self-efficacy, physical self-worth, self-esteem, self-confidence, aspects of social capital)?
2   Which sports, in what circumstances and through which mechanisms produce what impacts and for whom?

3　Even if sport interventions produce the desired intermediate impacts for some participants, in what circumstances do these contribute to the solution of wider social problems?

4　To what extent are sports programmes designed on the basis of an understanding of the nature and causes of the mostly complex problems to which they seek to offer a solution – lack of social cohesion, weak social capital, poor educational performance, anti-social behaviour and criminality, economic decline? (Coalter, 2007, p. 3)

Performance management in sport

Although there has been much research conducted analysing the performance of traditional (for-profit) organisations, the performance of non-profit organisations and in particular NPSOs is scarce. Of the few authors who have carried out studies in this field, the research has generally focused on the application of various models to determine performance dimensions (measurement) for NPSOs but has failed to address fundamental issues in a lack of performance management. Furthermore, all of these studies relate to a form of performance measurement which assesses an organisation's performance and none address the issue of performance management which is creating a sustainable management system/technique/tool for improved performance (O'Boyle & Hassan, 2014). For instance, Papadimitriou and Taylor (2000) apply a multiple-constituency approach to measuring Greek NPSOs' performances. The quantitative nature of this study provides an adequate overview of organisational performance within these organisations but does not describe or analyse core issues related to a lack of performance within these entities. Papadimitriou and Taylor's research does, however, point to the importance of a multi-dimensional approach to assessing an NPSO's performance which, given the emergent diverse range of performance pressures placed on these organisations, is an appropriate method of conducting such an analysis. The authors suggest that NPSOs should focus on the most important performance dimensions and "determine their relationship with the outputs of their organisations" (Papadimitriou and Taylor, 2000, p. 43). The study suggests that organisational performance can be determined by the level of satisfaction experienced by organisational stakeholders. Although there is a strong focus on stakeholders, the study fails to include a number of important stakeholder groups such as Greek NPSOs' relationships with the Greek Olympic Committee and international federations. Aside from this limitation, the suggestion that performance can be determined through the satisfaction of stakeholders is an interesting concept.

Papadimitriou and Taylor (2000) argue that in order to evaluate the indicators of an NPSO's performance it is essential to analyse the expectations of the organisation's various stakeholders. The authors suggest this is an integral part of the objective component of the performance measurement system. It may also unveil the imbalance between expectations of stakeholders and the actual results achieved by the organisation, allowing for better understanding of the organisation's dysfunctions (Spriggs, 1994). These expectations allow the organisation to identify the implicit or explicit criteria for performance that give rise to the mechanisms for evaluating performance itself. The stakeholders of an NPSO have variable interests and expectations depending upon the position of the organisation and their relationship with it. It may be necessary for an organisation to place particular importance on satisfying the needs of one or a limited number of stakeholders based on the level of financing or support they are receiving from those stakeholders (Papadimitriou & Taylor, 2000). Furthermore, as the organisation grows and the network of stakeholders is increased, meeting the expectations of all the various stakeholders presents a very complex issue for the management team.

Bayle and Madella (2002) do not apply the same logic to measuring performance as employed within Papadimitriou and Taylor's (2000) research. Their study argues that there are six major performance dimensions that French NPSOs must focus on (see Table 3.1).

Bayle and Madella (2002) use qualitative research methods to establish performance indicators for NPSOs that can aid in the construction of various performance profiles of organisations. In a complex study, the authors established a performance score according to the average of indicators utilised for each dimension. Statutory performance was divided into two main variables – elite performance and performance according to the number of licensed athletes – in order to study the correlations more accurately. The study found that the development of one area of performance can lead to the detriment of others and affect the overall performance of the organisation. For example, if a sporting entity has a substandard organisational and societal performance; this can explain issues of economic and financial performance degenerating over time.

The six performance profiles that the study establishes are as follows.

Powerful

This category of organisation typically achieves high scores on performance across all dimensions within the organisation. The authors argue that powerful organisations will often possess large financial resources and establish a priority to perform at a high and effective level. In their study, they suggest that some sport organisations are not in control of every performance aspect of their organisation. For instance, the cycling and athletic organisations in the study achieved promotional performance through competitive events that do not create any financial profit for the organisation and are often organised outside of their control.

Effective

Effective performance organisations are often effective on an elite performance level and operate at a satisfactory level of societal performance. A major problem area for these organisations is often promotional performance, and occasionally economic and financial performance.

Table 3.1 Bayle and Madella's (2002) performance dimensions

Type of performance	Strategies	Measurement
Statutory performance	• Obtaining the best sport result and developing the number of members.	• Sport results at high level and the number of licensed athletes.
Internal societal performance	• Improving the social climate and the involvement of all actors concerned.	• The degree of satisfaction of the actors.
Societal performance	• Contributing, by achieving their statutory objectives, towards a better functioning society.	• The societal legitimacy and the impact of the organisation's activities on society.
Economic and financial performance	• Obtaining the resources necessary to achieve the statutory objective and also managing their financial dependence.	• The capacity to obtain financial resources, diversification of resources and the capacity for self-financing.
Promotional performance	• Improving the media impact of the discipline among those practising the sport and the public.	• The organisation's reputation and image.
Organisational performance	• Organising, internally at headquarters and within the system, to respond to their statutory mission, the strategic plan and the requirements of the environment.	• The quality of functioning and the organisational reactivity.

Dilemmas

The size of this type of organisation can vary greatly and they are given the name 'dilemmas' due to the fact that they do not appear to make the best use of their media, economic and financial potential, or their base of practising athletes. These organisations also can be described as being involved in major structuring or restructuring or to have encountered a specific problem.

Atypical

These organisations can still operate at an effective level but have a clear gap in overall performance levels in comparison with other organisations. Boxing organisations, for example, have two major performance weaknesses: performance related to number of licensed athletes and societal performance. This group comprises organisations that exhibit various levels of overall performance.

Deficient

Organisations in this category are those that experience severe problems in relation to performance. They show low scores on all dimensions of performance across the entire organisation, and in particular societal performance. The finances of these organisations are often particularly precarious.

Problematic

These organisations are those that are in difficulty relating to performance in at least two specific areas. These areas are often economic and financial performance, as a result of restructuring or being in a phase of strategic reorganisation.

Bayle and Madella's (2002) study provides a number of descriptions for the performance of organisations, but the terminology used and the lack of identification of where these performance failings lie result in a confusing study that provides little insight into the actual management of organisational performance within NPSOs. Perhaps the major benefit of the methodology employed in their research is that the study allows for the comparison of performance between organisations, albeit only within French National Governing Bodies (NGBs). The major limitations of their study are that their approach to performance measurement is largely descriptive, limited to a specific time point and does not provide any evidence to identify a lack of organisational performance.

Madella, Bayle and Tome's (2005) study attempts to measure the performance of swimming NGBs in Spain, Portugal, Italy and Greece. Within their research, they take a broad perspective of performance, much like the perspective of performance taken within this book. The authors define performance in terms of resource dependency theory and state that it is "the ability to acquire and process human, financial and physical resources to achieve the goals of the organisation" (Madella, Bayle & Tome, 2005, p. 207). Their study defines performance within an NGB as compromising five different dimensions: human resources, finance, institutional communication, partnership and inter-organisational relations, volume and quality services, and athletes' international performances.

Madella *et al.* (2005) use numerical indicators of various performance issues to attempt to create an image of organisational performance which cannot uncover the true factors behind performance successes or failures. In order to address this use, they also employ a case study methodology to qualitatively analyse and compare areas of performance within these organisations, which is deemed to be a more effective approach in terms of uncovering key performance dimensions.

A "key problem for NGBs" raised within the study is described as "the relationship between professionals and volunteers and its impact on organisational performance" (Madella *et al.*, 2005, p. 217). Further important points that the study alludes to but does not discuss in major detail include the commercial ethos of the organisations and the issue of centralisation of the NGBs and how this may impact upon overall performance within the entities. The centralisation of NGBs is becoming a major issue for many organisations, such as the Gaelic Athletic Association (GAA) within Irish sport and the New Zealand Rugby Union (NZRU) within New Zealand, particularly in terms of the much-documented underperformance of regional bodies within the latter organisation. Madella *ct al.*'s (2005) study states that "it is not clear how much decentralised allocation of funding contributes to the overall effectiveness or efficiency of the organisations or it is rather a source of additional and non-productive spending" (p. 217).

Bayle and Robinson's (2007) study is perhaps the first to provide a "holistic" (p. 250) view of organisational performance within sport, as opposed to previous studies which simply conducted a measurement of organisational performance through the identification of various performance dimensions. Their study employs a survey and qualitative, semi-structured interviews to uncover management practices or tools used by NGBs within French sport. The authors divide the survey into four main components: strategy (the environmental context of the organisations and long-term planning), governance (the professional ethos of the organisation and the roles and calibre of the board), stakeholder relationships (strategic partnerships with public and private entities), and control and evaluation (processes or individuals responsible for managing and evaluating performance). One of the major benefits of Bayle and Robinson's study is that the authors apply two different types of perspectives to organisational performance: performance at the strategic level and performance at the operational level. However, one of the major omissions within this approach is that the study does not assign weight to either of these performance perspectives. It is clear that operational performance cannot be at a high level if performance at the strategic level is not at similar levels, therefore the study should refer to the importance of establishing a high level of performance being driven from the strategic (board) level downwards. In relation to the organisation's performance at strategic level, Bayle and Robinson (2007) suggest that there are three principles that performance depends upon: the system of governance, the quality of the organisation's network (affiliations, supporting bodies), and the positioning of the organisation within its particular sport. The study refers to these principles as the 'Strategic Performance Mix'.

At the operational level, Bayle and Robinson's (2007) study suggests there are three further performance issues that facilitate overall organisational performance:

1   Forms and levels of professionalisation – this refers to the delegation of responsibility which must be supported by a suitable organisational structure, accountability, and reporting mechanisms between paid and unpaid staff and board members and senior management.
2   The presence of a participatory organisational culture – refers to the ability of the organisation to have all stakeholders (mainly the board, professional staff and volunteers) contributing to a system of participatory management in order to share accountability for its performance.
3   Adopting a partnership approach – the study correctly states that organisations must form vertical and horizontal relationships with entities such as clubs and leagues, other NGBs, and ministries or agencies of sport.

In a more recent study, Winand, Zintz, Bayle and Robinson (2010) identify five main dimensions of performance: sport, customer, communication and image, finance, and organisation. These performance dimensions are analysed through adopting a quantitative approach which gives an adequate overview of performance. The study also includes finance and participation (sport) as two out of the five main performance dimensions.

Winand *et al.*'s (2010) study uses the same methodology as Madella *et al.* (2005), who propose seven basic steps for the development of a measurement system. Although measurement of performance is important, it does not necessarily show where specific failings of performance occur or how these failings can be better managed. An important aspect of the research methodology employed by Winand *et al.* (2010) is the comparison between the results of their quantitative research and the strategic goals and priorities of the selected organisations. This is an approach that is also utilised within this book as it is widely accepted that the performance of any organisation must be driven by and compliment the specific objectives as identified within that organisation's strategic plan.

In conducting an analysis of strategic and operational goals, Winand *et al.* (2010) suggest that, in general, the performance dimensions in their study are relatively independent of each other, in direct contrast with Bayle and Madella's (2002) study. However, Winand *et al.* (2010) do suggest that some relationships were able to be identified within their performance dimensions, most notably – and of significant importance to this book – a positive correlation between their financial dimension and sport for all (participation). This point is further

elaborated upon by the authors when claiming that not all organisations that performed well in the financial dimension did so in terms of their strategic
objectives. This would clearly suggest an absence of a performance management
approach or a clear failing of some performance dimensions. The authors
acknowledge this limitation and suggest that future research focus on "qualitative judgements ... in order to assess organisational performance" (Winand *et
al.*, 2010, p. 305). Although Winand *et al.*'s (2010) study allows for some insight
into organisational performance and may benefit the board in relation to forming
strategic imperatives, their model does not provide analysis of fundamental
issues behind a lack of performance, being congruent with the majority of
previous studies within this field (see Table 3.2).

Performance management and sports policy

As many NPSOs rely heavily – or in a number of cases solely – on public funds,
government policy in relation to sport can have a large impact of the functioning
of these organisations. Due to government intervention, many NPSOs are
required to implement certain strategies and initiatives in order to satisfy the
demands of the public funding authorities. Increasingly, governments are beginning to take more notice of the power of sport and have become aware of the
impact sport has in terms of both economic and social perspectives (Bergsgard,
Houlihan, Mangset, Nodland & Rommetveldt, 2007; Irish Sports Council, 2010;
Dalziel, 2011). The culture that surrounds sport in many nations is very significant, as evidenced by the media attention that national team sports receive and
the support for the construction of major sporting infrastructural developments
within many countries. Governments also perceive sport to be a major political
asset in delivering non-sporting objectives, such as conveying political power,
addressing social exclusion, promoting health initiatives, sparking economic
development and aiding with urban regeneration (Green & Houlihan, 2005). For
instance, the economic and social value of sport has been well documented in a
number of research studies (Delaney & Fahey, 2005; Irish Sports Council, 2010;
Dalziel, 2011). Therefore it is clear sport is used by governments to achieve a
variety of objectives, including those outside the realm of direct sport policy that
is concentrated on instrumental components of sport, such as achieving better
results in international competition and developing the base of active participants within a country.

Much debate surrounds issues of sport policy and sport development, including attempts to increase participation levels in sport (Coalter, 2007; Houlihan &
White, 2002; Hylton & Bramham, 2008). It is clear, however, that governments
implement policy relating to sport not only in order to regulate and guide sport
within their nation but also to use sport as a catalyst to achieve other non-sport-
related goals. Houlihan (2005) notes that "sport is a focus for a growing volume
of state regulatory activity" (p. 164) and "the increasingly prominent role of the
state as variously promoter, regulator, resource provider, manipulator and
exploiter of sport is beyond challenge" (p. 182). All policy decisions that are

Table 3.2 Extant literature: performance management in NPSOs

Author(s)	Design	Sample	Major results and findings
Papadimitriou and Taylor (2000)	Quantitative	20 Greek National Sport Organisations (NSOs)	• Provides five dimensions of performance: stability of the board and key strategic partnerships; athlete development; internal processes; strategic planning; use of emerging sport science.
Bayle and Madella (2002)	Quantitative and qualitative	40 French NSOs	• Provides six dimensions of performance: institutional; social internal; social external; finance; publicity; organisational.
Madella, Bayle and Tome (2005)	Quantitative and qualitative	National swimming federations in Portugal, Greece, Spain and Italy	• Provides five dimensions of performance: human resources; finance, institutional communication; partnership and inter-organisational relations; volume and quality of services; athletes' international performances.
Bayle and Robinson (2007)	Quantitative and qualitative	11 French NSOs	• Provides five dimensions of performance: system of governance; position in industry; quality of the operating network; facilitators; inhibitors.
Winand, Zintz, Bayle and Robinson (2010)	Quantitative	27 Olympic sport governing bodies in Belgium	• Provides five dimensions of performance: sport; customer; communication and image; finance; organisation.
Winand, Rihoux, Qualizza and Zintz (2011)	Qualitative	18 NSOs in Belgium	• Discusses performance from three perspectives: focusing on elite sport; developing innovative activities; the use of a broad range of volunteer expertise.

made at the governmental level can have a profound impact on NPSOs at almost every level which can ultimately affect their overall strategic objectives and performance, especially when these organisations are regulated by the state, as in countries like Ireland and New Zealand (see Table 3.3).

Houlihan (2005) supports the argument that not enough focus has been allocated to the area of sports policy by claiming that "it remains on the margins" (p. 163), while other policy areas are often intensely scrutinised to ensure best practice and results. The reasons for this issue are typically unclear as governments are often quoted as claiming that sport is an integral area of policy within any country. Houlihan (2005) also states that although "few governments in the 1960s gave any explicit budgetary or ministerial recognition to sport, by the mid-1990s sport was an established feature in the machinery of governments in most economically developed countries" (p. 163). As a result of this evolution, academic and government interest in the area of sport policy has increased dramatically, as governments are beginning to understand the power that sport can exert and its relationship with economic and other social issues within a nation.

The literature firmly supports the synopsis that sports policy in western nations has evolved to encapsulate two main aims. The first is to enhance elite sport within the country and the second to increase participation numbers in sport across the entire sporting spectrum (Bergsgard *et al.*, 2007; Green & Houlihan, 2005; Stewart, Nicholson, Smith & Westerbeek, 2004). However, two important 'sub-areas' of sports policy are also at the fore of international scrutiny: (1) 'Fair play' in sport in relation to the use of performance enhancing substances; and (2) the development of an adequate community sport system. The issue of performance management within NPSOs is of particular importance to the latter as the need for increased "capacity of the community sport system ... has generally been conceptualized as management improvement in the sport

Table 3.3 Governmental sports policy (Houlihan, Nicholson & Hoye, 2010)

Sport policy foci	• Elite sport development • Anti-doping or drug control • Increasing mass participation • Increasing the capacity of the community sport system
Regulatory intersections	• Organisational practices adopted by sport • Sport activity • Protecting members of sport organisations • Wagering and sports betting • Sport broadcasting • Physical education policy
Wider policy areas	• Using sport to address poor physical activity levels and ameliorate community health issues • Using sport for urban regeneration and economic development • Using sport to improve social inclusion and facilitate community development

sector, and has primarily focused on national sport organisations and clubs" (Houlihan *et al.*, 2010, p. 4). Elite sport is often criticised for issues surrounding the use of performance-enhancing drugs that can attract more media attention than actual results and 'on-field' performance. In relation to management improvement for NPSOs, many governments have encouraged the adoption of new initiatives to protect their investment. Processes and systems such as performance management became popular in the for-profit sector in the 1980s and early 1990s. Given the calls for a more professional ethos to be adopted within the NPSO sector, it is necessary that these organisations also adopt traditional management practices, such as performance management. This new approach to the management of NPSOs illustrates "the largely instrumental paradigm evident in government priorities and the subservience of other policy concerns to elite performance, rationality and professionalization" (Houlihan *et al.*, 2010, p. 4).

State sport agencies invest heavily in NGBs and other types of NPSOs. This investment comes directly from government who make this funding available but not without a cost. The impact that goes along with receiving such funding from a state sport agency has been well documented (Green & Houlihan, 2005). "Once an organisation has adjusted to high public subsidy, the extent of resource dependence can leave little option but to follow the shifts in government priorities" (Green & Houlihan, 2005, p. 179). As a consequence of receiving state support, NGBs can be subject to a number of requirements and must meet minimum criteria.

4 Individual performance management

Introduction

This chapter provides an in-depth analysis of theory and practice in relation to individual performance management processes. It is widely accepted that the performance of individuals within an organisation has a direct impact upon overall organisational results. In addition, NPSOs in particular are heavily reliant on the support and willingness of volunteers to deliver various operational and strategic targets, which makes this area of research evermore imperative for these unique entities. This chapter examines traditional and contemporary forms of individual performance management, upon which it is argued that the more contemporary process of '360-degree feedback' is the most appropriate to be used within the NPSO sector.

The role of the individual

All organisations, including NPSOs, consist of individuals brought together in order to assist in the achievement of certain strategic objectives. The combined performances of individuals working together will have a major impact on the capability of any organisation in achieving its strategic objectives (Van Emmerik, 2008). The role of management is to get individuals working together, to ensure that all employees' roles and responsibilities are aligned with overarching strategy, and that individuals are aware of how their performance impacts upon this. If employees are moving in opposite directions, it will ultimately have a detrimental impact upon the organisation achieving its objectives.

As the individual employee contributes to improving the performance of the organisation, it is essential that an individual performance management system is in place that helps them understand their role in achieving strategic objectives. McCarthy and Garavan (2001) suggest employees must receive constant support and feedback on their own performance, and have opportunities to gain more expertise in their roles through defined learning and development programmes. They add that performance management can only be successful if each section manager truly understands how to motivate and provide adequate learning and development resources to their employees, so that each individual or section can be sufficiently measured by the success of their direct reports, not simply by business results. The setting that surrounds behaviour – for example what people say and do that is praised or criticised over time – can also help in supporting patterns of success. The level of success an organisation experiences in applying the elements of performance management originates in the capability of its staff in serving stakeholder needs, meeting objectives and creating a culture where the focus is aimed at building long-lasting habits of success (McCarthy & Garavan, 2001).

As described in the previous chapter, monitoring overall organisational performance allows for the effective delivery of operational and strategic goals. Previous research has confirmed a distinct correlation between applying performance management models or systems and enhanced organisational results (Kennerly & Neely, 2003; Senior & Swailes, 2004; McNamara & Mong, 2005). Employee involvement is a critical component of any successful performance management system. The individual employee must play a prominent role in the design phase of any performance management system, as they are most aware of what measures must be taken in order to ensure the alignment of the system with the organisation's strategic goals (Greasley, Bryman, Dainty, Price, Soetanto, & King, 2005; De Jong & Den Hartog, 2007). Greasley *et al.* (2005) add that empowerment of individuals should apply to senior management and individual departments but also be extended to all employees within an organisation. Each individual or team must contribute and in return 'own' the performance management system themselves.

If an NPSO can employ a suitable performance management process, it can help the organisation to get the best out of every department and employee under its control. Weldy (2009) argues this is done by setting out clear steps on how to improve performance that are based on the principles of individual learning. He claims that the philosophy that is fundamental to individual performance management is derived from the science of 'behaviour analyses' commonly referred to as 'the psychology of learning'. Van Dyk and Conradie (2007) suggest learning relates to collecting and analysing information and then assessing this information to bring about a positive change, and that learning from one's own activity and from others are equally important. For the learning process to be successful, a willingness to be challenged over actions and achievements must be established within the workforce. For individuals to fully take part in the learning process they must understand why there is a need to do so. Management must convey that learning can drive improvement and performance within the organisation and also impact upon the development of the individual, resulting in organisational success along with opportunities for promotion (Van Dyk & Conradie, 2007).

Within the literature, performance management is often associated with the processes and structures of human resource management (HRM), for example issues surrounding compensation, appraisal, selection, recruitment and retention (DeNisi & Pritchard, 2006). Although these are significant fundamentals of an effectively designed workplace, they are systems, processes and procedures that disregard the knowledge of individual behaviours. They frequently stem or ignore the ways in which motivational issues can be established in the workplace to produce increased performance for the correct objectives, processed in the correct way and for appropriate reasons (Douglas & Morris, 2006).

Van Emmerik (2008) believes a critical component of successful performance management implementation is that performers gain excellence in their own performance and contribution. This is achieved by developing strong high-performance habits that can be applied across similar or different areas for effective problem solving and work habits. Regardless of the task, the goal at the individual level is to produce work that is of a high standard and to establish a real sense of pride in the work that they do (Chauvel & Despres, 2002). An integral component of adopting performance management practices within an NPSO is to ensure that these methods are successful in motivating the individual employee within a number of realms, including improving employee engagement, as they are required to see how their contribution directly affects the organisation's high-level goals (McBain, 2007). Furthermore, it is imperative that each individual's job description is intrinsically linked to strategic objectives in order to facilitate this situation. It is clear that organisational performance is directly associated with performances at the individual level and therefore must be managed effectively. As a consequence, it is necessary to examine how organisations manage individual performances and to establish a 'best practice' approach around this issue which can be adopted by the NPSO sector.

The performance appraisal

There is a clear gap in the literature concerning the assessment and evaluation of individual employee performances' within NPSOs. In traditional business organisations the performance appraisal has been widely used as a method of evaluating employee performance, setting goals for future performances and identifying areas of professional development required by the individual (DeNisi & Pritchard, 2006; Manasa & Reddy, 2009). Typically, a formal appraisal process will be conducted for an employee minimally twice per year. DeNisi and Pritchard (2006, p. 255) state:

> The goal of the performance management process is performance improvement, initially at the level of the individual employee, and ultimately at the level of the organisation. The ultimate goal of performance appraisal should be to provide information that will best enable managers to improve employee performance. Thus, ideally, the performance appraisal provides information to help managers manage in such a way that employee [and organisational] performance improves.

Many traditional business organisations also use the performance appraisal as a means of assessing an employee's eligibility for performance-based pay as well as possible promotion opportunities (Cleveland, Murphy & Williams, 1989; Landy & Farr, 1980). Manasa and Reddy (2009) suggest that the goal of any performance management system is to ensure alignment and effective management of all organisational resources in order to facilitate optimal performance. They add that the manner in which performance is managed within organisations is a key indicator of its overall success or failure. As the individual is clearly an integral resource impacting upon organisational performance, it is essential that performance appraisal processes are adequate and create value within the broader performance management system (Muczyk & Gable, 1987). There are a number of benefits associated with the effective use of performance appraisals, most notably improved communication between management and employees. Conversely, challenges such as employee dissatisfaction with the process and potential legal issues, if implemented incorrectly, have also been highlighted more recently within the literature (Schraeder, Becton & Portis, 2007; Manasa & Reddy, 2009). An additional challenge in relation to the performance appraisal process is that a system which is deemed to be effective within one country or culture may not be as appropriate in another. Given the globalisation and multinational operations associated with many modern organisations (both sport and non-sport), this has also been noted as a challenge associated with performance appraisals (Hofstede, 2001). Furthermore, although academic research relating to performance appraisals is well established, DeNisi and Pritchard (2006) argue that there is often disconnect between this research and actual practice. They suggest that "one possible explanation is that academic research has provided answers, but that practitioners are simply not aware of the relevant research findings" (p. 254). This situation has been noted as a problematic area within management research in general (Rynes, Brown & Colbert, 2002), and it can be assumed that it is affecting the area of performance appraisals as well.

The frequency that performance appraisals should be conducted is a source of constant debate within both research and practice. Many organisations simply conduct performance appraisals on an annual basis. However, Schraeder *et al.* (2007) argue that conducting performance appraisals on a more regular basis (quarterly) can yield positive outcomes both for the employee and their employer. Furthermore, Sudarsan (2009) suggests that more frequent appraisals result in reducing the extent of unexpected or surprising feedback on the part of the employee, occasionally typical of year-end reviews. A logical argument to the frequency of performance appraisals would suggest that the nature and role of the employee's position is a determining factor in this decision. For instance, annual performance appraisals may be suitable for employees who are involved in the manufacturing industry and whose main objective may be performance maintenance. For employees in other industries, such as those within NPSOs, this book argues that six-monthly performance appraisals are more appropriate due to the various objectives and timeframes in which they must achieve or make progress towards particular goals.

Benefits of performance appraisals

NPSOs could experience various benefits as a direct result of implementing effective performance appraisal processes. The general consensus in the literature is that performance appraisals are an important mechanism involved in performance management within all types of organisations, and have the potential to increase an organisation's effectiveness (Pettijohn, Parker, Pettijohn & Kent, 2001; Spinks, Wells & Meche, 1999). At a fundamental level, if performance appraisals are conducted within organisations then individuals will receive feedback on their performance and have the opportunity to become even more productive based upon that constructive feedback (Schraeder *et al.*, 2007). However, there are also a number of other benefits that are associated with the implementation of this management initiative:

1   Improved communication – the issue of poor communication has been identified as one of the major concerns within the management literature (examples include Schraeder *et al.*, 2007; Spinks *et al.*, 1999). As performance appraisals involve direct discussion, feedback and an opportunity to comment on issues with management, they contribute positively to eradicating employees' concerns, often relating to uncertainty. Furthermore, Schraeder *et al.* (2007) claim that feedback from management relating to individual employee performance is of crucial importance in guiding individual performances.

2   The establishment of trust between employees and their managers – developing mutual trust between employees and management has been noted as being an important factor in assisting individual performance within an organisation (Kanfer & Ackerman, 1989). Schraeder *et al.* (2007) add that distrust between employees and management can negatively impact upon performance and result in a lack of engagement on the part of the employee against organisational objectives. Mayer and Gavin's (2005) article discussing the issue of 'trust' within organisations claims that effective performance appraisals can contribute to increased trust within the organisation and therefore impact positively upon individual performance.

3   Linking individual performance to strategy – best practice in terms of organisational management, supported by literature (Schraeder *et al.*, 2007), suggests that individual employee roles and responsibilities should be intrinsically linked to overall organisational objectives. This allows both the individual and management to see exactly how the employee contributes to the organisation and how their performance can directly impact upon strategic imperatives. Performance appraisals create an ideal situation for both employees and management to discuss individual roles and responsibilities, set specific future performance criteria, and provide opportunities to establish 'line of sight' between individual performance and organisational goals.

4   Identification of training and professional development needs – as individual performance is clearly a central factor in determining organisational

performance, it is important that employees are given access to training and professional development opportunities in order to better serve the organisation. In order for the performance appraisal process to be complete, the individual must be presented with opportunities to address areas of required development that are identified within the appraisal itself. In addition, using performance appraisals to identify the development needs of new employees in particular has been shown to be most effective (Broady-Preston & Steel 2002).

5   Finally, the performance appraisal process is an instrumental tool in facilitating performance improvement, which is the ultimate goal of any performance management practice either at individual or organisational level. In support of this, Schraeder *et al.* (2007) claim there is a general consensus in the literature that effective human resource practices such as performance appraisals are positively related to individual and organisational performance improvement.

Challenges of performance appraisals

Although, as argued above, there are clear positive implications for organisations that are successful in implementing an effective performance appraisal system; the practice is also fraught with a number of challenges which must be acknowledged in order to ensure the process is not to prove ultimately counterproductive. For instance, in terms of linking strategy to individual employee performances, it has been noted that this can be a difficult task to undertake, particularly in large organisations with a high volume of employees (Twomey & Harris, 2000). Within NPSOs this issue may not be as prevalent as the number of employees within these organisations is generally less than those within their traditional business counterparts. Ultimately, problematic issues relating to performance appraisals arise as a result of two main factors: the performance appraisal process is not being implemented correctly, or the process is not suitable to the manner in which the organisation operates (Schraeder *et al.*, 2007). The challenges that arise from these issues are:

1   Advocates (both practitioners and academics) of Total Quality Management (TQM) claim that performance appraisals are unnecessary in most organisations and that TQM will ensure a high level of performance within all aspects of the organisation (Soltani, 2005). However, it is difficult to justify this argument in terms of NPSOs as TQM has mainly been applied within the manufacturing industry, which NPSOs are evidently not part of.
2   It has been noted that individual employees often have negative perceptions about the performance appraisal process. The evaluation and critique of an individual's performance can cause stress and discomfort (Spinks *et al.*, 1999) which may ultimately lead to a short- or long-term drop in performance. In addition, the anticipation of a performance appraisal meeting may cause tension between supervisors and subordinates.

3　The rating system used to evaluate employee performance must be appropriate and applied to all employees of a similar level within the organisation. The appraiser must be completely subjective in assessing the individual's performance, otherwise the performance appraisal process will serve little benefit to the organisation (Schraeder *et al.*, 2007). Furthermore, the appraiser must not provide skewed results to management and the employee about performance in order to please employees and avoid conflict.

4　If the performance appraisal process is not conducted appropriately and professionally, the organisation may be subject to legal issues that could arise as a result. Although not originally designed for this purpose, many organisations use the performance appraisal process as a tool to help in promotion decisions and disciplinarily actions (Spinks *et al.*, 1999). Therefore, if the process is implemented incorrectly, the organisation may be left open to legal action.

5　For organisations (such as the New Zealand Rugby Union, NZRU) that use a performance-based pay scheme, the performance appraisal is a significant factor in determining how much of the bonus an employee is entitled to claim. This further illustrates why the process must be implemented appropriately, as if it is not the benefits of other initiatives such as performance-based pay become completely undermined.

In addition to the various challenges set out above, research has suggested that individuals within organisations who operate a performance appraisal system are often not satisfied with the process (Sudarsan, 2009). This dissatisfaction generally relates to three major areas within the appraisal process: the subjectivity of the appraiser; the level of feedback supplied; and the frequency of the reviews undertaken, with employees suggesting (supporting this study's argument) that more regular reviews would prove beneficial (Sudarsan, 2009).

Although a central factor in assessing individual employee performance, traditional performance appraisals (a 'single rater' with a single person assessing performance) have become synonymous with a number of defects even when implemented correctly within organisations. A major theme within the literature relates to the negative associations around the performance appraisal interview, with both the employee and interviewee viewing this process as a stressful event and a chore that must be carried out to satisfy senior management. Furthermore, Folger and Cropanzano (1998) claim that managers are not good at supplying and dealing with negative feedback in relation to the performance appraisal interview and, as a consequence, the results of the appraisal interview can often be inflated. If this is indeed the case, as Folger and Cropanzano would suggest, then any performance management system operating at the individual level will be flawed and will ultimately create a negative impact upon organisation-wide performance. Additionally, as a result of inflated appraisals from their line manager, employees' expectations of pay and promotion may not be congruent with their actual performance and position within the organisation. Finally, a major area of concern in relation to the performance appraisal of managers/department heads, as outlined by Lepsinger and Lucia (1997), is that these individuals' performances may be judged on the efficiency/productivity of their department as opposed to their leadership skills and other behaviours that actually constitute individual performance. Due to these difficulties associated with the traditional performance appraisal process, it is clear that a new method is required to ensure individual performances are being managed and assessed accurately and appropriately. In response to this growing concern over the potential defects within the performance appraisal process, some organisations have successfully redeveloped the process to eliminate issues of appraiser bias and provide robust feedback to the individual (and the organisation) on various aspects of job performance. This process has been labelled '360-degree feedback'.

360-degree feedback

360-degree feedback is a performance appraisal process that takes the opinions and feedback of various groups and individuals into account when determining the overall performance of an individual employee. This can be contrasted with more traditional performance appraisal approaches which simply rely on a line manager's discretion in determining employee performance. In organisations that employ a vast number of individuals, this process has typically been utilised for managerial positions only due to the complexities involved in carrying out the process. However, smaller organisations have used this process for all their employees and, given the generally small staff numbers in NPSOs, it is argued that 360-degree feedback could well be conducted for all individuals within such organisations. Furthermore, a unique aspect of the 360-degree process is that the employee also carries out a self-assessment of their performance which can be compared and contrasted to the views of the other "raters" (McCarthy & Garavan, 2001) involved in the process. McCarthy and Garavan claim that a structured evaluation report is sought from various internal and external stakeholders of the organisation who can comment on the performance of the individual being appraised. The same structured evaluation is also sent to the employee for the purposes of self-evaluation. Lepsinger and Lucia (1997) suggest that the process involves a collection of perceptions about the individual in terms of their performance from a number of suitable 'rating' sources. They go on to claim that the purpose of the 360-degree feedback process is to show management and the individual concerned exactly how their behaviour (performance) impacts upon other organisational members and the organisation's objectives.

360-degree feedback has been seen under a number of different guises both within the academic literature and in practice. All of the terms refer to a number of individuals or groups contributing to the feedback and appraisal of the individual employee. They include: stakeholder feedback, group performance appraisal, full-circle assessment, and multi-rater feedback. For the purposes of this book, 360-degree feedback is defined as an appraisal process involving a number of different sources as opposed to traditional performance appraisals undertaken by a sole line manager. Figure 4.1 shows the various potential raters

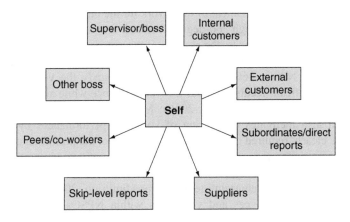

Figure 4.1 Potential raters in 360-degree feedback (adapted from McCarthy & Garavan, 2001).

within a 360-degree feedback performance assessment. Although external groups and individuals add greater depth to the appraisal process, the most common raters within the 360-degree feedback process are the line manager, subordinates, peers and self (i.e. the individual concerned).

Volunteers and 360-degree feedback

It is well known that volunteers play a major role in assisting NPSOs achieve various strategic objectives, and in some instances an NPSO may even have no paid employees whatsoever. Although research has been conducted relating to the recruitment, management and retention of volunteers (Cuskelly, Hoye & Auld, 2006; Cuskelly *et al.*, 2006), literature relating to the assessment or evaluation of volunteer performance is rare, and documented instances of this process taking place in practice are equally scarce. It can be assumed that the assessment of volunteers' performance rarely occurs due to the difficulties in assessing an individual's performance when s/he does not receive any direct financial gain through their work for the organisation. Doherty (1998) suggests that as NPSOs rely so heavily on volunteers it can also be assumed they do not wish to discourage volunteers from involvement in any way through the negative connotations associated with formal traditional performance appraisal processes. However, when motivations for volunteer involvement in sport are explored, it becomes apparent that individuals volunteer to learn new skills, 'give something back' and to help develop the sport, amongst other motivations (Sport NZ, 2006a). In addition, in order to facilitate the learning of new skills and contribute to the development of the sport, the Sport NZ (2006a) report also suggests that feedback and better communication were sought by volunteers to improve their volunteer experience. Therefore, based on volunteer motivations and expectations, it appears that NPSOs are making the mistake of assuming volunteers do not wish to receive feedback or assessment of their work for the organisation.

As documented above, although 360-degree feedback is an appropriate means of assessing individual performance, the essence of the process lies in the development and performance improvement of the individual concerned. If applied to volunteers within an NPSO, 360-degree feedback can satisfy the volunteers' desire to receive significant feedback about their performance while also identifying areas for development (Sport NZ, 2006a; McCarthy & Garavan, 2001). Subsequently, it also facilitates monitoring of volunteer performances by the NPSO, which is clearly required given the significant impact the performance of volunteers has on a wide range of NPSO strategic and operational imperatives. Finally, a 360-degree feedback approach applied to volunteers within an NPSO may contribute to easing the emerging tension (Papadimitriou, 2002) that may develop between paid employees and volunteers within NPSOs. A common assessment practice consisting of anonymous feedback may help to illuminate some of the causes of this tension and contribute to a more harmonious working relationship between these two groups of individuals.

360-degree feedback vs. traditional performance appraisal

When employing a 360-degree feedback approach, the multi-rater feedback approach proves useful as it is anonymous and therefore succeeds in removing the potential for over-inflated results associated with providing negative feedback to the employee, unlike the traditional approach. In addition, the stress/confrontational aspects of the appraisal are removed as line managers are not required to carry out an in-depth interview with the employee. A further barrier to conducting effective appraisals, as noted by Longenecker (1997), is the lack of information available to the appraiser to adequately assess the true performance of the employee. As 360-degree feedback provides opinion from a number of different sources, greater information and a more complete view of the employee's true performance can be presented. It is important to note that identification of training and development needs is still possible and perhaps more effective within 360-degree feedback, as this has been identified as one of the core necessities within any individual performance management system (DeNisi & Pritchard, 2006; Van Emmerik, 2008).

There are a number of significant differences between a traditional performance appraisal approach (single rater) and a more-modern 360-degree feedback approach (multi-rater). Traditional approaches are largely focused on providing an evaluation of the employee's performance and are generally linked with pay and promotion prospects (London & Beatty, 1993). Although this is not necessarily a detrimental technique, performance improvement and development are often understated and there is a large focus on past performance as opposed to creating a context for improved future employee performance. In contrast, and in line with 'forward looking' principles of performance management, 360-degree feedback places more emphasis on employee improvement and development by supplying the individual with robust feedback in relation to their behaviours and actions within the workplace. It is clear that the most obvious difference between the two approaches lies in multi-rater feedback as opposed to a single-rater appraisal, and as such 360-degree feedback takes the complexities of working in a modern organisation into account. Furthermore, the various individuals and groups that the employee interacts with are clearly a more appropriate source of feedback rather than a sole line manager who the individual may not necessarily interact with on a regular basis (McCarthy & Garavan, 2001).

Table 4.1 summarises the differences between 360-degree feedback and traditional performance appraisals.

Benefits of 360-degree feedback

360-degree feedback essentially encompasses all of the same benefits as traditional performance appraisals but also adds a number of 'unique' benefits. The reliance on one individual to assess an employee's performance, as in traditional appraisals, is widely considered to be a flawed process and the multi-rater feedback of the 360-degree approach is now being regarded as best practice within the traditional business environment (Maylett, 2009). Colleagues and peers of the individual, along with the line manager, have the ability to provide a more comprehensive overview of the employee's performance as opposed to single-rater feedback. This type of appraisal is especially relevant within NPSOs where the roles and responsibilities of individuals can vary greatly and the line manager may not have the opportunity to observe all areas of the individual's performance (Maylett, 2009). In addition to the above, there are a number of associated benefits with the successful implementation of a 360-degree feedback approach:

1   The process can address a number of performance dimensions that may not have previously been addressed under traditional performance appraisals or that have been neglected by the organisation. Furthermore, by collecting feedback from a number of raters, sources of conflict may be uncovered or resolved, in turn leading to a more effective workforce. Also, through seeking feedback from a number of sources, management are demonstrating to staff that they value their opinions within the organisation (London & Beatty, 1993).
2   Garavan, Morley and Flynn (1997) suggest that 360-degree feedback facilitates increased employee involvement within the organisation and improved workforce relationships. In terms of benefits for the individual, Garavan *et al.* (1997) claim the feedback from the appraisal process is more valid as it is generated from multiple sources. The authors go on to suggest that this feedback helps the individual become more "self-aware" (p. 141) which is an important step in terms of learning and development.
3   The anonymity aspect of 360-degree feedback allows co-workers to praise or criticise individuals without fear of repercussions or confrontation. This also has benefits for the individual as it illuminates their weaknesses within

Table 4.1 Traditional performance appraisals vs. 360-degree feedback

Criteria	Traditional performance appraisals	360-degree feedback
Why?	• To provide an evaluation on past performances from a single source.	• To provide an evaluation and feedback on behaviour and development needs from multiple sources.
Raters	• Line manager.	• Peers, subordinates, self, line manager, external individuals and groups.
Feedback	• The line manager cannot have anonymity.	• The multiple sources of feedback are able to remain anonymous.
Assessment	• Both quantitative and qualitative methods are employed.	• Generally only quantitative methods are employed.
Outcomes	• Salary, promotion, transfer, demotion, training and development.	• A strong focus on training and development in order to improve future performance. Can also be linked to compensation.
Frequency	• Annual event.	• Continuous, not limited to specific timeframes.
Applicability	• All employees.	• All employees (unless staff numbers too vast).

the workforce and gives them an opportunity to identify specific areas for performance improvement.

4 Through engaging with external entities during the feedback process, individuals must place a large emphasis on providing a good customer service. If the individuals or indeed the organisation is not providing a high-quality service to its customers, this will become apparent through the feedback process from external involvement.

5 Finally, Hoffman (1995) argues that, where there is no set standard of performance within an organisation in relation to certain tasks or activities, feedback from multiple sources can help create such a standard through conveying expectations of different facets and dimensions within the organisation.

Challenges of 360-degree feedback

Although there are clear benefits, as detailed above, to the implementation of a 360-degree feedback approach, as with almost all management initiatives there are also a number of limitations and challenges. Traditionally, organisations – and NPSOs in particular – are not good at providing feedback either in top-down (performance appraisal) or bottom-up (360-degree) systems. It may take a number of attempts at implementing a successful approach where raters are comfortable with providing the feedback required to make 360-degree feedback a success. Furthermore, the individual being assessed may not initially be accepting of the feedback as they may not understand that it is simply used as a method of improving performance standards. In time, individuals must understand that the appraisal system is not solely about criticism, but rather about identifying areas for improvement which in turn will increase potential for salary progression and promotion. The reluctance to accept feedback may be more evident where performance-based pay is based on the 360-degree feedback approach (Maylett, 2009). Similarly, a further challenge in relation to this is that raters may not be as willing to criticise the individual if they are aware that the employee's salary or promotion prospects may be adversely affected as a consequence. Some further challenges associated with 360-degree feedback include the following:

1 Inevitably, feedback will not always be positive and in certain circumstances the individual may receive a large amount of negative feedback. Kaplan (1993) claims this may cause a defensive reaction within the employee and lead to demotivation within their organisational role. This will ultimately cause a decrease in individual and therefore organisational performance.

2 When 360-degree feedback is introduced as an organisation-wide appraisal system, the potential for 'survey fatigue' exists due to the possibility of individuals filling out a number of feedback reports about their peers, subordinates or managers (Bracken, 1996; Kaplan, 1993; London & Beatty, 1993). This situation may result in less-than-accurate evaluation reports. The organisation should make an effort to ensure that no employee is charged

with filling out an excessive number of reports to create an 'even spread' across the entire workforce.

3   A further limitation of the 360-degree approach is that the feedback obtained from the multiple raters is most commonly quantitative. This does not allow the raters to discuss specific areas or performance tasks where the individual may have performed well or poorly. The adoption of some qualitative measures within the process would appear to address this issue to a certain extent.

4   Schneier, Shaw & Beatty (1992) suggest that many 360-degree feedback systems are not directly linked to strategic imperatives within the organisation. This must be a fundamental concern for all organisations as, in the first instance, it is imperative that employee roles and responsibilities are directly aligned with strategy, and therefore the evaluation of those roles and responsibilities must also be strategically aligned.

5   Finally, 360-degree feedback requires a significant increase in cost and administrative responsibilities on the entire workforce as almost all employees are involved at some stage of the process (London & Beatty, 1993). Traditional performance appraisals can often be conducted at far less cost to the organisation. However, organisations must be willing to sacrifice both cost and time in the short term in order to reap the rewards of a successfully implemented 360-degree feedback approach, which can provide significantly more benefit to the organisation in increasing overall performance as compared with the traditional approach.

It is clear that there are a number of associated benefits and challenges that are synonymous with the 360-degree feedback approach. It is also clear that this approach can offer significantly greater benefits and more accurate assessments of employee performances when compared with the traditional performance appraisal approach. It is important to note that 360-degree feedback can be used as both a development tool and as a performance appraisal tool. For the purposes of this book, it is suggested that the process be used as a performance appraisal tool to be implemented within NPSOs, superseding any existing process (if there is one in place). In comparison to the traditional approach, 360-degree feedback still allows management to assess target achievement, performance in relation to strategy, and any other performance criteria sought by management. The contrasting aspect between the two is that 360-degree feedback provides a far greater insight into the individual's overall performance as multiple aspects and responsibilities of their job are critically appraised from sources that have an intimate knowledge of those areas. Finally, the 360-degree feedback approach can also be linked to performance-based pay, which appears to be rare in NPSOs, based on the literature, but may have significant consequences in terms of performance. Performance-based pay can be linked to the achievement of particular goals within the process rather than an overall performance rating, which makes the award of such compensation more valid. However, the focus of the process should still remain on performance improvement through the identification of areas for professional development (Maylett, 2009; McCarthy & Garavan, 2001).

It is clear that the individual is a major factor in determining overall organisational performance standards, and as such it is imperative that an appropriate performance appraisal and improvement system is in place. This book argues that 360-degree feedback is the most appropriate system in terms of managing this imperative aspect of organisational performance for NPSOs.

5 Fundamental performance dimensions for NPSOs

Introduction

This chapter examines the extant literature related to fundamental areas of performance within an NPSO. Areas of research that have been reviewed in Chapter 2 and Chapter 4 have focused on general performance dimensions impacting upon all types of organisations (both organisational performance management practices and individual performance management practices). Therefore, the focus of this chapter is to identify performance dimensions that are of critical importance to NPSOs in particular and have a somewhat unique significance within these entities.

The chapter begins by examining issues within the broad area of 'sport governance' focusing on the performance of the board within NPSOs. The competencies and practices of board members in relation to 'financial management' are also addressed, as effectively managing the financial component of an NPSO clearly has a direct impact upon overall organisational performance. Following this analysis, the performance dimension of 'participation' in sport is thoroughly explored and the practices and processes of NPSOs in relation to this fundamental dimension of performance are examined – this section largely focuses on the interventions that NPSOs adopt to stimulate participation and how these interventions are evaluated to indicate their effectiveness.

Governance in sport

NPSOs in modern society are faced with multiple performance challenges and pressures from various stakeholders, such as the general public, players and athletes, coaches, media and the organisation's own members. Combined with these new and existing performance pressures, there is a call for NPSOs to be more transparent and accountable amid ever-growing levels of finances garnered through evermore divergent streams that exercise a major influence upon the sector. The contemporary NPSO must meet these challenges alongside their desire to produce elite athletes and coaches, while also recruiting and retaining a strong membership base. Governance is clearly a key focus for NPSOs as it relates to the development of policies and strategy, which directly affects organisational performance (Hoye, 2006; Hoye & Auld, 2001; Ferkins, Shilbury, & McDonald, 2005).

If an organisation adopts suitable systems of governance, this can translate into a level of high performance and the creation of an achievement culture throughout the entire organisation. A lack of a proper structure of governance can ultimately give rise to shortcomings within an organisation, resulting in inadequate strategic planning and policy making, and poor decision making. Aside from these internal issues that can arise from 'improper' governance, external consequences such as withdrawal of funding, sponsorship, membership and possible intervention from external agencies, such as government departments, may arise (Hoye, 2006; Mason, Thibault, & Misener, 2006).

A single and agreed definition of sport governance is yet to be established, confirmation perhaps that the issue of governance within any organisation is a multi-faceted and divergent concept. It has previously been defined as "the exercise of power and authority in sport organisations, including policy making, to determine organisational mission, membership, eligibility, and regulatory power, within the organisation's appropriate local, national, or international scope" (Hums & MacLean, 2004, p. 5). In contrast, sport governance has also been described as "the structure and process used by an organisation to develop its strategic goals and direction, monitor its performance against these goals and ensure that its board acts in the best interests of the members" (Hoye & Cuskelly, 2007, p. 9). Within these definitions some core themes present themselves, principally direction, power, regulation and control.

For the purposes of this book, governance within a sport organisation is understood as: offering a clear *direction* that aligns with the mission and vision for the organisation; the delegation of *power* is critical in order for each area of the organisation to operate and achieve results at the desired level; the issue of *regulation* in terms of sport governance is required to establish clear rules, guidelines and procedures for members and governed entities to adhere to; and the concept of *control*, like direction, is to ensure that any decisions and activities undertaken by the board are strictly aligned with the overall objectives and best interests of the organisation. In relation to regulation and control, a good system of governance should incorporate the power to impose penalties on individuals or groups who are not meeting compliance responsibilities (Slack & Parent, 2006; Hums & MacLean, 2004; Ferkins *et al.*, 2005).

Employing this definition of governance in sport, it is clear that the role of the board is to act in the best interest of the NPSO and its stakeholders, and therefore it is argued that the manner in which these activities are conducted should be scrutinised regularly to ensure best practice (Hoye & Cuskelly, 2007). Moreover, the key to any successful system of governance lies in the composition, roles, activities and decision-making capacity of the board. Board members must have appropriate previous experience and knowledge of how these unique entities operate, combined with expertise to address the various performance pressures and challenges that they face. It will be evident that a system of 'good' governance (Hassan, 2010) is in operation within an organisation that has been effective in making real progress towards the organisation's various objectives and overall vision, and is providing a valuable service to its membership. In order to fully understand how the board impacts upon the issue of governance in an NPSO, it is essential to conduct an analysis of previous research within this area.

The board: extant research

NPSOs such as the case study organisations within this study are central to the development of participation in sport, and fostering the development of sport in general, within their jurisdiction. These entities not only foster increases in participation but are also responsible for coaching development, staging events and competitions, volunteer training, and other important aspects of sport management and development. Government agencies, both sport and non-sport, are beginning to fully realise the importance of having effective structures and systems of governance in place within these entities (Hoye & Doherty, 2011). Furthermore, the negative impact that 'bad' governance practices can have on these organisations has been documented by a number of agencies (Australian Sports Commission, 2005; Sport NZ, 2004, 2006b; UK Sport, 2004). As noted above, Hoye and Cuskelly (2007) have suggested that the board is a central feature of the governance system and structure that operates within these organisations. The calibre of board membership, in terms of their knowledge of both sport and traditional business practices which are required to govern such an organisation, is clearly an important factor in facilitating overall board effectiveness and thus organisational success (Papadimitriou and Taylor, 2000; Papadimitriou, 2007). This has been further highlighted by Bayle and Robinson (2007), who state that "the system of governance, most notably the permanence and position of the main executives, are one of the keys to an NGB's success" (p. 258). Supporting Bayle and Robinson's (2007) study, Herman and Renz (2008) noted that research has confirmed that board performance is directly related to organisational performance.

Although it is widely claimed throughout various studies in the literature that board performance is related to organisational performance (Bayle & Robinson, 2007; Papadimitriou & Taylor, 2000; Herman & Renz, 2008), there are only a limited number of empirical studies that have been conducted to confirm this hypothesis. Hoye and Auld's (2001) research applied a specific board performance scale, Self-Assessment for Non-profit Boards Scale (SANGBS), which had previously been developed by Slesinger (1991). In their research, by employing the SANGBS scale they were able to empirically measure NPSO board performance by distinguishing between 'ineffective' and 'effective' boards. This scale has also been used in later studies, specifically those undertaken by Hoye and Cuskelly (2003, 2004) and Hoye (2004, 2006).

Other studies have analysed issues that are directly associated with the performance of the board in NPSOs. These studies largely focus on the internal workings of the board in relation to the extent of authority between the board and the CEO (Hoye & Cuskelly, 2003), the relationship between staff members and chairpersons of the board (Hoye & Cuskelly, 2003), the relationship between board chairpersons, board members and staff (Hoye, 2004, 2006) and issues of board cohesion (Doherty & Carron, 2003). Central to the arguments put forward in this book, in exploring the composition (calibre) of the board and recruitment of board members Hoye and Cuskelly (2004, p. 95) state:

> board members who do not possess appropriate skills, who are unsure of their role due to the absence of individual role descriptions, or have not been adequately orientated to an organisation, may find it difficult to contribute optimally to the board and thereby impact negatively on board [and organisational] performance.

As noted above, there is consensus in the research that board performance is directly related to organisational performance and, in addition to this, Hoye and Doherty (2011) argue that "expectations of board performance are tied to how well a board undertakes its role" (p. 274). Furthermore, Bayle and Robinson (2007) and Papadimitriou (2007) suggest that how effective the board is in performing its role is related to organisational performance and success. Given the impact that the role of the board can have on overall organisational performance, it is also necessary to examine the literature relating to this important field of NPSO governance.

The role of the board

Academics and some government sport agencies have attempted to develop governance guidelines in order to help NPSOs implement effective systems to improve their governance capacity. The majority of these guidelines focus on defining and providing clarification of the role of the board within such organisations. For instance, Walters, Tacon and Trenberth (2011) suggest NPSO boards "consider their most important roles to be financial, strategic and legal" (p. 14). The Australian Sports Commission (2005) describes the board's role in a legal, strategic, financial and moral capacity. In addition to this, the agency suggests that the board has the responsibility of recruiting the CEO, conducting analysis of organisational and financial risks, and being accountable to stakeholders through periodic reporting. Sport NZ (2006b) provides a more vague definition of the role of the board, advocating that it involves advancing and protecting "the long term interests of the organisation as a whole, which it holds in trust" (p. 19). UK Sport (2004) also provides four fundamental roles of NPSO boards: "(1) to set the organisation's strategic aims; (2) to provide the leadership to put those aims into effect; (3) to supervise the management of the entity; and (4) to report to members on their stewardship" (p. 6). Interestingly, the Irish Sports Council has not defined the role of the board within non-profit sport organisations in any of its publications. Agencies such as the Australian Sports Commission, Sport NZ and UK Sport have shown leadership and realised the need to

define the board's role within NPSOs in order to implement effective governance structures and systems. By not doing the same, the Irish Sports Council is
arguably acceding to poor governance within Irish sport, which can "have a
significant negative impact on the NGB and the sport: withdrawal of sponsorship; decline in membership numbers and participation; and possible intervention from external agencies" (UK Sport, 2004, p. 7).

It is also important to note that the role of the board in an NPSO can be different to boards that operate in another sector. From an analysis of the literature,
it is clear that the role of the board differs greatly between the for-profit sector,
the non-profit sector and the sport sector.

As Table 5.1 suggests, board members have a variety of roles within the
organisation in which they govern. However, little research has been conducted
offering empirical evidence of these roles (Inglis, 1997; Shilbury, 2001). Of the
research that has been conducted relating to roles of board members in NPSOs,
four different factors can be identified. According to Inglis (1997) these are:

1   Mission – ethics within the organisation, not deviating from agreed direc-
     tion, developing policy which relates to overall vision.
2   Planning – strategic planning, risk management, financing, staffing, com-
     pliance with relevant legislation.
3   CEO – recruitment and retention, assessing performance, establishing joint
     leadership.
4   Public image – establishing ties with the community, sourcing funding and
     sponsorship, ensuring relationship with the general public is positive.

Perhaps a significant point worth noting in relation to Inglis' (1997) research is
that the perceived performance of the board varies greatly between members of
the board and employees within the subject organisations, and major discrepan-
cies in board roles and performance are also noted between male and female
members. Inglis (1997) concludes that "understanding additional explanations
for varying perceptions of the roles by gender should be a focus for further
research" (p. 174).

The size of the board

The size of the board within NPSOs is an area of research that few studies have
addressed, even though this may potentially be an integral issue in determining
board and organisational effectiveness. For the purposes of this analysis, a large
board is described as having more than 10 members. Conversely, a smaller board
is described as having less than 10 members. Miller-Millesen (2003) suggests
the size of the board should be large enough to ensure that the CEO or managers
within the organisation do not possess complete control of decision making and
strategic direction within the organisation. In addition, Chaganti, Mahajon and
Sharma (1985) claimed that a larger board size reduces the control function of
the CEO over the board and provides greater depth of leadership. Furthermore, it

Table 5.1 Roles of the board in different sectors

Type of sector	Roles of the board
For-profit sector	• Create vision and policies • Approve strategic decisions • Recruitment and retention of suitable CEO • Assess CEO performance • Report to investors • Establish a reputable public image • Ensure compliance with necessary legislation • Ultimate control of capital finance issues (McNulty & Pettigrew, 1999; Lynall, Golden & Hillman, 2003; Blair, 1995; Clarkson, 1995; Huse, 2005)
Non-profit sector	• Create vision and policies • Develop ongoing strategic direction • Evaluate essential services and activities • Recruitment and retention of suitable CEO • Assess CEO performance • Ensure compliance with necessary legislation • Lobby for funding and sponsorship • Self-appraisal (Pointer & Orlikoff, 2002; Cadbury, 2002; Carver, 1997; Houle, 1989)
Sport sector	• Create strategic direction and vision • Form suitable organisational policies • Develop a reputable public image • Assess management performances • Report to stakeholders • Recruitment and retention of suitable CEO • Ensure compliance with necessary legislation • Lobby for funding and sponsorship • Ensure risk management practices are in place • Self-appraisal (Australian Sports Commission, 2005; Hoye & Auld, 2001; Hoye & Doherty, 2011; Michie, 2000; Michie & Oughton, 2005; UK Sport, 2004)

has been argued that the size of the board should be large enough to attract various valuable resources required by the organisation, in addition to availing itself of the experience, knowledge and skills that are accessible through the establishment of larger boards (Goodstein, Gautam & Boeker, 1994). Pfeffer and Salancik (1978, p. 172) stated: "The greater the need for effective external linkage, the larger the board should be." If an NPSO is largely concerned with satisfying external individuals and entities, then a larger board may facilitate this through creating a diverse range of knowledge and expertise (Abzug, 1996; Luoma & Goodstein, 1999). A notable study carried out by Zahra and Pearce (1989) used empirical evidence to claim that financially viable for-profit organisations had larger boards (between 10 and 15 members) in comparison with organisations that were less profitable.

Although there appears to be evidence that suggests a large board provides greater benefit to an NPSO, not all researchers agree over this issue. Goodstein *et al.* (1994) and Herman (1981) claim that larger boards can be ineffective in a number of areas mainly because constructive meetings and efficient decision making becomes less likely. This scenario arises due to board fragmentation, contention and factions within the board, resulting in delays in the decision-making process. The cohesiveness and participation of large boards may also be negatively affected, further impacting on the board's effectiveness. Moreover, communication may be an issue within large boards and a failure to keep all board members informed of important information within the organisation may affect the contributions of various board members (Goodstein *et al.*, 1994; Dalton, Daily, Johnson & Ellstrand, 1999). In direct contrast with studies that show large boards increase organisational performance, Jensen (1993) claims that smaller boards are a mechanism which can help an organisation perform at the optimum level. Empirical studies have also been conducted which suggest that greater financial performance can be achieved through the implementation of a smaller board (Daily, Certo & Dalton, 1999; Yermack, 1996).

From the studies listed above, it can be easily determined that research findings concerning the relationship between board size and effectiveness are mostly inconsistent. However, some valuable information can be extracted from these studies. Most research would suggest that boards within non-profit organisations, typical of NPSOs, are large (Unterman & Davis, 1982; Callen, Klein & Tinkelman, 2003; Provan, 1980; Cornforth & Simpson, 2003) with as many as 30 members in some cases (Oster, 1995). It can be assumed that this large board size is a direct result of the NPSO's need to attract valuable and diverse resources, experience and knowledge into the organisation. Studies have also been conducted attempting to establish a relationship between board size and board performance within the non-profit sector. Again, the evidence to support either side of this argument is inconclusive. Research has suggested a direct correlation between donations to a non-profit organisation and larger boards (Olson, 2000), while a number of contrary studies have shown that there is no notable relationship between board size and organisational performance (Bradshaw, Murray & Wolpin, 1996; Miller, Weiss & MacLeod, 1988).

Although there is still much debate surrounding the issue of best practice in terms of board size, a general consensus within the body of literature available would suggest that large boards are currently necessary within NPSOs due to their dependency on attracting donations, funding, experience and knowledge to the organisation (Yeh & Taylor, 2008). However, for-profit organisations with a professional board of directors can rely on a smaller board membership by adopting a suitable recruitment and retention strategy in order to ensure the composition of the board is directly aligned to the specific needs of the organisation. Therefore, given the need for NPSOs to 'professionalise', this book subsequently argues that NPSOs should adopt a small professional board of directors to ensure that board composition directly aligns with performance challenges for the organisation in terms of having the correct mix of knowledge and expertise. As a result, the need for larger boards and the negatives associated with their size can be removed.

The independence of the board

For the purposes of this book, board independence refers to two types of scenarios within a governance system. Firstly, board independence refers to the situation where the CEO of an organisation is classed as a board member and has equal voting rights as other board members. As one of the major roles of the board is to monitor the performance of the CEO, this is clearly not a healthy governance structure as it undermines the board's ability to carry out this function. Secondly, an independent board also refers to the establishment of a board that does not contain representatives who are current members of the organisation, such as those from affiliated regional associations. Parochialism has been identified as a major issue that impacts upon the performance of many sport boards and the selection of independent board members is now regarded as 'best practice' in organisational sport management (Hood, 1995; Walters *et al.*, 2011). Furthermore, the selection of an independent board should be carried out following a national open recruitment campaign to ensure the best possible candidates are selected to lead the organisation.

Research suggests that if the board is composed of individuals who are former employees, or even individuals who have an internal vested interest within the organisation, then the CEO/management's performance is less likely to be monitored on a continual basis, and an independent board is far more likely to scrutinise CEO/management performance at an adequate level (Fama & Jensen, 1983; Dalton, Daily, Ellstrand, & Johnson, 1998). Another benefit of selecting board members from the external environment is that they may bring an understanding and 'voice' to stakeholders of the organisation that may have not been heard previously (Yeh & Taylor, 2008). Furthermore, with the adoption of an independent non-executive board, it can be ensured that appropriate knowledge and expertise is present within the board in order to deliver on strategic imperatives, a situation which cannot be guaranteed with the election of a 'dependent' board.

In contrast to the body of literature which is divided relating to board size, there is a clear consensus that board independence is positively related to board effectiveness (Dalton *et al.*, 1998). According to Jensen (1993), a completely independent board may be an unrealistic ideal, as the CEO and senior managers are routinely required to sit on the board due to their knowledge of the daily operations and this knowledge can aid the organisation in the decision-making process. Aside from this sometimes necessary exception, as stated previously, this book argues that an NPSO should strive to implement an independent professional board of suitable external directors. Although there has been little research conducted analysing the relationship between board independence and organisational performance in NPSOs, within the traditional business environment it has been proven to be effective. Zahra and Pearce (1989), Rhoades, Rechner and Sundaramurthy (2000) and Dalton *et al.* (1998) all found there to be a positive relationship between board independence and financial performance.

Board conflict

In the absence of a clearly defined and articulated role description, members of boards or committees can occasionally feel it is necessary to become involved in the daily operations of the organisation in order to exercise their control-and-supervision function. This practice inevitably leads to conflict with management and other employees whose role within the organisation is to carry out those very same tasks (Kilmister, 2006). Adding to this, it is almost always outside the board's remit to become involved with operational plans being executed within the organisation. The board's role in planning is at the strategic level, and it is important for an NPSO to differentiate between strategic and operational plans. The operational plans within an organisation are the responsibility of the CEO and staff. When a board or committee wrongfully become involved in operational planning within an organisation, they are often stepping outside their area of competence and becoming involved in problematic issues that are not their responsibility. This practice becomes even more problematic as it draws the board away from their strategic planning responsibilities (Garratt, 1996). It is also likely within this situation that the board will anger and de-motivate specialist staff employed precisely for their operational expertise. Furthermore, when the board within an NPSO empowers itself to establish operational plans instead of allowing management to do so, it denies itself the opportunity to hold employees accountable for the role that they are employed to carry out (Kilmister, 2006).

It is a relatively recent practice for boards within NPSOs to establish clearly defined boundaries between their governance role and the role of management. While it is common practice and a relative necessity for CEOs to have a detailed job description outlining the reporting line to the board, the board itself can often fail to clarify the nature of their own roles and responsibilities (Kilmister, 2006). Examples of this occur when there is confusion over the CEO's role in the organisation in relation to finance, setting salary levels for staff or in relation to the power of the board to make operational decisions within the organisation.

Unless boundaries and specific role descriptions are set in place, conflicts will inevitably arise relating to such issues. When boundaries have been drawn up, it is important for board members to remove themselves from operational functions and allow the CEO to carry out his/her responsibilities. Intrusion and interference across agreed boundaries can result in a loss of trust and contain the potential for diminished performance.

Furthermore, new members to boards within NPSOs can be poorly informed of what their role is in relation to the organisation, and "regrettably, most new board members just drift with the tides" (Chait, Holland & Taylor, 1996, p. 1). The fact that very few boards within NPSOs have role descriptions or terms of reference results in little attention being paid to the introduction of new members into the board's affairs (Walters *et al.*, 2011). In addition, in terms of individual performance management, it is a rare occurrence for a board to establish a budget for its own development requirements. Training for board members takes place 'on the job' which can result in wasting potential contributions from new board members, and does not allow for constructive criticism of current practices or exploring new methods of conducting the board's responsibilities.

A further problem that exists within sport governance is the potential for the board and its members to focus either on the past or the near future for the organisation, instead of conducting its role of creating an achievable strategic vision for the NPSO. While monitoring the financial and non-financial performance of the organisation is an important function of the board, it is not the exclusive component. The board will inevitably be required to expend some time and energy analysing these issues, but it must not lose focus of its true value to the organisation, which lies in its collective creativity and wisdom to ensure the long-term vision of the organisation is being strategically aligned with the ever-changing external environment.

Best practice

"Good governance" (Hassan, 2010) is not something that can be easily achieved, much like the development and maintenance of the management–governance relationship which exists within NPSOs. By definition, managers within NPSOs are typically goal-driven, focused and often practical. They are expected to be highly motivated to make an example to staff within the organisation. In contrast, good governors should be thinkers. They are required to focus on the long-term aspects of the organisation in relation to outcomes, values, vision and "high level strategic direction rather than operational strategies and goals" (Kilmister, 2006, p. 173). Good governors should establish a clear relationship with the CEO and make them accountable for their performance in that role. Boards that operate effectively within NPSOs add value to the organisation that is greater than what the CEO or general staff can contribute. Good boards must make a difference through valued contributions to the life of the organisation that is shown in the delivery of superior outcomes to those stakeholders on whose behalf the board exists. Hoye and Cuskelly (2007, p. 178) have commented:

The statutory requirements, corporate and non-profit governance codes and guides to principles and standards, including those specific to sports governance, stipulate how sports organisations should determine their governance structures, systems and processes and what sort of behavioural standards are expected of those in charge of fulfilling the governance role.

In addition to these codes and guides, NPSOs are also subject to a number of other performance pressures from agencies and organisations to develop and adapt their own codes of behaviour with a goal of improving governance standards. With such a diverse range of pressures and accountability being placed on NPSOs, the need for adequate performance management systems and processes to be in place is now a necessity in order for core competencies such as the governance issue to be implemented most effectively.

The board must play a vital role in ensuring an NPSO is effective in delivering benefits and contributing to the overall sustainability and success of the organisation. As one of the core competencies of the board lies in effective decision making, it is clear that the impact the board can have on an NPSO is substantial. From the literature relating to the roles, composition, size and independence of the board it is possible to gain a greater understanding and perhaps develop a best practice structure of governance to be implemented within this unique sector.

In terms of performance management, this book argues that current boards within NPSOs should be disbanded in favour of the selection of suitable external candidates to form a non-executive independent board of directors to lead these organisations. This will remove the issue of parochialism and ensure the correct mix of knowledge and expertise is present within NPSO boards. For efficiency purposes and in line with best practice from the for-profit sector, it is argued that the size of these new boards should be between seven and 10 members. Furthermore, no CEO within any NPSO should be a member of the board as it clearly undermines the board's ability to monitor and assess the performance of this individual. The CEO's role should be limited to the daily operations of the organisation, allowing for regular feedback to the board on operational issues. Finally, this book argues that role descriptions should be in place for all board members to ensure they do not become involved in management functions and are meeting their obligations. In addition to this, training and professional development opportunities should be established in order to ensure that board members are providing the best possible service to the organisation.

Financing sport organisations

The ability of NPSOs to attract and retain adequate sources of finance is an imperative performance dimension for their sustainability and survival (Cordery & Baskerville, 2009). NPSOs are "expensive to run: requiring good quality playing surfaces, coaching, equipment, well maintained premises, and administration" (p. 27) so that stakeholders' have a positive experience. Securing funds from various sources is becoming increasingly competitive and the amount of funding that various sources can provide is also limited. A further complex issue exists in relation to the expectations of funders and the requirements of NPSOs that receive funding often being disconnected and potentially causing dysfunction. In NPSOs such as the case study organisations addressed in this book, the various revenue streams include: government funding, subscriptions/levies from members, loans and grants from public and private bodies, sponsorship, and other commercial activity. These income streams combined with any retained earnings the organisation may have enables them to deliver their service to their sporting stakeholders and provides the organisation with the potential of long-term sustainability (Stewart, 2006). Cordery and Baskerville (2009, p. 2) state: "Each funding stream's strengths and weaknesses need to be considered by these organisations to ensure that they receive sufficient cash to meet expenses and repay liabilities."

Many organisations, from all types of industries, have had to adjust to the changes in the current economic climate, including organisations from the NPSO sector. The 'income mix' that an organisation employs must be balanced against necessities in expenditure and any liabilities that may be associated with following a particular income stream. Little research has been conducted analysing how NPSOs plan to develop additional revenue streams to fund expansion or increased expenditure within their organisations. Kearns (2007) claims that research is also scarce relating to the internal trade-offs made by the boards concerning various funding streams and the analysis that is conducted relating to potential new income streams. It is imperative for the board of NPSOs to have an intimate and educated knowledge of how the various revenue streams impact upon their organisation, and the level of expenditure and liabilities related to various revenue streams must be analysed before the board can benchmark their performance.

Income generation

It is clear that NPSOs must receive income in order to fund necessary expenditure in the delivery of their services and ultimately attain organisational goals. Stewart (2006) suggests that securing continual long-term funding is a crucial performance dimension and should be a major focus of the board's responsibilities. The competitiveness, limit on funds and current global financial situation makes this issue even more imperative for the modern NPSO. Cordery and Baskerville (2009) claim that the challenge for the board within a sport organisation in relation to finance is to achieve positive cash flows, giving the organisation the best opportunity to attain its mission. Subscriptions/levies from members are often a major source of revenue for NPSOs. Kearns (2007) claims that income from member subscriptions/levies is the revenue within the organisation that is most aligned with strategy, objectives and mission, and therefore must be highly valued. He adds that the financial charge placed on members should be reviewed annually to ensure equality across the various aspects of the organisation and alignment with similar NPSOs. Although this investment does not pay out a dividend, members receive associated benefits through service, provision of facilities and the organisation of the sport by the NPSO. As financial dividends are not distributed to members of NPSOs, these entities will often retain a base of financial reserves for future expenditure, often for capital projects such as infrastructure and facility development or the purchase of new equipment. Fried, Shapiro and DeSchriver (2008) claim the constitution within the organisation will ultimately determine how financial assets are distributed amongst its investors and member organisations. Traditionally this occurs in the dispersal of income or other tangible assets such as new facilities to member organisations, including regional or local bodies. It is therefore expected that members who have paid subscriptions to the NPSO will receive their return on investment through the use of assets such as community assets, usually in the form of sport facilities.

It is important that NPSOs have the ability to attract income from a range of sources other than member subscriptions/levies. These revenue streams can be an important part of the 'income mix' and include donations, philanthropic grants, commercial sponsorship and other commercial activities such as 'pay for play' initiatives. The reality of these various income streams is that each one comes with associated benefits and costs. In terms of membership subscriptions, Steinberg (2007) argues that this source of revenue should be a steady revenue generator, especially within NPSOs, giving stakeholders the ability to make use of goods and services they would otherwise be unable to avail of. However, Steinberg (2007) adds that members' subscriptions/levies must also be affordable to potential members in order to attract and retain an adequate base of annual subscriptions. Income from commercial sponsorship and grant funding are becoming increasingly important to NPSOs as funding from government sources begins to decrease, or at best stabilise, within many countries (Irish Sports Council, 2012). It is imperative that modern NPSOs have the ability to attract commercial sponsorship and grant funding; however, these arrangements can be costly to administer, and the trade-off of conditions associated with such revenue streams must be analysed to ensure the organisation is not removed from focusing on its mission to the detriment of its stakeholders.

NPSOs can receive income from sources such as the organising/hosting of competitions, rental income, trading activities and interest from retained earnings. Depending on the size, scope and financial health of the organisation, interest from reserves in bank accounts could be a significant revenue stream and may allow the organisation to reduce the cost of subscriptions/levies placed on its membership. However, the global financial situation has resulted in low interest rates for investments within financial institutions, which has compromised an organisation's ability to receive substantial returns on this aspect of financial management. Irrespective of the current low interest rates being offered by financial institutions, Cordery and Baskerville (2009) claim that many NPSOs have established "investment trusts" (p. 18) in anticipation that future interest rates will rise, allowing the organisation to benefit in the long term. The emergence within sport management of innovative financial management practices such as this points to the need for diversification in relation to income generation and a shift from solely relying on funding from government sources. The need for diversity in funding NPSOs has been previously examined by Chang and Tuckman (1990), who concluded that diversification in the income mix is directly associated with overall financial strength within NPSOs. However, Kearns (2007) does note that income sources must not remove the focus of the organisation from its core mission, should not restrict the organisation from receiving other forms of income, and should not compromise the organisation's independence or autonomy.

Income from commercial sponsorships and donations can be a major revenue stream for NPSOs, providing they can convey their suitability as a potential sponsored entity (Berrett & Slack, 2001; Doherty & Murray, 2007). Cordery and Baskerville's (2009) study concluded that NPSOs are not good at attracting high levels of sponsorship and, although it is highly sought after by many NPSOs, "it is very hard to come by" (p. 19). The board can be an integral part of the sponsorship process (Doherty & Murray, 2007) by utilising their networks to attract commercial sponsorship to the organisation. Cordery and Baskerville (2009) concur that "board members should bring with them networks in order to make connections to new sponsors for the organisation" (p. 19). Some NPSOs employ a tiered sponsorship approach where a sponsor will invest in a certain aspect of the organisation that fits with their own business aspirations or image. For smaller NPSOs this can often be a successful approach as they will rarely have the capability to attract 'big name' sponsors who can invest sufficient funds to support all aspects of the organisation. Research (Berrett & Slack, 2001; Doherty & Murray, 2007) suggests that the key to implementing a successful sponsorship agreement is to establish the expectations of both parties and ensure that there is transparency and agreement in relation to various issues within the sponsorship arrangement. Following on from this, it is also important that constant communication is maintained with all sponsors and they are invited to attend any organisational events or activities so they can view their investment 'in action', potentially securing renewed investment within the organisation.

As alluded to by Kearns (2007) above, a further complex issue in relation to developing the 'income mix' within organisational sport management is that choosing one income stream in preference to others may "crowd out" (Weisbrod & Dominguez, 1986) other potential sources from the organisation. An example of this occurs when an NPSO may own a facility that it receives rental income on. Grant-giving bodies may analyse this situation as though the organisation does not require additional funds due to their potential to create funding through their rental income (Weisbrod & Dominguez, 1986). In comparison, if the organisation is successful in attaining grant funding from an awarding body, members may expect a reduction in annual subscriptions/levies due to this additional influx of revenue (Weisbrod & Dominguez, 1986). Little research has been conducted into this issue of 'crowding out' in relation to choosing a certain income source over another and it is difficult to decipher behavioural drivers in relation to this, but nonetheless it is apparent that this indeed should be a concern for the board within the modern NPSO.

Liabilities and debt

Literature relating to NPSOs and debt is scarce, even given the fact that many organisations continually operate on an annual loss and others have built up large debts to various forms of creditors (McCárthaigh, 2011). Yetman's (2007) research suggested that over 60 per cent of non-profit organisations within the United States were in debt to a variety of creditors. His research claimed that the ratio of accumulated debt to total assets within non-profit organisations was 33 per cent, which rose to 38 per cent upon removal of medical and educational non-profit organisations. It can be assumed, given the unique qualities of NPSOs and the tradition of under-resourcing within the sector, that the ratio would be even higher for these entities (Jegers & Verscheuren, 2006). Yetman (2007) suggested that non-profit entities had knowledge of various long-term financial options but lacked adequate knowledge of the consequences and costs that employing such a financial strategy could have upon the organisation. 'Financial leverage' (the ability of an organisation to repay its debts), as described by Yetman (2007), is different in non-profit organisations in comparison with for-profit organisations. Due to the absence of shareholder equity in almost all non-profit organisations, the financial leverage of these organisations is severely limited. Cordery and Baskerville's (2009) study also analyses financial leverage in terms of NPSOs. Their study states that "the notion of leverage ... ignores the fact that, although members will seek non-financial returns from the organisation, equity in non-profit organisations does not have a financial cost as it does in the for-profit sector" (Cordery & Baskerville, 2009, p. 28). Taking into account the concept of 'financial leverage', it is important for NPSOs to analyse the ratio of total liabilities to total assets within the organisation and to make sound financial judgements in terms of its ability to repay debt based on this assessment.

Many NPSOs rely on loans from financial institutions to fund short- and long-term projects. This debt must be repaid through future cash flows and as a result the board must ensure that future income levels will rise within the organisation, ideally resulting from the project that the loan has been used for (Stewart, 2006). The board can often be forced to develop new revenue streams, restructure the debt or, in extreme cases, default on the loan due to the lack of foresight into how exactly the organisation could repay the loan in the first instance. A common cause for this situation is the production of overly optimistic forecasts or lack of forecasts being accepted by members and financial institutions when considering this route of financial investment. Detailed business plans, transparent financial reports, the development of organisational policy on debt, and peer review of any loan applications would assist the board in making financial decisions that would not damage the long-term financial and non-financial credibility of the organisation.

Some NPSOs receive loans from members that are non-interest bearing, although Cordery and Baskerville (2009) suggest this practice can vary widely from sport to sport. Their research claims that "one of the benefits of these loans is that members were considered likely to gift the funds [to the NPSO] after a number of years, thus obviating the need for repayment of these loans" (Cordery

& Baskerville, 2009, p. 32). If an organisation finds itself in this cost-effective situation, it is important to ensure there is legal compliance with any such dona-tion. There are a number of laws which affect 'deposit takers', as the NPSO would be in this case. If a board member does not have the appropriate expertise in terms of this aspect of financial management, it is important for the organisa-tion to seek external advice in relation to this matter.

A further loan option for some NPSOs is to enter into an arrangement with local, county and city councils and authorities to secure funding with terms that may be more favourable than financial institutions, due to a lower interest rate and access to additional funds (Fried, Shapiro & DeSchriver, 2008). For instance, if an NPSO borrows money from a financial institution it will often be disqualified from applying for funds from any philanthropic trust associated with that commercial entity. NPSOs may also pursue the sale of assets to local, county and city councils in order to release funds tied up in these assets. A leasing or renting agreement is often subsequently arranged with the local authority, allowing the organisation to retain use of the facilities but lifting the obligation of the organisation to maintain upkeep and administration responsibil-ities. The negatives associated with an arrangement such as this is that the organ-isation may lose priority within the facility, and the future of the facility and therefore the sport organisation may be uncertain.

Best practice

James and Young (2007) suggest that very few NPSOs set target levels of income they wish to derive from various revenue streams, instead increasing the financial burden on their members in line with inflationary rises and making use of either grants or loans to make up the required deficit to run their organisation. However, Cordery and Baskerville (2009) suggest that proactive and innovative NPSOs are in fact beginning to diversify in terms of their revenue streams, even though these adjustments may prove to be minor in a lot of cases. They make recommendations that organisations should share facilities with other sports and non-sport organisations who could contribute to running costs, particularly in the 'off-season'. Likewise, their research claims that the NPSOs should develop out-of-season codes of the sport to ensure year-round usage (and therefore income) of all facilities. Further best practice recommendations include the establishment of trusts through donations, bequests and fundraising to ensure the future financial viability of the NPSO; the establishment of businesses within the organisation's premises such as cafes, bars, shops and gyms, and the creation of an external business, such as renting properties or leasing premises on land owned by the NPSO. Membership fees are an issue that must be constantly revised by the organisation to ensure fairness and equity with NPSOs that provide similar ser-vices (Stewart, 2006). Sponsorship can be a key revenue stream for an NPSO providing both the sponsor and the sponsored entity have clear and agreed-upon expectations of the terms of the sponsorship contract. All NPSOs should be aware of the various grants that they are eligible to receive; however, this income source should not divert the board's focus from exploring other potential revenue streams. Finally, Cordery and Baskerville's (2009) research suggests that NPSOs should take the opportunity "to re-evaluate current income streams to build up those that are performing poorly into a steady income and a successful link to members and sponsors" (p. 20).

NPSOs are complex entities that require expert governors, managers and financial structures to ensure their sustainability (Thibault, Slack & Hinings, 1991). In order for NPSOs to survive, cash flows must remain positive over time. In times of economic hardship, many of these organisations are suffering from the reduction or withdrawal of government funding and as a result must explore additional revenue streams using a best-practice approach. State agencies for sport, such as Sport NZ and to a lesser extent the Irish Sports Council, have produced numerous documents and resources to help NGBs and other NPSOs establish appropriate mechanisms for attracting necessary financial resources to their organisations. Sound financial management in relation to budgeting, income targets and cash flow forecasts are often non-existent in many NPSOs, even at a the NGB level. NPSOs that do not have these imperative practices in place will inevitably be consistently reliant on external sources of income to support their on-going operations, as a result of incapacity to raise sufficient 'year round' income to fund their sport. Organisations that are solely reliant on government or grant support, which can often be unguaranteed and variable, will be unable to successfully create budgets for periods greater than a number of months (Cordery & Baskerville, 2009). In contrast, financially viable NPSOs, which are not solely reliant on government or grant support, have the ability to set specific income targets from various applicable sources and can accurately budget as a result.

Sport NZ's publication *Nine steps to effective governance* (Sport NZ, 2006b) suggests that board members should have a broad base of expertise in relation to financial management in order to establish practices and protocols that are practiced within traditional business environments. Hoye and Doherty's (2011) research further supports this claim, suggesting that the "calibre" (p. 272) of board members within NPSOs is an important determining aspect of the financial viability of the organisation. Organisations that have elected members rather than appointed members to the board will often lack the required financial management expertise or spread of appropriate knowledge due to the absence of an assessment of board member's skills and abilities during the election process. Ideal board members within NPSOs are those who understand the sport or sport in general, but most importantly have experience within the traditional business environment, particularly in relation to financial management and ideally within a similar governing role. In addition, board members should be able to exercise their contacts and abilities to attract additional revenue streams, especially in relation to commercial sponsorship for the organisation (Sport NZ, 2006b). It is clear that one of the most imperative role of the board lies in planning income and expenditure within the organisation and, in support of Sport NZ's (2006b) and Hoye and Doherty's (2011) research, it is also clear that the board is a crucial determinant of financial and therefore overall organisational performance.

Participation in sport

Increasing participation in sport is one of the primary objectives of many NPSOs, both in Ireland and abroad. All of the case study organisations within this book have listed this performance dimension as imperative to their operations. This is perhaps seen as being of crucial importance due to government policy, and therefore (state) funding being intrinsically linked to the growth of participation numbers in the sport and recreation sector. This performance dimension is central to the mandate of state sport agencies (government) but is also imperative to other organisations such as NGBs and local sporting bodies. Creators of policy, funders of sport and indeed government acknowledge the importance of increasing physical activity within nations (Driscoll & Wood, 2001). Stephenson, Bauman, Armstrong, Smith and Bellew (2000) suggested that over 60 per cent (on a global basis) of adults do not undertake an adequate amount of physical exercise or involvement in sport. In this instance, an 'adequate' amount of participation in sport or physical activity is described as 30 minutes of moderate activity at least five days a week.

The consequences and implications of prolonged physical inactivity have been discussed widely by many researchers (Stephenson *et al.*, 2000) and it is suggested to be one of the most preventable causes of disability, mortality and morbidity in the developed world. Conditions and diseases that physical activity can have a direct positive effect on include heart disease, various forms of cancer, depression, stroke, obesity and diabetes. Adding to this, research suggests that individuals who partake in adequate exercise on a regular basis live longer than those who are mostly inactive (Stephenson *et al.*, 2000; United States Department of Health and Human Services, 2002).

Non-physical benefits

Although, as stated above, there are clear physical benefits related to active participation in sport, benefits are not strictly limited to the physical dimension. Sports participation plays a pivotal role in the social and psychological development of individuals (particularly children), facilitating mental health and community well-being (Steptoe & Butler, 1996; Stone & Hughes, 2001; Irish Sports Council, 2010; Dalziel, 2011). Active membership of sport organisations and regular physical activity has been demonstrated to: affect thoughts on empowerment and achievement (Nies, Vollman & Cook, 1998; Brunton, Harden, Rees, Kavanagh, Oliver & Oakley, 2003); be an important component of creating self-esteem and developing respect for others; act as a natural stress relief; and instil competencies such as team work, self-discipline and mechanisms for coping (Brunton *et al.*, 2003). The social aspect of sports participation is also an important by-product of involvement and can have significant benefits for the individual. Community well-being, as outlined above, is increased due to participants forming bonds of friendship and increased socialisation, resulting in the reduction of isolation for many individuals or groups within the community environment (Driscoll & Wood, 1999).

An important part of participation in sport, which derives little physical benefits but still encompasses a social and psychological dimension, is the non-active
sport participant. These individuals assume the roles of coaches, officials, managers, administrators and various other volunteer positions within sport and
NPSOs. Cairnduff (2001) claims that within many demographics both non-active
and active involvement in sport has a direct impact on crime rates, self-harm,
substance abuse and social cohesion. In further supporting research relating to
sports participation, the Council of Europe provides a definition of sport as "all
forms of physical activity which, through casual participation, aim at expressing
or improving physical fitness and mental well-being, forming social relationships
or obtaining results in competition at all levels" (Council of Europe, 1993).

The benefits of sports participation clearly have a significant impact on the
physical, cultural and social dimensions of nations, and as such it is important
that NPSOs establish maximising participation in sport as a crucial area of performance. Active participation in sport can vary widely depending on the
internal demographics of a country, the culture of sport and the economic development of a nation. The Irish Sports Monitor, a tool established by the Economic
and Social Research Institute (ESRI) and the Irish Sports Council, claims participation in Irish sport increased from 30.8 per cent in 2008 to 33.5 per cent in
2009. In New Zealand, the 2007–2008 Active New Zealand Survey claims 79
per cent of adults partake in at least one sport or physical activity on a weekly
basis. In an Australian context, 43 per cent of the population are involved in
sport at least three times per week (Standing Committee on Recreation and
Sport, 2006). In Canada, participation in sport appears to be declining with a 45
per cent active participation rate in 1992 (Salmon, Owen, Crawford, Bauman &
Sallis, 2003) changing to just 31 per cent in 2004 (Bloom, Grant & Watt 2005).
Sport England's (2004) report suggests that rates of participation in sport within
an English context have experienced little change since 1984.

Barriers to participation

It is apparent from literature and reports available relating to participation in
sport that not only do percentages of participants vary from country to country,
but also certain demographic groups participate far less than others. Men participate in sport and physical activity more than women; as people get older participation in sport decreases; and individuals and groups from indigenous or
culturally diverse backgrounds also participate less (Armstrong, Bauman &
Davies, 2000). Research conducted in the UK claims that men who hold profes-
sional/managerial positions in employment are more active in sport and physical
activity (47 per cent) in comparison with those in other forms of employment
(33 per cent) (UK Department of Health, 2004). Further research conducted in
South Africa would suggest that 30 per cent of the population is involved in
regular physical activity; however, lower socio-economic groups are still largely
excluded from mass sport participation (Sport Recreation South Africa, 2007).
Indeed, the literature confirms that cost is a major barrier to participation in

sport, along with employment and family responsibilities, pressures on time, and concerns over safety (Booth, Bauman & Owen, 2002; Brunton *et al.*, 2003; Salmon *et al.*, 2003). Other significant barriers to participation in sport as outlined in the literature include lack of transport to facilities/venues, dependent children and the cost of childcare (Richter, Wilcox, Greaney, Henderson & Ainsworth 2002), and limits on participation opportunities most commonly associated with rural communities (Brunton *et al.*, 2003). Richter *et al.* (2002) also suggests that language barriers, cultural differences, racism and prejudice from a participant's previous experiences within sport impact upon their decision to continue involvement in sport and physical activity. Oliver (2006) further supports these conclusions, claiming that intimidating club cultures for women, the elderly and individuals from diverse backgrounds are significant causes for discontinuation of sporting activities within these groups. Further issues, such as inclement weather for outdoor sports (Salmon *et al.*, 2003), self-consciousness and fear of embarrassment or failure (Brunton *et al.*, 2003), and perceived or actual risk (Booth *et al.*, 2002), are also factors that negatively impact participation in sport.

Interventions

Numerous studies have been conducted attempting to accurately assess the benefits of participation increases in sport and physical activity (Brunton *et al.*, 2003). The gap in the literature exists in the analysis of the role of NPSOs in developing successful strategic initiatives to facilitate increased non-active and active involvement in sport. An examination of the interventions utilised by NPSOs for best practice in increasing participation rates is non-existent within the literature. Interventions such as policy shifts, media campaigns, alterations to existing initiatives, volunteer encouragement campaigns, 'come and try' programmes, educational and informational sessions, and using role models as campaign leaders are well documented, but the results and effectiveness of such interventions are not.

The lack of an evaluation of interventions used by NPSOs to stimulate involvement in sport is alarming. The conspicuous absence of literature relating to this topic may be due to a number of causes: the collection of data in relation to such interventions is held by the sporting bodies who have conducted the research; it is possible that interventions are simply not evaluated by the sporting bodies to measure their effectiveness; or perhaps the results of studies that have been conducted have been withheld from publication (by the NPSO) due to negative outcomes. Howes, Doyle, Jackson and Waters (2004) argue that researchers should always seek publication of research regardless of positive or negative results; however, it is conceivable that results of such studies within NPSOs are withheld from publication for fear of stakeholder reactions.

As it is clear that a number of strategies and initiatives are being utilised by NPSOs to stimulate involvement in sport, it is imperative that an analysis of these interventions is conducted to establish best practice. Within the literature relating to participation growth interventions, the most popular initiatives include: 'come and try' days; age-, ethnic- and gender-specific programmes; alterations to traditional rules/equipment; and flexible delivery of the NPSO's product/service. Furthermore, Eime, Payne and Harvey (2008) conclude that 97 per cent of NPSO CEOs in Victoria, Australia, believe that the creation of welcoming environments within local clubs and associations would increase participation. However, the study also refers to the limitations of NPSOs in relation to this issue and suggests this is a difficult environment to create. Further research conducted through Sport England (2004) suggests that NPSOs must do better at understanding the barriers to participation faced by potential participants. The report concludes that motivational factors must be intrinsically linked to the participant's motives for involvement, along with an acknowledgement of lifestyle preferences and common pressures (time, family, cost) faced by potential participants. Qualitative studies relating to barriers of participation, such as the Sport England (2004) report, are abundant in the literature and therefore should be examined by NPSOs to create interventions most suitable for their target participation group. Furthermore, a high-performing NPSO should solicit their own research to become informed of sport-specific issues that must be addressed in matching interventions with their target group.

Best practice

Due to the lack of analysis relating to interventions by NPSOs to increase participation, identifying a best practice approach can be difficult. The various techniques and methods that NPSOs use to increase participation are well documented; however, the cost effectiveness and impact that such interventions produce on the rate of sport participation is not yet understood on a broader scale. An examination of the effectiveness of these interventions should be incorporated within the funding/budget for the initiative and as such can help the organisation analyse the impacts these programmes are creating. Payne, Reynolds, Brown and Fleming (2003) claim an NPSO's ability to measure and critically evaluate interventions such as participation drives is limited. They therefore suggest that NPSOs should work in collaboration with academic institutions to ensure an appropriate and unbiased evaluation of interventions is carried out. They further argue that experienced researchers will be familiar with appropriate data collection/analysis methods, and summarises by suggesting that sport practitioners should be proactive in forming positive relationships with the tertiary education sector.

Although there is a lack of adequate analysis of the effectiveness of participation interventions used by NPSOs, Priest, Armstrong, Doyle and Waters (2008) outline a number of best-practice approaches to the design phase of such interventions. The authors suggest that for any programme/initiative that is used within a certain demographic, a further control group should be developed to compare and contrast actual results of the intervention. When no control group is utilised, NPSOs should conduct repeat data collection exercises pre- and post-intervention to account for "normal" fluctuation in numbers (Ukoumunne,

Gulliford, Chinn, Sterne & Burney, 1999). Furthermore, a follow-up, longer-term collection should be conducted to measure the prolonged success of the intervention. If organisations are implementing mass-participation campaigns spanning all forms of participant, the evaluation of the campaign should involve a qualitative assessment of the various outcomes for each participation group, along with a quantitative assessment of the campaign's success as a whole. Priest *et al.* (2008) also suggest that any evaluations conducted should report against the context for the intervention (cultural, political, social setting for the intervention and its evaluation). If the initiative to increase participation is to be an on-going process, the sustainability of the intervention must be evaluated, particularly analysing its sustainability if funding is reduced or withdrawn. As volunteers are the drivers of sport, organisations must ensure that this participant group is well established (as they are often the leaders of participation drives) before recruiting other forms of participant.

In order for NPSOs to create evidence-based interventions, it is imperative that they carry out research prior to the design of any such initiative. Ideally they will have the capability to conduct this research internally, but if not this should be done in collaboration with institutions from the educational sector, as stated above. Furthermore, as government policy is clearly in support of increased rates of participation in sport and physical activity, it is important that state agencies also conduct research examining the effectiveness of various interventions, rather than simply reporting on increases or decreases within participation rate assessment tools. Corti, Brimage, Bull and Frizzell (1996) argue that the lack of sufficient literature relating to the effectiveness of participation interventions is consistent with a lack of literature relating to evaluation of initiatives within the sport sector in general. Focusing on sport participation specifically, aside from a need for evaluation of initiatives, further research is required relating to supportive environments to remove actual and perceived barriers to participation, and the role that sport encompasses as a "culturally appropriate vehicle" (Priest *et al.*, 2008) for integration of minorities and people from diverse backgrounds within society.

Summary

The literature review within this book began by examining research related to performance management practices, theories and tools employed within the traditional business environment. This was followed by a review of the extant literature in the area of individual performance management. It became apparent that the concept of performance management is central to the overall success of any organisation in relation to the attainment of strategic goals and objectives. These practices appear to be well developed within the traditional business environment, but little research has shown these practices to be equally as embedded within the cultures of NPSOs.

The literature review continued by examining research that specifically related to 'performance' within NPSOs. A relatively small number of studies have been conducted attempting to quantify 'performance' within these organisations. Of these studies, the majority have employed quantitative research methods which have provided an overview of performance dimensions within selected NPSOs but have failed to uncover the cause of any underperformance within these entities. Research relating to the use of performance management tools specifically within NPSOs, such as the Balanced Scorecard, is currently absent from the sport management literature.

This chapter concluded the literature review within this book by examining fundamental performance dimensions that impact upon NPSOs (governance, financial management, participation). Research relating to corporate governance within NPSOs is a growing field with a number of studies focusing on various aspects of this performance dimension. These areas include the size of the board, the independence of the board, and the calibre of the board – all of which are of particular significance to the focus of this book.

The area of financial management within NPSOs is a less well-developed area of research. However, it is clear from the extant literature that the calibre of the board within an organisation and the ability of NPSOs to attract a diverse range of income streams are imperative for a sustainable, financially viable NPSO. In contrast, the performance dimension of 'participation' has received the attention of an abundance of scholars from various fields as the literature crosses into areas of health, sociology and policy, in addition to the sport management discipline. However, there is a clear gap in the literature which relates to the analysis of the effectiveness of participation interventions employed by NPSOs.

6   Case study organisations
Context

Introduction

This chapter provides a detailed description of the primary case study organisations selected to be examined within this book. Qualitative research and case study methodology in particular requires a robust analysis of the selected organisations as a whole, and this has been carried out largely through interviews with key participants who work within or closely with these organisations, and document review that has been either supplied by the organisations to the author or that has been made publicly available through the organisations' websites or through other mediums. The primary documents used to analyse the activities and objectives of the case study organisations were their strategic documents which contained information relating to the mission, vision and strategic objectives of each organisation. Strategic management and performance management are intrinsically related and therefore the analysis of these documents is imperative to examine this relationship further within each case study organisation.

Justification of case study countries and NPSOs

Interviews

The participants chosen for this study were individuals who had an intimate knowledge of the way particular NPSOs operate in the primary case study populations of the Republic of Ireland and New Zealand, and secondary case study populations of Australia, the UK and Denmark. Participants had various levels of power and responsibility within these organisations, ranging from the executive and board level down to middle and lower management levels. The rationale behind choosing the countries of the Republic of Ireland and New Zealand as the primary populations for this study was based on a number of factors as shown in Table 6.1.

For the primary case study organisations in Ireland, three organisations were chosen: the Irish Sports Council, the Gaelic Athletic Association and Basketball Ireland. Comparable with these organisations, within New Zealand the organisations chosen were: Sport NZ, the New Zealand Rugby Union and New Zealand

Table 6.1 Justification of case study countries

Criteria	Ireland	New Zealand
Population	4,588,252 (Central Statistics Office, 2012)	4,433,369 (Sport NZ, 2012a)
Central government sport expenditure	€618.3 million (Irish Sports Council, 2010)	€313.2 million (Dalziel, 2011)
Central sport agency budget	€44.5 million (Irish Sports Council, 2012)	€72 million (Sport NZ, 2011)
Delivery of sport	NGB, LSP, volunteer led	NGB, RST, volunteer led
Culture of sport	Dominant sport=GAA	Dominant sport=rugby

Cricket. A minimum of five individuals from each of these organisations (15 from Ireland, 15 from New Zealand) were interviewed about various issues surrounding the broader area of performance management in contemporary NPSOs. The rationale behind choosing these organisations was as shown in Table 6.2.

Ireland

The Irish Sports Council

The Irish Sports Council (ISC) is a state agency that was established in 1999 to deal with all sport related matters on behalf of the Irish government. The mandate of the Irish Sports Council includes the following:

- Create policies and strategies which facilitate the promotion of sport within Ireland.
- Encourage increased participation in all sports and coordinate the efforts of sport bodies involved in the delivery of sport services and facilities
- Encourage initiatives related to 'fair play' in both recreational and competitive sport.
- Assume responsibilities for anti-doping practices in Irish sport
- Conduct studies related to Irish sport in order to facilitate research-led decision making.
- Encourage research in areas of both recreational and competitive sport (Irish Sports Council, 2009a).

Table 6.2 Justification of case study organisations

Criteria	Ireland	New Zealand
Central sport agency	Irish Sports Council	Sport NZ
Dominant/cultural sport	Gaelic Athletic Association	New Zealand Rugby Union
Emerging sport	Basketball Ireland	New Zealand Cricket

The ISC board consist of a chairperson and 10 board members that are 'hand-picked' by the government minister that the Council is responsible to. Before the economic crisis beginning in 2009, the Council was employing 31 full-time staff members. The number of staff and the budget for the ISC has been reduced substantially since that period. As part of its mandate, it is required to produce strategic plans and submit these to the Minister for Transport, Tourism and Sport. To date the ISC has produced five strategic plans with specific goals outlined within these strategies. The manner and methods in which these objectives will be measured or deemed to be achieved is unclear. There is no referral to any form of performance management within the ISC strategic plans.

The ISC states that its vision is to: encourage people to feel valued within sport; establish sport as an important component of young Irish people's lives; ensure people have adequate access to facilities and coaching and are only limited by their commitment and talent; and facilitate world-class performances by Irish sportspeople, fairly (Irish Sports Council, 2009a). The ISC also states that its operations are underpinned by certain values which are shown in Table 6.3.

The mission of the ISC is to "plan, lead and coordinate the sustainable development of competitive and recreational sport in Ireland" (ISC, 2009a). In order for the ISC to achieve its mission and role in Irish sport, it uses a variety of mechanisms in relation to various sporting areas:

- Developing policy within the ISC statutory remit.
- Allocating funding to various individuals and NPSOs.
- Lobbying of sport-related issues supported by research.
- Creating direct policy affecting the sport industry such as 'codes of ethics'.
- Attempting to increase NGB and other NPSO capability to help the ISC deliver on its mission.
- Acting as a regulatory body relating to issues such as disputes and anti-doping.

Ultimately, the various objectives of the ISC can be broken down into two strands:

1   Increasing participation numbers in sport.
2   High-performance sport.

Table 6.3 Values of the Irish Sports Council (Irish Sports Council, 2009a)

Promote inclusiveness and integration in sport	Be based on transparency and accountability
Commit to measuring and reviewing its programmes and initiatives	Be open to innovation in the organisation and delivery of sport
Develop ties with other relevant sporting entities within Ireland	Recognise the role volunteers have in Irish sport
Recognise the role sport can have on health and well-being	Recognise the commitment and dedication of Irish Sport Council staff

Increasing participation numbers in sport

According to the ISC strategy, the organisation argues that increasing participation numbers in sport can have a positive impact on the health and well-being of people within a country. In response to this, the ISC has established a Participation Unit which is supported by research which the Council conducts. As outlined within the strategy, the ISC see Local Sport Partnerships (LSPs) as the crucial mechanism in the achievement of an increase in participation numbers on a national scale. The 33 LSPs operating throughout the country have the responsibility to use the resources provided by the ISC to stimulate an increase in participation. Along with facilitating an increase in the general population, LSPs are also required to focus on minorities who are not normally represented within sport, such as the elderly, the disabled and individuals from disadvantaged communities.

As noted in the literature review for this study, participation in sport also includes volunteerism, and within the context of Irish sport the volunteer is a crucial component of sport delivery. Over 270,000 individuals volunteer in a sport-related capacity each year (Irish Sports Council, 2010) and this is something that the ISC must strive to maintain while introducing policies to recruit additional volunteers. The Participation Unit has developed strategies and policy in an attempt to facilitate the desired increase in participation within Irish sport through the recruitment of new players, coaches, volunteers and administrators.

High-performance sport

Aside from increasing participation numbers in Irish sport, the other main role of the ISC is to facilitate the development and success of elite Irish athletes and teams on the international sporting stage. Operating under the ISC's control is the Irish Institute of Sport (IIS), whose aim is to provide valuable services to Ireland's athletes and foster the development of high-performance sport within Ireland. The success of any high-performance programme can be easily quantified by measuring the success of Ireland's athletes at European and global sporting events such as the European Championships and the Olympic Games. The ISC attempts to stimulate this success by providing funding for various elite Irish athletes and creating competition pathways for those athletes. Strategy documentation which the ISC has produced in order to support high-performance sport include the high-performance strategy (2001), the foundation strategy for the IIS, and a review of the Athens (2004) and Beijing (2008) Olympic Games in relation to the success of Irish athletes. From 2005 to 2008, €34m was invested in high-performance sport in Ireland which the ISC claims has improved Irish athletes' performances at international competitions (Irish Sports Council, 2009b).

Current challenges facing the Irish Sports Council

In order for the ISC to achieve the goals and objectives set out in its strategic plan, it will be required to attract substantial investment into the sport sector within Ireland, both from a financial and non-financial perspective. As participation growth is a key performance area for the ISC, they will have to establish a working relationship with individuals and groups from various departments and entities who can help them deliver on their goals in relation to this area. Entities from the healthcare and educational sectors cooperating with the council will be integral to this objective being achieved. The ISC must convey to these stakeholders that increases in the numbers of participation can have a positive impact in servicing their own objectives. The ISC must translate 'interest' in sport into participation in sport by establishing clear pathways and outlets for people to become involved in sport, with a focus on those individuals who have been traditionally unrepresented within participation statistics such as the elderly and individuals or groups from disadvantaged backgrounds.

The relationship the ISC has with its 'partner' NPSOs within Ireland is another complex challenge facing the organisation. A more dynamic and efficient working relationship must be created between all these entities in order to deliver on specific and general strategic objectives of the ISC. This must be done by ensuring LSPs and NGBs have the required resources and capability to work on behalf of the ISC. The role the ISC plays in the operations of their partner NPSOs must also be addressed to further enhance capability and strategic success. Issues such as governance structures, auditing and other internal business processes must be examined by the ISC to ensure best practice is being applied within their partner agencies.

Many stakeholders within Irish sport see the ISC as an agency that contributes towards research and implements policy related to sport, such as anti-doping. The ISC must improve its function of conveying its role as a leader in stimulating growth in participation throughout all levels of sport and physical activity within Ireland. However, anti-doping must continue to be an important part of the ISC's function, and as the pressures and continuing battle against doping in sport grows it is crucial that the anti-doping unit with the ISC – in collaboration with the World Anti-Doping Agency (WADA) – is capable of carrying out its roles and responsibilities to ensure an equal, level playing field within both domestic and international sport.

Finally, the recruitment and retention of volunteers in sport is a major challenge for any agency involved in the sport sector. Volunteers are often the mechanism that facilitate the development of sport, and the ISC must attempt to attract suitable individuals who are willing to volunteer in order to stimulate participation numbers in sport or contribute to some competency-based elements of managing sport within Ireland, where applicable. If volunteer numbers decrease dramatically this will ultimately limit the capability of all NPSOs within Irish sport, and in particular damage the desired objectives of the ISC in relation to both participation and high-performance sport.

The Gaelic Athletic Association

The Gaelic Athletic Association (GAA) is Ireland's largest sporting, cultural and community organisation. Founded in 1884, the Association has grown to have over one million members representing 1,650 clubs.

The vision of the GAA as defined in its Strategic Action Plan and Vision Plan 2009–2015 is "that everybody has the opportunity to be welcomed to take part in our games and culture, to participate fully, to grow and develop and to be inspired to keep a lifelong engagement with our Association" (Quinn, 2002). The aims of the GAA are:

- Strengthening of the national identity of a 32-county Ireland through the preservation and promotion of Gaelic games and pastimes.
- Actively supporting the Irish language, traditional Irish dancing, music, song, and other aspects of Irish culture, fostering awareness and love of the national ideas in the people of Ireland, and assisting in promoting a community spirit through its clubs.
- Promoting its aims amongst communities abroad through its overseas units.
- Supporting the promotion of camogie and ladies' Gaelic football.
- Supporting Irish industry – all trophies and playing equipment must be of Irish manufacture and the penalty for non-observance is €200, while Irish paper shall be used for all official documents and correspondence (GAA, 2009).

The GAA promotes the sports of Gaelic football, hurling, handball and rounders. The Association at central level also has strong links with the Ladies' Gaelic Football Association and Camogie Association, which govern the female versions of both Gaelic football and hurling.

The GAA's mission as outlined in its most recent strategic plan is as follows:

> The GAA is a community-based volunteer organisation promoting Gaelic games, culture and lifelong participation. The GAA is a volunteer organisation. We develop and promote Gaelic games at the core of Irish identity and culture. We are dedicated to ensuring that our family of games, and the values we live, enrich the lives of our members, families and communities we serve. We are committed to active, lifelong participation for all, and to providing the best facilities. We reach out to and include all members of our society. We promote individual development and well-being, and strive to enable all our members achieve their full potential in their chosen roles.
>
> (GAA, 2009)

The organisation operates almost on an entirely voluntary and amateur basis, and while the GAA has a small number of professional staff, its members and players participate in the Association's activities without financial reward. One of the participants interviewed in this research highlights the importance of values:

> Each of the one million GAA volunteer members are "owners" of the GAA. These members carry out the work of the Association on a voluntary and democratic basis. As such, the executive staff and leadership of the Association have a responsibility to adhere to a clear set of values and principles.

The values of the GAA are highlighted on all GAA communications, including the Association's website, strategic plans and resources. They are shown in Table 6.4.

GAA structure and governance

The GAA's structure is complex and unique in comparison with other NPSOs within Irish and indeed international sport. The structure of the organisation (illustrated in Figure 6.1) comprises the following democratic units:

- Clubs (1,650)
- County Committees (32)
- Provincial Councils (5)
- Central Council (1)
- Annual Congress

The GAA clubs

The club is the basic unit of the Association and organises GAA games and activities on a local level. Membership of the GAA is operated through the club structure, therefore all members of the GAA must have an affiliated club. Each club elects its management committee at the annual AGM. The make-up of

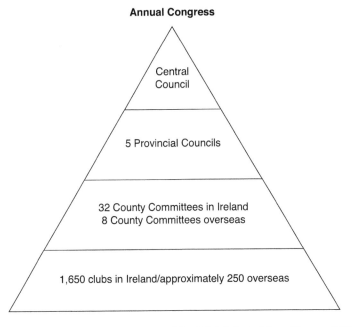

Figure 6.1 Governance structure of the GAA (adapted from Feeney, 2009).

Table 6.4 Values of the GAA (GAA, 2010)

Community identity	Respect	Amateur status	Player welfare	Inclusiveness	Teamwork
• Community is at the heart of the Association. Everything done helps to enrich the communities that are served. • Fostering a clear sense of identity and place.	• Respect each other on and off the playing fields. • Operate with integrity at all levels. • Listen and respect the views of all.	• A volunteer-led organisation. • All members play and engage in games as amateurs. • Provide a games programme at all levels that meets the needs of all players.	• Provide the best playing experiences for all our players. • Structure games to allow players of all abilities to reach their potential.	• Welcome everybody to be part of the Association. • The Association is anti-sectarian. • The Association is anti-racist.	• Effective teamwork on and off the field is the cornerstone of the Association.

management committees may vary. However, officers usually include chairperson, vice-chairperson, secretary, treasurer, public relations officer, cultural officer, children's officer, youth officer, coaching officer, players' representative, delegate to County Committee, and no more than five committee members without portfolio (Quinn, 2002).

The GAA County Committees

A County Committee is a geographic region of control in the GAA based on the relevant county of Ireland. The County Committee is responsible for organising GAA club fixtures, and the promotion of GAA games and activities at county level, including the management and organisation of county teams. The County Committee elects officers to be members of a County Management Committee, which has executive responsibility for the governance of the GAA in the county.

Officers of a County Committee who are elected at the annual county convention include chairperson, vice-chairperson, secretary, treasurer, public relations officer, delegate to the GAA Central Council, two delegates to the Provincial Council, coaching officer, development officer, and youth officer. The Management Committee meets on a monthly basis, can make decisions on day-to-day issues, and make recommendations on major decisions to the larger County Committee (with representatives of each of the county's clubs) which usually meets on a bi-monthly basis (Quinn, 2002).

In most cases the county secretary is a full-time post, appointed by the County Committee, who operates as a de-facto CEO for the GAA in the county. The county secretary is responsible to both the County Committee and has a broken line of responsibility to the director of the relevant Provincial Council (GAA, 2009).

Provincial Councils

Provincial Councils are regional bodies within the GAA and are comprised of several GAA County Committees. The Provincial Councils are responsible for the organisation of club and inter-county competitions, and the promotion of GAA games and activities within their region. There are five provincial councils: Connacht, Leinster, Munster, Ulster and Britain. The European County Committee is also aiming to become a full Provincial Council in due course (GAA, 2009).

Quinn (2002) claims that the core functions of a Provincial Council are:

- Management of inter-county and club championship fixture programmes.
- Club and community development.
- Coaching and games development.
- Development of physical projects to enhance the Gaelic games.
- Training of volunteer county and club officials.
- Educational sector development.

Each Provincial Council comprises two County Committee delegates, delegates from the GAA education sectors, and delegates from ladies' Gaelic football, camogie, handball and rounders. A Provincial Management Committee oversees the day-to-day affairs of the Provincial Council and is comprised of the following officers elected at the Provincial Convention: chairperson, vice-chairperson, provincial director and secretary, treasurer, and public relations officer. The President can also appoint three more members of the Council as voting members of the Management Committee. The provincial director is the chief executive and accounting officer of the Council, and also acts as a member of the GAA Central Executive Committee (GAA, 2009).

Central Council

Between Annual Congresses, responsibility for the on-going operation and development of the GAA is vested in the Central Council (Quinn, 2002). The main role of the Central Council is to oversee the implementation of policy on behalf of the members, provide leadership and direction to the Association, direct operations, manage and develop resources, and facilitate communications with Provincial Councils, County Committees and clubs. Day-to-day responsibility for the running of the GAA is delegated to a Management Committee chaired by the President (Quinn, 2002). The Management Committee also serves in the same role as a board of directors in a public company, overseeing the work of the Association, with Central Council setting policy. On a day-to-day basis the President oversees the work of the Director General (GAA, 2009).

The GAA's strategic document (GAA, 2009, section on 'Senior Management Team of the Association') claims the Director General is responsible to the GAA Management Committee and Central Council, and is responsible for the paid staff of the GAA as directed by an Executive Committee. The Executive Committee of the GAA includes the Director General (chair), Director of Finance, Director of Games, Marketing and Commercial Director, Director of Communications, Croke Park Stadium Director, and the provincial directors.

Annual GAA Congress

The GAA Congress is the main policy-setting forum of the GAA. Quinn (2002) claims the functions of Congress are:

- Reporting to members on the stewardship of the Association during the preceding 12 months.
- Election of a President of the Association every three years.
- A forum for debate on the issues affecting the Association which should inform Central Council in its decisions on strategic issues.
- Determination of policy for the Association in relation to specified reserved rights, such as:

- The strategic direction and role of the Association, including its ethos and especially its voluntary ethos;
- The structure and administration of the games;
- Playing rules.

Basketball Ireland

Basketball Ireland (BI) is the national governing body for the sport of basketball throughout all 32 counties on the island of Ireland. Although the sport does not have a similar profile within Ireland as GAA, soccer or rugby, in participation terms basketball is Ireland's third largest sport with the ISC estimating playing numbers in excess of 300,000 (Irish Sports Council, 2009c). There are over 300 clubs and 1,200 teams competing at local, regional and national level within Ireland, with particularly comparatively high numbers on the women's side of participation. Broadly, the organisation exists in order to develop and promote basketball within Ireland through increasing levels of participation and to provide appropriate leagues, administration and services to the basketball playing public within Ireland. The organisation operates with a number of stakeholders involved with the sport at various levels. Such stakeholders include the Department of Transport, Tourism and Sport, the ISC and LSPs, along with stakeholders from the private sector including legal entities, auditors, financial institutions, the media and a small number of sponsors.

At the beginning of 2009 it became apparent that BI was suffering from a large financial deficit which had accumulated over a number of years. This debt was reportedly caused by a failure of management in relation to financial irregularities and the impact of the economic climate within Ireland at that time. The estimated €1.2m worth of accumulated debt forced the withdrawal of both men's and women's senior national teams until the organisation can address its financial situation and rebuild its image and reputation as an entity worth investing in from both an ISC and commercial sponsorship perspective. On 23 December 2009, then BI CEO Debbie Massey tendered her resignation to the board of BI following revelations of the financial turmoil and controversy the organisation was facing. The organisation essentially operated without any management leadership for 16 months until current CEO Bernard O'Byrne was appointed in April 2011. O'Byrne had previously been CEO of the Football Association of Ireland (FAI) and had been involved in a number of private ventures, both sport and non-sport related, prior to his appointment within BI.

As of 2011, there are two major administration groups that operate within BI: the board and the National Council. The board of BI is made up of eight individual members who have responsibility for the overall governance and leadership of the organisation. The board is responsible for ensuring adequate performance of the organisation at various levels, developing and deciding upon strategic direction, and complying with all relevant legislation in relation to Irish company law. The board also liaises with an independent finance committee that provides information to the board relating to the financial aspects of strategic

goals and that offers advice or suggestions where deemed appropriate. This independent committee was established following the failings of management in
relation to the apparent abundance of financial errors and irregularities men-
tioned previously.

The second major administrative group operating within BI is the National
Council. This is a representative group of individuals who are involved within the
game at all levels and within all capacities. The type of groups represented on the
National Council include the regional boards, officials, primary and secondary
schools, senior league representatives, colleges and international affairs. BI and the
National Council are strategically linked through an operational agreement.

Strategy 2011–2014

BI has placed emphasis on a number of aspects of both on- and off-court objectives which the organisation aims to achieve or make progress towards by 2014.
Broadly, these strategic priorities include those outlined in Table 6.5.

IMPROVING MANAGEMENT AND GOVERNANCE

In order for BI to improve upon the previous failings of management and the
issues surrounding governance within the organisation, there are a number of
issues which must be addressed. The National Council must be effective and
have the capability to make informed decisions based on adequate information
supplied by the board and other facets of the organisation. Within the representative bodies on the National Council it must be ensured that all groups involved
in the game have a voice to express concerns and offer opinions – a current
obvious omission within the National Council is a representative from the
players of basketball within Ireland, for example. The various committees who
operate under the scope of the National Council must have clear terms of

Table 6.5 Basketball Ireland strategic priorities (Basketball Ireland, 2011)

• Work to improve the management and governance aspects of BI	• Develop domestic leagues into attractive competitions for both teams and supporters
• Develop strategies for increased participation of women in basketball	• Facilitate the development of clubs at all levels and age groups
• Facilitate the successful performance of elite teams	• Increase participation levels at educational institutions (primary, secondary and tertiary)
• Develop new revenue streams and improve marketing communications	• Be more accountable to stakeholders through transparency and better communication
• Increase numbers of officials/ commissioners and other technical members	• Facilitate the involvement of underrepresented groups within the game in Ireland

reference and understand their roles and functions in relation to their particular committee focus, and also submit yearly budgets and regular activity reports to the National Council. Individual National Council members should also lobby various issues related to the game within other organisations and entities that could have a positive impact on an aspect of basketball within Ireland, such as policy development and funding. Furthermore, it is imperative that BI retains a strong working relationship with the ISC and the Department of Transport, Tourism and Sport. Individual members of the National Council should also be forward thinking in their approach to developing the game and should seek out new initiatives and strategies for achieving this, even if this requires the adaptation of successful initiatives from other NPSOs.

SUCCESSFUL ELITE TEAMS

Although senior national teams are not presently competing in international competitions, it is imperative that the organisation continues to foster the development of elite players to ensure the future success of these teams. There are currently no mechanisms in place to identify talented basketball players at any level within the game. The senior men's and women's national teams have both achieved moderate success in the past but it would appear that little has been done in order to learn from these successes and adopt a model that could repeat such results.

DEVELOP REVENUE STREAMS THROUGH EFFECTIVE MARKETING AND COMMUNICATIONS

In recent years, basketball has received little to no coverage within the national media aside from one weekend during the year when the National Cup final is broadcast on national television. The organisation must address this urgently if it wishes to attract commercial sponsorship into the game. As a minimum, a weekly presence in national media through radio, print or television is required if BI are to successfully attract new revenue streams through commercial sponsorship. The organisation has recently updated its online presence through a reconstruction of its website. It must continue to seek out new ways of using its online presence to operate more efficiently and improve communications with its various stakeholders. BI has set targets of increasing commercial revenue by 20 per cent and 'online store' revenue by 33 per cent annually (Basketball Ireland, 2011).

INCREASING NUMBERS OF TECHNICAL MEMBERS

New development plans are required for increasing the numbers of table officials, commissioners, referees and other technical members. This is often a side of participation that is overlooked in sport but is integral to the successful operation of the on-court aspects of BI. The organisation has set up committees made up of members and non-members of the National Council, and it is their responsibility to ensure that development plans are in place and are effective to stimulate these aspects of participation in the sport.

IMPROVEMENT OF DOMESTIC LEAGUES

The domestic leagues in Ireland have decreased in standard, media coverage and attendances since the early 2000s. At its height, the men's league had between 15–18 teams competing each year, with that number now reduced to a mere eight teams. BI must work with clubs and the league committees to assess how they can make the league a more attractive venture, not only for sponsors but also for supporters and the media. With a focus being placed on participation of women in the sport over the course of the current strategic plan, growing the women's league is also imperative to establish an elite standard of the game for developing players. The organisation must also analyse the formats for leagues at various levels, from underage to senior level, to ensure they are appropriate and that all levels of the game are being catered for.

FACILITATING THE DEVELOPMENT OF CLUBS AND INCREASING
PARTICIPATION

BI should play a more active role in helping clubs develop appropriate systems of governance, strategic plans, developing revenue streams, and many other functions of management. Lines of communication with clubs must be constant, and any information which BI receives relating to potential grants or funding for clubs should be relayed back to the various clubs and representative individuals.

Although basketball is played widely at the secondary schools level, there are few initiatives to encourage participation at the primary level and also a large drop-off in participation occurs at the tertiary level. BI is strategically developing an initiative at the primary school level to increase participation numbers to 40,000 (Basketball Ireland, 2011). The success of this will depend on how effectively the organisation can liaise with the various schools and individuals who will be delivering the initiative 'on the ground'. College basketball in Ireland is generally focused around one four-day tournament during the year where most universities play a 'blitz style' competition. The tournament is well attended by tertiary institutions and BI should capitalise on this area of participation to grow the game at the tertiary level by creating attractive competitions throughout the year for colleges to compete in.

Furthermore, if BI can achieve strategic success in attracting new streams of revenue to the organisation, a sizeable portion of this should be invested directly into growing the current numbers of female participants within the game. The Women in Sport programme launched by the ISC has had some positive outcomes for female participation, and BI should look to repeat initiatives which proved to be successful under this programme and investigate other strategies for growing participation within the female demographic. In order to successfully assess whether participation is growing, the organisation must implement effective measurement and evaluation systems (as highlighted in the literature) across all levels of participation, from primary schools through to elite level senior national league teams. One of the ways that BI can boost participation numbers is to establish a close relationship with the LSPs and attempt to influence them to implement programmes promoting participation and involvement in playing and coaching, aligned with BI's strategic objectives.

ACCOUNTABILITY AND TRANSPARENCY

Given the history relating to mismanagement of finance within the organisation, BI must repair its tarnished image and ensure complete transparency and accountability in all aspects of its operations. The development of the new strategic plan must be achievable financially and relevant to the current issues facing the organisation, and BI should seek feedback and input from all stakeholders within the game relating to this plan. Internal financial reporting within the organisation must be transparent and reported regularly to the board, using the services of external auditors if necessary. As there are a relatively small number of employees within the organisation, BI can easily ensure accountability of roles and responsibilities of staff to ensure an efficient workforce. Constant communication with the ISC and other stakeholders is required to enhance feedback and successful collaboration relating to a variety of strategic initiatives and objectives. The implementation of an independent finance review committee within the organisation has been a positive element of BI's attempt to ensure mistakes of the past are not repeated, and the organisation must continue to seek advice and collaborate with this committee to create a transparent financial situation within the organisation.

PROMOTE INTEGRATION OF UNDERREPRESENTED GROUPS

With an ever-changing demographic within Irish society, BI must take account of individuals and groups that are currently underrepresented within the sport. Such groups include foreign nationals, the elderly, individuals from disadvantaged communities and individuals with disabilities. The organisation should seek to form partnerships with various agencies and entities that interact and represent these groups in order to successfully address the issue of underrepresentation in Irish basketball. The organisation should also seek to develop initiatives with local county councils and LSPs that must also address the common issue of these underrepresented groups within Irish sport.

New Zealand

Sport NZ

Sport NZ, formally Sport and Recreation New Zealand (SPARC), was created in 2003 as a response to the growing demand from the sport sector to establish a single agency responsible for the creation of relevant policy, coordination, delegation of government resources and establishing a direction for the future of New Zealand sport. Within the original mandate for Sport NZ, particular areas of concern were also highlighted, mainly being the need for policy development and leadership in the areas of coaching and regional development, and growing the active volunteer base within sport in New Zealand. The creation of Sport NZ essentially combined the work of three agencies that had previously played a part in sport at various levels: the Hillary Commission's major concern had been to boost participation numbers in physical activity and sport; the Sports Foundation was responsible for funding high-performance sport; and a section of the Office for Tourism and Sport created policy concerning sport-related issues within New Zealand. An independent review of the organisation by Deloitte (2006) showed that Sport NZ was operating efficiently and had achieved greater success and sector capability as a single entity in comparison with the previous model of three different organisations playing major roles within the sport sector.

The broad functions of Sport NZ cover a variety of sport-related issues. The organisation is responsible for investing in sport (mainly high performance), increasing participation numbers in sport and physical activity, facilitating increased capability of its partner NPSOs (NGBs and Regional Sport Trusts), and providing policy advice to the Minister for Sport in New Zealand. It is a unique function of a Crown entity in New Zealand that Sport NZ carries out operational functions within the sport sector and also has a role in policy development. The main functions of Sport NZ are summarised in Table 6.6.

The Sport NZ delivery model

Sport NZ works with various partner agencies involved in the sport sector throughout New Zealand. These NPSOs provide the groundwork for building participation in sport and developing sporting talent. It is estimated that there are over 15,000 clubs and organisations driven by over 750,000 volunteers at a local level within New Zealand sport (Sport NZ, 2009b; Dalziel, 2011). As a result of the broad range of clubs and organisations at local level, Sport NZ's delivery model involves working with NGBs and Regional Sport Trusts (RSTs) who then interact directly with the sporting public. Sport NZ is required to strategically invest in these entities to ensure that they have the capability to make progress towards Sport NZ's objectives related to grassroots and community sport. Ultimately, Sport NZ is not responsible for the delivery of sport provisions; rather, it is responsible for the strategic investment and creation of direction by influencing partner NPSOs. Sport NZ is seen to be a relatively small investor in community sport and, although it provides substantial funding to NGBs and RSTs, only a portion of this makes up the funding sources of community/grassroots sport. Funding for this area of sport in New Zealand mainly comes from territorial agencies, such as local and city councils, and gaming and community trusts; these contribute $660m and $167m per annum respectively (Sport NZ, 2009a). The organisation has attempted to work with these entities to coordinate investment in community sport but at best it can

Table 6.6 Functions of Sport NZ (Sport NZ, 2009a)

Investing in sport	Policy development	Participation	Partner agency capabilities	Arbitrary
• Developing appropriate investment strategies to develop the sport sector. • Inclusion of both NGBs and RSTs in investment decisions. • Liaising with other investment agencies within the sport sector.	• Creating policy to enhance sport at all levels, from grass roots to elite level. • Conducting relevant research within the sport sector in relation to participation, elite sport and other relevant research-related areas.	• Developing national and local initiatives to boost participation. • Providing advice to NGBs on how to recruit and retain sport volunteers, coaches and officials. • Playing an active role in sport development within the education sector.	• Delivering valuable advice and consultancy with partner agencies, mainly NGBs and RSTs. • Assisting partner agencies implement appropriate governance and organisational structures.	• Assisting the Sports Tribunal in New Zealand with any dispute resolution case.

only try to influence these organisations to align their investment with Sport NZ's broader strategic objectives.

There are approximately 80 NGBs that operate under Sport NZ's jurisdiction within New Zealand sport. Although these NPSOs are recognised by Sport NZ, in order to receive funding they must satisfy a number of requirements such as showing the ability to increase participation levels in sport and achieve high-performance results. Gaming trusts are also more likely to invest within NPSOs if they are recognised by Sport NZ. Since its inception, Sport NZ has struggled to have a major impact on the recreation sector within New Zealand for sports such as cycling, walking, running, tramping (hiking) and fishing. The organisation does recognise a number of recreational entities, such as Outdoors New Zealand, the Mountain Safety Council and the Sir Edmund Hillary Outdoor Pursuits Centre, and has set a priority to play more of a role in this area of physical activity.

The other partner NPSOs that Sport NZ invests in are the RSTs. The 17 RSTs within New Zealand have a direct impact on grassroots and community sport within their locality. Sport NZ predominantly invests in these organisations to increase participation numbers in sport, and occasionally will allocate funding for specific initiatives such as establishing governance and leadership capability within RSTs, or constructing regional sports houses where various NPSOs can use a single facility in an attempt to reduce overall operational costs.

As stated above, territorial agencies, gaming trusts and other government agencies invest significantly more in community-level sport in comparison with Sport NZ. The organisation has attempted to strengthen and develop its relationship with these entities in order to facilitate coordination between RSTs and the various agencies listed above. Gaming and community trusts alone invest over $167m annually within community sport (Sport NZ, 2009a). This is a unique aspect of sport provision which very few countries throughout the world have adopted. The funding and grants provided by these organisations is traditionally allocated for the provision of sport and community facilities. It is imperative that Sport NZ creates a strategic alliance with these entities to utilise them as a mechanism of achieving objectives related to community sport. However, a potential conflict of interest arises with this situation as Sport NZ also provides advice and policy on the impact, challenges and trends with gaming grants. Other government agencies that may have a substantial impact on the success or failure of Sport NZ objectives are the Department of Conservation (recreation in the outdoors), the ministries of Education and Health (joint initiatives, participation in school sports), the Department of Internal Affairs (gaming and community trusts), and the Accident Compensation Corporation (sport-related injuries).

Increasing sector capability

One of the functions of Sport NZ is to provide advice and support relating to organisational effectiveness within NGBs and RSTs. There are a range of initiatives that the organisation uses in an attempt to carry out this function, including the establishment of CEO leadership programmes, workshops on organisational performance, and workshops for effective governance and strategy implementation. Additionally, the organisation has developed tools and models that are applicable to various NPSOs, not just NGBs and RSTs. These initiatives are predominantly aimed at community NPSOs and deal with issues such as people management, applications for grant funding, risk management, sponsorship resources, and health and safety. Sport NZ aims to further develop these initiatives across the broader sport sector in New Zealand and place a focus on the issues of good governance and leadership, particularly within the RSTs (Sport NZ, 2009a).

Research in New Zealand sport

A further function of Sport NZ is to conduct valuable research that provides an insight into participation and high-performance sport within New Zealand, allowing the board and the Minister to make informed decisions relating to these areas. *The active New Zealand survey* (2009) was carried out to provide an insight into participation numbers in sport of individuals aged 16 and over. This particular survey addressed issues such as what types of physical activity people are engaged in, for how long and how often, and how regularly individuals volunteer with a sport-related event or situation. Research such as this provides Sport NZ with the ability to make informed decisions relating to participation, such as the 'Push Play' programme. This initiative has been designed to create an awareness of the benefits of participation in sport and physical activity, and is implemented through the networks of NGBs and RSTs. The results of *The active New Zealand survey* 2007–2008 suggest that 80 per cent of individuals take part in some form of sporting or physical activity on a weekly basis, and that only half the adult population meet the minimum recommendation for physical activity of 30 minutes at least five times per week (Sport NZ, 2009b). Informed research allows Sport NZ to focus on specific areas within the development of its strategy and can potentially illuminate other areas where investment of financial or non-financial resources may be required. Finally, research that Sport NZ carries out not only provides them with information but also provides their partner NPSOs with insight into how successful they are at stimulating participation and physical activity within their area of interest.

Current challenges facing Sport NZ

In keeping with an international trend of decreasing numbers of participation in sport and physical activity, Sport NZ is facing a challenge to recruit and retain players, officials, coaches and volunteers within all types of sport, and to attempt to reduce the increase of sedentary behaviour within the New Zealand population. Research carried out by the organisation in 2008 suggested a relatively stable base of participation in sport and physical activity but the reliability of this data must be questioned given Sport NZ's inability to access data from the recreation sector within New Zealand (Sport NZ, 2009a).

Sport NZ's 2009–2015 strategy document suggests NGBs in New Zealand have traditionally been under resourced and have had a limited capability within the sector. This has resulted in sub-standard infrastructures and delivery networks for regional and local affiliated NPSOs. Aside from attracting investment, NGBs have developed on-going problems of recruiting and retaining a competent workforce. Individual employees involved in community-level sport are generally under paid and undervalued, resulting in a high turnover rate within this sector. The ability of NGBs to attract financial and non-financial resources to their organisations has become a constant struggle for many (Sport NZ, 2009a).

Sport NZ must take into account that a large part of the sport and recreation sector takes place on an informal or irregular basis through tramping, walking, cycling and running or 'pay for play', and the traditional club structure is having less of an impact on New Zealand sport than it has in the past. The organisation must address the fact that the traditional club is finding it difficult to function in the new sporting environment, and commercial entities are now becoming a major player within the sport and recreation sector.

Sport NZ's (2009) review of the 2008 Beijing Olympic Games suggests that investment in high-performance sport in New Zealand has been successful, with substantial improvement with New Zealand athletes finishing in the top 16 of their respective sports. However, developing the success of elite athletes and teams is still a constant issue for the organisation with New Zealand – like Ireland – being a relatively small country, resulting in a smaller talent pool and reduced access to the necessary resources and expertise that is prevalent in larger competitor nations. Although Sport NZ is a major investor in high-performance sport, the pathways and development of the talent pool requires improvement and analysis in order for New Zealand to produce elite-level athletes on a sustainable basis.

New Zealand Rugby Union

The New Zealand Rugby Union (NZRU) was created in 1892 in order to govern and develop the game of rugby at a national level within New Zealand. As part of a number of functions within the mandate of NZRU, it is responsible for fostering the development of the game, promoting and administering the game, and organising regional and national competitions of behalf of the rugby community within New Zealand. The organisation employs over 80 individuals at the organisation's headquarters, in a number of roles and responsibilities. These individuals are responsible for management functions, stimulating participation, administration, marketing and sponsorship, and managing high-performance rugby teams such as the All Blacks and Black Ferns (women's rugby). The NZRU is one of the larger NPSOs in New Zealand and has adopted a professional approach in the manner in which it conducts its operations (New Zealand Rugby Union, 2012).

The functions of the NZRU can be compared with those of a traditional business in that the NZRU has specific departments and staff employed to deal with management issues commonplace to traditional business environments. Such comparisons can be made with communications, finance, IT, human resources, marketing and sponsorship, risk management, legal, and performance management. The degree to which these functions are carried out within the NZRU is rare compared with most other NPSOs within New Zealand sport and further supports the professional ethos the organisation has adopted.

From a legal perspective, the NZRU is an incorporated society which declares that any profits that are made cannot be distributed to its members, other than to achieve the objectives of the NZRU constitution. The organisation does distribute profits to the provincial unions to achieve results relating to community rugby, high-performance rugby, and for hosting and organising national and international rugby events, where appropriate. As an incorporated society, the law requires the organisation to have a constitution and on a broad scale the NZRU must adhere to the objectives and regulations as laid out in this constitution. The regulations within the constitution relate to the governing of: provincial unions and other affiliated organisations, directors and officers, limitations of power by the NZRU directors, financial processes, dispute resolution, and the regulation of the game of rugby. NZRU has a President and Vice President, much like any large NGB, who represent the organisation at national and international events and functions and are elected for a term of two years. These officers may also attend meetings of the board but are not entitled to vote on board decisions.

The CEO of the NZRU is supported by executive and management teams which cover the entire scope of the organisation's operations. In line with the functions of most NPSO CEOs, he is responsible for the delivery of the strategic objectives and goals as laid out by the board in the strategic plan. Executive team members within the organisation are the general managers for corporate services, public affairs and professional rugby. The remainder of the general managers sit on the management team and include the general managers for business development, grassroots and provincial rugby, the All Blacks manager, and the financial controller. The roles and functions of the various 'teams' within the NZRU are illustrated in Table 6.7.

Strategy and vision

The NZRU released a new vision in 2008, designed to "inspire and unify New Zealanders" (New Zealand Rugby Union, 2008), which incorporates all aspects of rugby from grassroots level, to provincial rugby, to elite level competition. Each year the organisation sets specific goals and priorities for initiatives and outcomes to be achieved relating to its strategic plan. These objectives are assessed and measured with the use of a Balanced Scorecard (Kaplan & Norton, 1992) which NZRU has renamed 'Scoreboard'. This management tool breaks down the individual goals and objectives of each department within the organisation and is assessed as a percentage of total actual outcomes versus total desired outcomes. The elements contained within the Scoreboard are directly

Table 6.7 Functions of NZRU 'teams' (New Zealand Rugby Union, 2008)

Provincial union and grassroots rugby	Corporate services	All Blacks	Public affairs	Professional rugby	Commercial
• Supporting players, coaches, referees and volunteers at local and regional levels. • Providing funding for coaching initiatives. • Managing databases of participants.	• Delivering support functions in HR, IT, finance, general management and board support. • Organising corporate hospitality and hosting events such as annual awards and capping of All Blacks. • The NZRU legal department also sits within corporate services.	• Liaising the media. • Providing necessary equipment and resources. • Dealing with medical issues. • Employing and consulting with specialist coaches and trainers.	• Communicating with government agencies, media and the general public. • Working with NZRU charitable trusts. • Managing the New Zealand Rugby Museum.	• Managing high-performance rugby players, coaches and referees. • Organising elite level national competitions and international matches. • Being aware of the latest developments in sports science relevant to rugby.	• Managing marketing and sponsorship arrangements. • Delivering the NZRU commercial agenda. • Negotiating broadcast rights. • Seeking out new revenue streams. • Merchandising and endorsement management.

related to the vision for the organisation and can be measured accurately to reflect the organisation's success in making progress towards that vision.

In order to establish a clear and comprehensive vision for the NZRU, the organisation consulted with all major stakeholders, from community rugby through to high-performance and professional rugby. Unlike many NPSOs, the NZRU has not produced a summarised vision statement but instead has developed a detailed illustration of each component of the organisation and where it wants these components to get to in the future. There are six components contained within the vision of the NZRU, shown in Table 6.8.

As stated above, the NZRU sets various priorities for the calendar year as to what specific outcomes it wants to achieve in relation to its strategic objectives. These objectives translate the long-term vision into real-time and measurable outcomes. It is the NZRU board's responsibility to monitor and evaluate the organisation's progress towards the strategic vision, and the responsibility of the management team within the organisation to deliver on the operational initiatives and processes in order to achieve that vision. The management team are also charged with regular reporting to the board on the progress of the various outcomes as laid out in the strategic plan and set priorities for the given year. The priorities the organisation sets focus on unique, large-scale or strategically imperative initiatives and outcomes. Issues such the management of the All Blacks and hosting and organising test matches or other on-going processes are generally not listed as priorities despite their important relevance to the overall success of the organisation.

New Zealand Cricket

New Zealand Cricket (NZC) has previously been known as the New Zealand Cricket Board and is responsible for governing and developing the game of cricket within New Zealand. NZC is the second largest NGB in New Zealand, after the NZRU, and cricket is a highly popular sport within New Zealand, particularly in the summer months. New Zealand is one of 10 countries that compete in Test match cricket and, although the domestic competitions are not followed as widely as rugby, international Test matches receive a large portion of interest and media attention within New Zealand. The fact that domestic competition is not widely followed can be compared with the majority of the cricket-playing nations (excluding India), as the majority of media and supporter interest in these countries is generated from international Test matches and tournaments. The domestic competition which NZC organises includes six teams that compete for the Plunket Shield, the State Shield and a 'Twenty20' competition. At an international level NZC is responsible for producing both men's and women's' national teams. Although cricket is a popular sport within New Zealand, traditionally the national cricket team has not experienced the same measure of success as other popular sports such as rugby. The women's team have experienced success at the international level by winning the Cricket World Cup in 2000.

Table 6.8 Components of NZRU's vision (New Zealand Rugby Union, 2008)

Strong grassroots rugby	High-quality competitions	Success for the All Blacks	Developing global rugby	Internal processes	2011 Rugby World Cup
• High-quality playing and participation at club, school and provincial levels. • Access for all demographics to be represented within rugby. • Using rugby as a tool for teaching respect and commitment. • Developing rugby as a positive influence within communities.	• Competitive, enjoyable and inspiring levels of competition play. • Creating player and coaching pathways and development initiatives. • Creating competitions that are respected and cherished by both players and supporters.	• Providing the necessary resources for the All Blacks to maintain winning expectations. • Be a leader in rugby development at all levels. • Support the game of rugby domestically and globally. • Act as an ambassador for the nation of New Zealand abroad.	• Consulting with developing rugby nations on best practice and share experience. • Creating opportunities for the growth of global rugby. • Having a strong working relationship with the International Rugby Board (IRB).	• Staying current with international best practice. • Ensuring management and organisational structures are appropriate. • Creating clear roles for individuals and organisations.	• Ensuring the legacy of the tournament has a profound positive effect on rugby and the nation of New Zealand. • Using as a catalyst for participation and infrastructure development. • Learning from the experience of hosting the tournament for future events.

Aside from organising domestic cricket and producing national teams, NZC is also responsible for the development of cricket at all levels throughout New Zealand. The organisation has a high-performance centre located at Lincoln University and also runs various initiatives to promote and encourage the game within community cricket. 'MILO Kiwi Cricket' is a community-development cricket programme introduced within schools in order to stimulate participation in the game from a young age. NZC operates a number of cricket academies which are most commonly based at educational institutions, and these facilities provide teams and players the opportunity to train in pre-season camps and prepare for international competitions. In 1998, NZC launched a national development programme with the aim to get people involved in the sport and retain those individuals who already participate in cricket through playing, coaching, officiating or volunteering. This initiative focused on all levels and demographics within cricket and programmes were designed at the school, club and recreational levels in order to increase interest and participation in cricket. At the same time, NZC implemented a 'player and coach pathways' system in order to provide clear direction and opportunities for aspiring players and coaches within the game. A major focus within the NZC development programme is at the primary school level in order to establish an interest with young people and encourage parents and teachers to become involved in coaching and volunteer roles, which lay the foundations for further initiatives at secondary school and club levels.

NZC has invested heavily in the development of cricket throughout New Zealand and the ability to do this has mainly come from revenue through broadcasting rights (New Zealand Cricket, 2007). When NZC hosts an international Test match it must absorb all expenses of the event, including the expenses of the touring team. However, in return for this it is entitled to the full amount of broadcasting revenue raised in negotiations with the broadcasting companies. The broadcasting deal which ended in 2012 was worth NZ$65.4m, in comparison with a previous four-year deal of NZ$14.4m negotiated in 2003 (New Zealand Cricket, 2008). Part of the reason for such a substantial increase was the tour of the Indian national team in 2009. For New Zealand, a home international tour by an Indian national team generates far greater income than any other touring team, such as Australia, England or the West Indies. The income generated from such a tour even exceeds the International Cricket Council (ICC) stipend received by NZC following an international cricket tournament such as the World Cup. The ICC has also signed a broadcasting deal with ESPN until 2015 which covers the Cricket World Cup, 'Twenty20' competitions and the Champions Trophy. This broadcasting deal is worth approximately US$1bn and under the constitution of the ICC all member organisations such as NZC will be entitled to a portion of the generated income (New Zealand Cricket, 2011).

Strategy 2007–2011

The NZC strategic plan entitled *Pushing beyond boundaries* was designed in order to facilitate the growth and success of cricket both domestically and internationally. The plan has a focus on advancing cricket on the field through higher levels of play and improving results of national teams, but also focuses on the development of the game off the field through organisational development, increasing revenue streams and increasing the capability of the six major cricket associations governed by NZC. The vision and objectives for NZC as an organisation require success and improvement in all areas of the game, from community cricket to elite levels. The four-year plan is broken down into yearly operational plans with specific objectives to be achieved within that timeframe. NZC developed the current strategic plan through a framework of linking the vision of the organisation to its purpose, goals and priorities, much like the principles behind the Balanced Scorecard (Kaplan & Norton, 1992). The wording of the vision for the organisation rather vaguely states: "Cricket is a vibrant game, inspiring New Zealand through outstanding performance" (New Zealand Cricket, 2007, p. 7). The *2007–2011 strategic plan* contains the purpose, goals and priorities for the organisation, as shown in Table 6.9.

Each of the priorities listed in the organisation's strategic plan are underpinned by specific operational plans, as set out in the following sections.

CULTURE OF EXCELLENCE

The organisation wishes to establish a culture of excellence relating to playing performances and the internal performance of NZC itself (NZC, 2007). NZC acknowledges that if it is to achieve such a culture of excellence, it will require substantial improvements in all areas of on-field performance from community cricket through to Senior National Teams. NZC proposes to create such a culture through: a review of lines of accountability and values; promoting behaviour that facilitates the implementation of a culture of excellence; working harder to improve communication with all stakeholders; creating a working environment where performance is robustly scrutinised; and attracting and retaining high calibre personnel within the organisation (NZC, 2007, p. 15).

NATIONAL TEAMS

NZC believes that in order for the organisation to have the ability to stimulate growth, attract sponsorship and increase revenue streams, the success of the men's and women's national teams is paramount. The high-performance programme that operates within NZC is strategically structured to facilitate the success of the national teams at international competitions. There are a number of issues that NZC must focus on in order to foster this development of high-performance at the international level:

•   Recruitment of players – the organisation must have structures in place which can identify suitable players who have the potential to compete at the elite level. Player development pathways must be in place and the appropriate services and facilities must be available to prospective elite players.

Table 6.9 NZC purpose, goals and priorities (New Zealand Cricket, 2007, pp. 9–14)

Purpose	Goals	Priorities
• Leading the direction of cricket at all levels within New Zealand. • Being a positive influence within the game both domestically and internationally. • Increasing the number of participants and supporters of cricket. • Establishing a culture of transparency and quality throughout all aspects of cricket in New Zealand. • Developing competitive national teams that have access to leading player-development systems and structures. • Hosting successful events and building on the commercial side of NZC.	• Men's and women's national teams ranked first or second in world and consistently winning international tournaments. • Increase in the support and media attention received by cricket. • Increase in participation numbers to over 100,000 individuals taking part in cricket each year. • Develop new revenue streams and increase reserves in line with set targets.	• Establish a culture of excellence. • Create high-performing teams at the domestic and international levels. • Communication with stakeholders. • Create a situation for sustained growth of cricket. • Develop and enhance the commercial aspects of NZC.

A strategic alliance with the New Zealand Cricket Players Association (NZCPA) is required in order to keep 'lines of communication' open between the two parties.

- Recruitment of coaches – likewise, for coaches it is important that identification and development systems are in place in order to grow the number of elite level coaches within New Zealand. Implementing a robust coaching review mechanism to establish accountability and provide coaches with the opportunity to identify areas for improvement is required.

- Elite services (recruiting and retaining high-calibre individuals capable of managing the needs of an elite level national cricket team) – the delivery of world-class sport science services to players and coaches is also a crucial element of success in modern sport. NZC must also ensure that all equipment, playing and practice facilities are of a standard suitable to an elite level national cricket team (New Zealand Cricket, 2007, p. 17).

STAKEHOLDERS

As a result of the implementation of a completely independent board (Hood, 1995), it is essential that NZC develops and improves clear lines of communication between the organisation and its various stakeholders. These stakeholders include provincial associations, clubs, schools and many other entities such as sponsors and the general public. It is crucial that the goals and objectives of cricket bodies, such as major and district associations within New Zealand, are aligned with the overall aims of NZC as laid out in their strategic plan. These organisations are the catalyst for NZC achieving or failing in its strategic direction. In order to successfully grow and develop cricket, NZC must also ensure there are good lines of communication between a number of other entities, such as cricket supporters, the ICC, umpire associations, Sport NZ, facility managers and volunteers (New Zealand Cricket, 2007, p. 19).

SUSTAINABLE GROWTH

In order to sustain an adequate level of growth in the game, NZC must recruit new players, coaches, officials and volunteers, and focus on retention strategies for those individuals and groups who are already involved with cricket at various levels. In order to facilitate an effective recruitment and retention strategy, it is imperative for the organisation to understand the needs and expectations of the various groups involved.

Increasing participation levels is a major area of concern for NZC, as with most NPSOs, and it must ensure that suitable structures to promote and attract new participants to the game are in place, particularly at the grassroots level. A particular demographic which the organisation must focus on is representatives from the Māori and Pacific Island communities, as these groups are currently under represented within cricket in New Zealand (New Zealand Cricket, 2007). Retention strategies must be introduced at school level to address the dropout rates when players leave secondary school education. A successful strategy would incorporate a link between leaving secondary school and a transition into the club cricket environment. Moreover, it is important for NZC to constantly assess the formats and organisation of the game at various levels to ensure it is an attractive and feasible sport for both supporters and players. Finally, volunteers must not be undervalued at any level within the game, and they should be provided with adequate training and resources to grow the game at the club and school level (New Zealand Cricket, 2007, p. 21).

COMMERCIAL SIDE OF CRICKET

NZC must continue to explore new revenue streams that can give the organisation capabilities to achieve strategic goals. The management of existing commercial revenue streams, such as the negotiation of broadcasting rights, sponsorship arrangements, gate receipts and funding from the ICC, must be constantly evaluated and assessed to ensure stakeholder satisfaction and to provide security for financial health within the organisation. The organisation should also look to establish a secure base of financial reserves to protect the itself against unforeseen circumstances and ensure financial viability. In order to attract additional revenue streams, particularly from sponsors, it is important that NZC generates a public image of an organisation which upholds and promotes the values of cricket, acts as a transparent entity, communicates effectively with stakeholders, and has the capabilities to deliver entertaining and successful cricket events. These activities should be underpinned by appropriate governance structures, high-calibre governors and managers, and suitable performance management practices (New Zealand Cricket, 2007, p. 23).

7 Introduction to case study organisations and Ireland case study

Introduction to case study appraisals

This chapter, along with Chapter 8 and Chapter 9, provides analysis and discussion of the empirical research contained within the book. Each case study organisation from Ireland (this chapter) and New Zealand (Chapter 8) are examined as a separate entity. In Chapter 9, the findings from the international case study organisations are combined and synthesised to explore differences in their approach to the area of performance management in comparison to the Irish and New Zealand case studies. An introduction and summary of each case study (Ireland, New Zealand, and International) are provided to analyse similarities and contrasts within the area of performance management within these different geographical locations.

Within the literature (Neely, 2005; Bourne *et al.*, 2003) and in practice, performance management has been used as a broad term to describe many different facets of an organisation's performance. The literature review within this book has shown that it can be used in terms of overall organisational, departmental and individual performances. For the purposes of this study, performance management is defined by the identification of five perspectives of organisational performance management that are central to the overall effective performance of NPSOs. These perspectives have been identified following an in-depth analysis of extant literature relating to traditional performance management practices and organisational performance in sport. Broadly speaking, these perspectives encompass:

1 The use of traditional performance management tools such as the Balanced Scorecard or any of its derivatives.
2 An analysis of how the role of the employee and volunteer is managed within organisational performance, given their significant impact on overall organisational success.
3 The structures and systems of governance operating within the organisation, with particular emphasis on the calibre and independence of individuals within the board.
4 The organisation's ability to attract a diverse range of income streams and manage the financial aspect of the organisation.

5   The evaluation and effectiveness of participation interventions in the sport(s) that the organisation promotes.

First, the case study organisations (outlined previously) are examined for their use of traditional performance management tools or practices that are common within the traditional business environment. These practices have been proven to be effective for organisations operating outside the sport sector and as a result this study seeks to gain an insight into current practices of performance management in NPSOs. In the absence of such practices, reasoning and justification for their non-existence or deployment is sought. The Balanced Scorecard designed by Kaplan and Norton (1992) and its derivatives are the most-utilised performance management tools in the traditional business environment and have also been adopted by many non-profit organisations. Their use in NPSOs is as yet unknown and this book identifies whether or not they have been adopted within the NPSO environment. Following a review of the literature relating to both traditional performance management and performance within NPSOs, this book argues that performance management tools and practices are indeed appropriate for use within NPSOs and can be significant factors in assisting these organisations achieve strategic objectives.

Second, the role of the individual has been described as central to the overall success of any performance management practice (DeNisi & Pritchard, 2006), and indeed the overall success of organisations as a whole. The appraisal process of employees and volunteers, the linking of employee roles and responsibilities to strategy, the existence of adequate job descriptions, performance-based pay, and the training and professional development of both employees and volunteers have been identified as a crucial area of performance in the literature and are therefore assessed within the chosen case study organisations. Following a robust review of the extant literature and drawing upon empirical research, this book argues that the individual performances of employees within NPSOs should be evaluated on an on-going basis and not simply undertaken annually. This appraisal process should also involve 360-degree feedback on a continual basis. Furthermore, this process should also contain a significant element related to identifying areas of professional development and training required by employees and volunteers in order to deliver a better service to the organisation and its members. The book also argues that both employee and volunteer roles should have suitable job descriptions and that they should be intrinsically linked to the strategic direction of the organisation so there is 'line of sight' to illustrate exactly how the individual employee and volunteer contribute to overall organisational success.

Third, the governance system that operates within an NPSO has been shown to be an integral component of facilitating overall organisational success (Hoye & Cuskelly, 2007). In keeping with this, issues such as board composition, board size and board independence will be analysed within the case study organisations. In terms of managing the governance aspect of the organisation, this book argues that all NPSOs, particularly at the national level, should adopt an independent professional board of directors (Hood, 1995) following an open national recruitment campaign. One of the major failings of sport executive boards in the past, and indeed in a lot of cases presently, is that they do not possess the necessary knowledge and expertise to run national sport organisations. This book argues that this lack of knowledge and expertise is limiting the capability of NPSOs, particularly in the area of traditional management competencies such as adopting performance management practices. The adoption of professional independent boards within NPSOs would combat this issue and others, such as parochialism and nepotism (Niemann, García & Grant, 2011), which have too often been synonymous within some sports bodies in the past. The complexities and often-redundant nature of governance structures within the case study organisations detailed in this book, which may be hindering organisational performance, are also analysed to examine whether more streamlined organisations can be established.

Following on from this, one of the major performance areas as identified within the literature is the ability of an NPSO to attract a diverse range of revenue streams to fund its activities. As government funding and support for sport begins to decrease or at best 'flat line' (Cordery & Baskerville, 2009), it has become necessary for NPSOs to attract multiple revenue sources in order to continue to provide an adequate service to their stakeholders. The case study organisations will be examined for their ability to attract commercial sponsorship along with engagement in other commercial activity, such as the negotiation of broadcasting rights. Innovative ways in which the case study organisations have been able to add to the "income mix" (Cordery & Baskerville, 2009) within their organisations, such as the formation of strategic partnerships, will be highlighted within this comparative analysis. It has also been noted in the literature (Stewart, 2006) that board members should have the appropriate knowledge and expertise in relation to the financial management of an NPSO, along with mobilising 'contacts' in terms of attracting commercial sponsorship. Supported by the extant literature (Chang & Tuckman, 1990), this book argues that multiple sources of income are a sign of financial health within an NPSO and the board's ability to attract additional revenue streams, instead of merely relying on government support, is a crucial performance area for NPSOs.

Finally, a performance field that is high on the priority list of all the organisations examined throughout the latter part of this book, as identified following document review and supported by existing literature (Driscoll & Wood, 2001), is the challenge of increasing participation in their sport(s). The evaluation practices of the selected NPSOs in relation to participation interventions and their effectiveness is examined. Both the ISC and Sport NZ are charged with leading and developing sport within their respective countries, and a large part of their remit focusses on increasing the rate of participation within these countries. The remits of NGBs in Ireland and New Zealand are also largely focused on increasing participation in sport and as such it is imperative that this performance area is similarly addressed. This book argues that NPSOs should set specific targets in terms of participation and must have adequate interventions in place, supplemented by appropriate monitoring and reporting mechanisms, to deliver results within this performance area. Furthermore, the book argues that NPSOs must assess the effectiveness of various interventions used in order to determine their impact upon participation, as this has previously been highlighted as a major weakness of many NPSOs within the literature (Payne, Reynolds, Brown & Fleming, 2003).

Ireland

Introduction

The Irish NPSOs selected in this book are either solely reliant on or receive a significant portion of their funding from government sources. This may come in the form of grants through the ISC or directly from other government departments. Furthermore, the economic and social benefits of sport have been well documented and the potential positive return on investment for government and for the general population is rarely questioned. However, there has been little accountability in the past in terms of the performance of these organisations and this has resulted in some high profile cases of mismanagement and criticism of the underperformance of Irish sport in general. Most recently one on the major NGBs within Irish sport, Basketball Ireland, suffered an entire financial collapse due to a lack of accountability in the funding they were receiving from the ISC, compounded by suggestions of flaws in the governance and management structures that were operating within that organisation.

NPSOs such as the GAA have developed into bureaucratic entities that are also receiving criticism, often from within their own ranks, for not meaningfully engaging within their membership and essentially ignoring the foundations upon which such organisations were established. In the case of the GAA in particular, suggestions of an out-dated governance structure (Hassan, 2010) and lack of leadership, seemingly due to an absence of traditional business acumen within its decision-making bodies, is potentially impacting the organisation's performance along a number of levels. Furthermore, as sport in Ireland continues to develop amid a more professional ethos, it is essential that individuals in influential positions – such as board members of the ISC and major NGBs like the GAA and Basketball Ireland – demonstrate an adequate mix of sporting knowledge and traditional business acumen to lead sport in this new, modern, competitive and professional environment. Given the professional development of sport both on and off the playing surfaces, such high-calibre individuals are required in order to bring NPSOs in line with their mainstream business counterparts in terms of establishing traditional business practices such as performance management, which has seemingly been absent within these entities in the past. The following section provides analysis and discussion relating to the empirical research of the Irish case study.

The Irish Sports Council

Performance management practices

Winand *et al.* (2010, p. 2) state:

> Sport performance is a well-known concept. Everyone can judge if athletes succeed in their sport and their victories or medals are indicators that allow an assessment of their level of sport performance. Likewise, organisations often wish to improve their performance in achieving their goals; understanding of performance comes when managers use tools to assess their resources, their processes or their outcomes in order to ensure their successes.

There appears to be an agreed form of individual performance management system in place within the ISC, the organisation vested with overall responsibility for government intervention into Irish sport, although there are conflicting statements over how exactly this system operates and its overall benefit to the organisation. This will be explored in greater detail in the subsequent analysis offered during this part of the book. However, when interviewees – many of whom were or are employees of the organisation – were asked about an Organisational Performance Management System (OPMS) (Winand *et al.*, 2010), all confirmed that no such system was in operation: "There is no formal system in place; we don't use a balanced scorecard"; "There is no balanced scorecard operating within the ISC or an NGB that I am aware of"; "There is no formal performance management process used within the ISC. We do not use any form of balanced scorecard." If these practices are absent or at best deficient within this organisation, other NPSOs in Ireland are unlikely to be encouraged to adopt performance management practices.

One participant refers to "a review of objectives in the strategic plan", a Department of Transport, Tourism and Sport review, and "consultation with stakeholders" as methods through which the organisation measures and evaluates performance. While stakeholder management is an important aspect to any organisation's activities, none of the participants refer to an on-going method of measuring and monitoring organisational performance or the use of any well-known performance management tools, again such as Kaplan and Norton's (1992) industry-standard Balanced Scorecard. Another participant refers to the various performance targets that are outlined within the ISC strategic plan but again does not allude to any mechanism or system of monitoring and evaluating behaviour or results in relation to these targets. They suggest that the organisation is "not averse to performance management practices" but does not offer any reason as to why these practices have not been adopted.

Although the ISC is the sole major funder in the case of the majority of NGBs of sport within Ireland, it does not necessarily measure NGB performance in a formal and robust manner. The Basketball Ireland case is a relevant example of the need for the ISC to monitor and evaluate the on-going performance of NGBs in its key role as 'oversight' body for Irish sport. Winand *et al.* (2010) suggest that the non-profit status of sport organisations has in the past allowed management to avoid placing emphasis on managing organisational performance. However, Winand *et al.* (2010, p. 2) go on to claim "new pressures have emerged from the state, sponsors, members and other stakeholders that have required these sport organisations to become more performance oriented or to build their capacity in order to better manage their organisational performance". When asked how the ISC encourages increased organisational performance in terms of governance, financial management, participation and individual performance within NGBs, one participant stated: "NGBs have been asked to develop a strategic planning approach and to cascade that down into an individual level within their organisation; some organisations do a good job, some do not." Another participant states: "Funding reflects NGBs who are performing well and NGBs who are performing poorly." A further participant asserts: "NGBs are evaluated on their operational plans", a process that provides very little insight into actual performance results within an organisation. No mentions of specific performance management principles or practices are made. The ISC assists NGBs with strategy and development and provides feedback to the organisations on various initiatives through an 'NGB support kit' but "no support is given in terms of performance management". The ISC is "not looking for any information from NGBs in relation to performance management, we are just looking for outcomes of activities". A participant also claims that "NGBs are left to evaluate their performance as they see fit" and, although the ISC funds NGBs, "the running of the NGB is solely the responsibility of the board and CEO. The ISC makes recommendations to NGBs about certain topics but does not enforce." This is further supported by another participant, who argues that the ISC thinks it is "best to advise NGBs rather than force implementation of systems or processes".

It could be argued, however, that an effective performance management system operating within the ISC would incorporate a continuous monitoring, reporting and auditing system of the NGBs within Irish sport, and that emerging issues, such as a build-up of extreme debt, could easily be identified and addressed before becoming fatally unmanageable.

Although there does not appear to be any form of Organisational Performance Management System (OPMS) within the ISC, when asked if NGBs should adopt such practices the ISC interviewees almost unanimously agreed that they should: The ISC "wants to provide guidance on performance management to NGBs in the future"; "It would be a good idea to make NGBs and LSPs adopt performance management structures." It may be a challenge for the ISC to encourage NGBs and other sport bodies to adopt performance management systems and practices when, as an organisation itself, it may not be engaging with and adopting these principles in the execution of its own remit.

Individual performance management

Tinkham and Kleiner (1993, p. 5) suggest that "performance appraisals can be a motivating factor for employees; careful implementation of performance appraisal techniques will assure desired company goals are encouraged". According to participants of the ISC case study, there is a formal performance appraisal process in place within the organisation for individual employees. One participant describes it as a performance management review process which "all managers and staff must go through on an annual basis". The process is a competency-based assessment which analyses "achievement of objectives, setting objectives for next year, and the assessment of training and development needs". Another also describes the process as one in which "people set their objectives for the year and report on it. They also identify their training needs." They go onto state that there are "open discussions in terms of performance" with various staff. A participant claimed that "a performance management system was introduced within the broader civil service, which the Council is a part of. It is a legacy system." They go onto state that within this process there is "an element of appraisal and an attempt at development".

Rousseau and Wade-Benzoni (1994, p. 463) state that "organisations implement their business strategies through the human resource practices they use", such as linking individual performance to strategic imperatives. They suggest that "it develops a framework for understanding how each contract shapes employee performance, retention, cooperation with fellow employees and customer responsiveness" (p. 463). A successful and effective performance management practice acknowledges the pivotal role that individual employees have in meeting strategic objectives and the significance of aligning employee roles and responsibilities with those objectives. Within the ISC case study, one participant claims that the individual performance assessment process is not linked to ISC strategy: "It is meant to link to strategy but it is more focused on junior employees where it is operational based." They claim:

> Strategic imperatives do not play a major role in the conscious operations of the employees. They are more focused on the day to day. As the ISC is a grant-giving body, employees tend to focus on the administration of the grant process. It becomes more about repetition rather than reflection. Employees tend to focus on what forms need to be filled out rather than what it is the ISC is trying to achieve.

It is also apparent that there are not strong enough information systems within the organisation to underpin either an individual- or an organisational-based performance management system: "The idea is reasonably OK; in reality there is a deficit in its implementation." This participant goes on to state that the individual performance management process "does not work well with senior management. It is difficult to assess their performance with big, long-term strategic objectives." There is a substantial body of literature relating to the importance and application of performance appraisals, but Ammons and Rodriguez (1986) claim there is a gap in the literature examining the issue of performance appraisals for "upper management". As highlighted by the literature review in this book,

360-degree feedback is proposed as being best practice for assessing individual performances, including for those operating within senior management.

There is, however, an attempt to assess the individual performance of the CEO within the ISC. The board has the responsibility of carrying out this task. Until 2011, the CEO was appraised by the board for a performance bonus by the remuneration committee. This bonus was linked to the achievement of strategic objectives. O'Donnell (1998) argues that if the CEO is the only individual in the organisation eligible for performance-based pay it can create a number of problems within that organisational setting. He states that "linking pay to individual performance ... increases friction between those eligible for performance bonuses and junior officers excluded from the scheme" (O'Donnell, 1998, p. 28). Within the ISC, as of 2011 a bonus system is no longer in operation for the CEO at the request of the Irish government's Department for Transport, Tourism and Sport. One participant states that "the CEO's performance is assessed but it is not as robust as it could be". They claim that, in order for individual performance management systems to work well within the ISC, "it is imperative that senior managers are engaged as managers but also as individuals being assessed". Supporting Ammons and Rodriguez's (1986) conclusions, they summarise by stating that individual "performance management is not as strongly imbedded at the management level and even at the board level as it should be". Additionally, they state that "more accountability and responsibility is necessary around some form of performance management system. Not enough people are being held accountable for what they are delivering or contributing to strategic objectives. How do individuals add value to the organisation?"

Governance

Ferkins *et al.* (2005) suggest that organisational governance is directly related to organisational performance. Hoye and Cuskelly (2007, p. 4) claim that "...the people empowered to make decisions on behalf of the organisation (the board) act in the best interests of the organisation and its stakeholders". The failure to have suitable governance systems to oversee the performance of NPSOs "can result in withdrawal of sponsorship, decline in membership numbers and participation, and possible intervention from external agencies" (UK Sport, 2004, p. 5).

As within traditional systems of governance, the CEO of the ISC is appointed by the board and is responsible for delivering the objectives and goals of the organisation as established by that board (Ferkins & Shilbury, 2010), particularly those relating to the areas of "anti-doping, high performance sport, strategies for participation, codes of practice for sport and research and information". The CEO is appointed for a five-year term by the ISC board "pending approval from the sport and finance ministries", and is eligible for re-appointment at the end of that five-year term. As highlighted in the literature (Hoye & Doherty, 2011), it is imperative that leaders of NPSOs such as the ISC are of a high calibre and have a good mix of sporting and business acumen.

Goodstein *et al.* (1994) and Herman (1981) contend that within larger boards (greater than nine people), in-depth discussion becomes unlikely and factions are easily developed, therefore limiting the board's ability to work as a cohesive unit and conduct efficient decision making. Daily, Certo and Dalton (1999) also suggested that smaller boards may help an organisation improve its financial performance. Within the ISC, there are nine board members who are individually appointed by the Minister for Transport, Tourism and Sport with "no input from the ISC", and who are responsible for delivering the agenda of the Minister in relation to certain initiatives and creating an on-going strategic direction for the organisation. Although the board is charged with creating the strategic direction for the organisation (Ferkins & Shilbury, 2010), at times the Minister may develop policies or initiatives that are not in strategic alignment with the ISC. The provision of funds to the Gaelic Players Association (GPA) to cover expenses (for elite, but otherwise amateur, players within the GAA) is an example of this, where there was a large political dimension to that decision.

As the majority of individuals on the boards of Irish sport bodies come from sporting backgrounds, there can be little experience from the traditional or mainstream business sectors evident within Irish sport boardrooms. A participant states that "in the past people with business acumen have been on the board" and "you do need a bit of that". The same participant goes on to suggest that the ISC "needs people who are used to working with government departments" and that "access is hugely important". In addition to this, another participant claims "board members must have a passion for sport and understand Irish sport". Although it is important for board members to be familiar with Irish sport, this cannot be a sole criterion for appointment to such an influential position. In line with Papadimitriou and Taylor's (2000), Papadimitriou's (2007) and Hoye and Doherty's (2011) research relating to the 'calibre' of the board, only one participant stresses the true importance of having individuals with business acumen in the form of non-executive independents within the board. They state that "the appointment of the board needs to be looked at" and add that "of particular concern are the skillsets of the current board and its lack of competencies to manage sport in an evolving professional environment". When asked further about the competencies and composition of the board, one participant states that the "government may look to have open applications for board positions" in the future. This would be a positive development for the governance structure within the ISC.

Finance

Ninety per cent of the ISC's budget comes from the national lotteries system through the Department of Transport, Tourism and Sport. The remaining 10 per cent of this budget comes from non-guaranteed sources. One participant claims that funding from the Minister "comes with particular agendas on a yearly basis". However, another participant states that the ISC is given "free rein" to spend the money as they see fit but that occasionally some funding is ring-fenced for certain initiatives such as the 'Women in Sport' programme. This is supported by others: "Funding comes with the Minister's priorities but the ISC can spend the majority of funds as we see fit." This participant also details some smaller elements of funding that the ISC receives: "The Golf Trust has been set up to fund emerging professionals within the game and is largely supported by corporate sponsors. LSPs receive some funding through An Post for the running of cycles at various times of the year." These are essentially the only forms of commercial activity that operate within the organisation. Chang and Tuckman (1990) clearly state that an organisation should seek out various revenue streams and not rely solely on government support as appears to be the case within the ISC.

Berrett and Slack (2001) examined how NPSOs are positioning themselves to attract corporate sponsorship. They suggested that there are two major determinants in an organisation's ability to be successful in attaining corporate sponsorship: media exposure and participation numbers. These two determinants could be developed further by the ISC to convey to potential sponsors the attractiveness of investing in the organisation. Amis, Slack and Berrett (1999) suggest that an NPSO's ability to attract commercial sponsorship is directly linked to organisational performance and success. Currently the ISC does not receive any major funds from a corporate sponsor or collective of sponsors. During 2009–2012, the organisation experienced a "15% reduction which included a reduction in staff numbers". When asked about funding in relation to NGBs, one participant correctly makes the point that "funding is a major challenge in the current economic climate" and, supporting Chang and Tuckman's (1990) research relating to multiple revenue streams, suggested that "NGBs need to generate their own sources of funding and not solely rely on ISC funding".

The ISC itself has the responsibility for allocating funding to over 60 NGBs within Ireland. One participant summarises the view of the ISC in relation to their own provision of funding to the various sport bodies within Ireland as one in which ISC "must go with [its] strengths and the organisations that will deliver for you when funding is tight". Another participant suggests that "as the funding decreases for NGBs from the ISC, the ISC will have less influence" over sport bodies in seeking their alignment with ISC policy and direction.

Participation

Thibault, Slack and Hinings (1991) refer to the ethos of sport becoming ever more professional in nature, and the relationship between NPSOs, volunteers and employees within sport management becoming equally as complex. One participant states that a lot of "professionals were being employed in Irish sport and, now the money has dried up, it is beginning to go back to a more volunteer-led approach. Volunteers are now being asked to give more time and more expertise." As the number of employees within NPSOs such as the ISC and NGBs are reduced, the pressures placed on volunteers to have the time and expertise to manage NPSOs that were previously managed by professionals becomes intense. The ISC workforce itself has also been reduced. Ultimately this results in a lack of stability within the sector as the management of NPSOs reverts back to this volunteer-led approach. This situation "is challenging sport as people drift in and out of the volunteer approach". The situation becomes even more difficult as "people are now working longer hours which make it harder to get volunteers". The ISC has a responsibility to provide as much support as possible to Irish NPSOs in terms of recruiting and retaining a solid volunteer participant base within Irish sport. Cuskelly *et al.* (2006) suggest that once volunteers have been recruited it is important that they receive appropriate training and development in order to facilitate their success in managing various functions within a modern NPSO. A participant commented: "Volunteers must be invested in so they can return a good service."

The literature review in this book has highlighted the numerous benefits that are associated with participating and volunteering in sport. Within the ISC, all interviewees agreed that growing the numbers of participation within Irish sport is a major performance objective for the ISC: "it is the main function of the council. I see it as the priority. Generating a more active Ireland"; "We set long-term objectives in numbers and carry out research with the ESRI [Economic and Social Research Institute]." Stimulating participation numbers in sport is "a major research function" of the ISC. A major issue in relation to this area of performance is the organisation's ability to obtain reliable data from sport bodies and groups such as NGBs, LSPs and local authorities. This directly relates to the ISC's ability to communicate effectively with its many stakeholders and educate them on the need of supplying accurate information to the ISC in terms of participation.

Much like growing the volunteer base of groups and individuals within Irish sport, stimulating participation faces similar problems concerning, amongst other issues, a lack of time and competition from other forms of entertainment and non-sport related activities (Brunton *et al.*, 2003). One participant states that "the recession has helped in that people have more free time, so they will participate in sport". However, they fail to mention barriers to participation, such as the relationship between the increased costs of participating in sport and the reduction in disposable income on the part of the general public. Moreover, there is no suggestion that participation interventions are assessed for their effectiveness within the ISC, which would again represent best practice in the allocation and justification of scarce public funds.

An effective performance management approach within the ISC would consist of identifying and evaluating suitable interventions along with accurate annual reporting of participation rates in Irish sport, detailing variances in demographics and geographical locations. Finally, a further major flaw of the Irish Sports Monitor, the tool currently used to measure sports participation in Ireland, is that it only analyses participation in adult sport and fails to take into account the vast numbers of adolescents and children who also partake in sport on a daily and weekly basis. This is ultimately providing inaccurate results but is of course of use when measuring broad figures in relation to sports participation in Ireland.

The Gaelic Athletic Association

Performance management practices

From an organisational standpoint, the "GAA is new to the whole area of performance management" both at GAA headquarters and at lower levels of the Association. Participants suggest that the extent of performance management within the GAA is based on the assessment of targets detailed in the organisation's seven-year strategic plan. This would be considered a very basic management function and simply a by-product of the strategic management process rather than an accountable, transparent and robust analysis of crucial performance areas affecting the organisation. Participants do not refer to any formal templates or practices relating to a Balanced Scorecard (Kaplan & Norton, 1992) or any of its subsequent derivatives.

At county and provincial levels within the organisation it is also clear that no such practices or culture of performance management exist. One participant explains how the GAA is still attempting to encourage strategic planning at county levels and correctly points out that performance management systems cannot be implemented until strategic plans are in place. The fact that it appears that some county-level bodies are still operating without the guidance of a strategic plan is alarming and exemplifies how organisational management remains in its infancy in some parts of the Association. This participant adds that the GAA would like to see all county boards develop a strategic direction but as of yet this is not commonplace within the Association. A performance management practice adopted at GAA headquarters would help to ensure that all county and provincial bodies have, as a minimum, a strategic plan in place which aligns with the overall aims and objectives of the GAA's central operation. Again, the emergence of one of the core performance issues facing Irish sport is present in this situation, with participants conceding that there is often a lack of the required experience even at county level.

At the provincial level, organisational performance management is also largely non-existent. Again, supporting Papadimitriou and Taylor's (2000) and Papadimitriou's (2007) extant research, the issue of management expertise appears to be a factor in this case even though there are paid officials at this level within the organisation: "it is difficult to get the provinces to adopt performance management; they're not used to it; it will take years before the GAA gets provinces to be where we want them to be".

Another participant supports the above statement and concedes that there are no performance management tools or practices utilised at the provincial level. They state that the extent of performance management at provincial level consists of annual reports measured against strategic objectives. This practice, although necessary, would nevertheless be considered a very basic management practice within traditional business and does not provide any identification of key performance areas for the Association going forward. A further participant describes how GAA headquarters set key performance indicators (KPIs) for the provinces but do not provide them with any resources (other than financial) for how they can best achieve those performance targets. They go on to claim that the extent of performance management at the provincial level consists of monthly reviews of financial budgets and ensuring compliance through external auditors. Participants allude to a Management Information System (MIS) that records data in relation to games development within each county but do "not believe that any sport organisation [in Ireland] has really grasped performance management", including the GAA. One participant epitomises the need for performance management practices to be implemented across all levels of the GAA, and indeed other NGBs and NPSOs within Irish sport: "we must make sure we deliver against our targets; we are getting public money; we have to be accountable for that public money, so we have to have systems in place so we can report back on that".

The need for performance management practices in the GAA and Irish sport goes beyond simply being accountable to funders. Effective performance management practices also must be in place to manage issues such as the role of employees and volunteers in Irish sport and to establish a working relationship between the two groups which contributes to the growth and achievement of organisational objectives. Furthermore, with a growing number of stakeholders and performance areas which NPSOs must now manage, having no way of monitoring, reporting and managing these issues will ultimately lead to underperformance within NPSOs. Each organisation may have different barriers in place for the establishment of performance management practices. In the case of the GAA, it is evident that the major barrier is a lack of appropriate knowledge and expertise made more difficult by the disconnect between paid employees of the organisation and its volunteers, as further explored below.

Individual performance management

Some form of performance appraisal is now commonplace in most traditional business entities, allowing for evaluation of employee contributions to organisational success (Cleveland, Murphy & Williams, 1989; Landy & Farr, 1980). At GAA headquarters, one participant claims that there is a "firmly established" culture of individual performance management practices in place. However, they also acknowledge that this system has only "been in place over the last few years". They claim that the appraisal process is "in place at every level" within GAA headquarters and consists of setting individual objectives for the year and formally appraising employee performance biannually. Another participant simply claims that "individual employees are evaluated against objectives" but fails to go into detail relating to any robust performance appraisal processes. For senior managers within the GAA, "there is an element of salary based on performance", which is rare in Irish sport management for employees other than the CEO of an organisation. Interestingly, the provincial councils decided not to adopt this performance-related pay approach to individual performance management as they decided that they cannot be held fully accountable for their performance due to their heavy reliance on the work of volunteers. "If a volunteer decides not to do something, the kickback is on the employee ... sometimes volunteers will not work with you" because of time constraints, health and various other issues. Furthermore, another participant agrees that this is a major problem relating to individual performance appraisal within the Association: "[We] set goals and objectives for staff; the success of that depends on the cooperation of the volunteers." They provide an example, suggesting that if an employee is charged with "getting 200 clubs to develop a strategic plan" that ultimately this "is dependent on volunteer willingness, expertise" and so forth.

An important aspect of an individual performance management practice is that all levels of employees within an organisation are subject to similar performance appraisals (DeNisi & Pritchard, 2006). One participant claims that some form of individual performance appraisal "needs to be implemented at the provincial and county level" but at present there are no formal appraisal processes in place. However, other participants claim that an appraisal process does in fact exist, at least within the Ulster GAA Provincial Council. One claims that there are "one-to-one appraisal meetings on an annual basis" where work plans are set out for staff, which in turn form the basis for performance assessment. They also state that "monthly staff meetings" occur during which employees can offer and receive feedback on their work plans. They claim the Provincial Council previously held biannual appraisals but "moved to an annual approach" as a result of the longevity of some strategic objectives.

Performance appraisal should be an intrinsic component of the workforce (DeNisi & Pritchard, 2006) both within GAA headquarters and its Provincial Councils, and each employee should be able to explain exactly what the process entails. Further illustrating the problematic issues of combining professional and volunteer staff, one participant states:

> The problem with implementing [individual] performance management at the county level is that it is a volunteer-led system. It is difficult to have volunteers reviewing the performance of full time people. [The Chairperson of county boards is most often a volunteer.] Often volunteers do not have the expertise or know how to review performance or set objectives and targets.

With this statement, this participant correctly identifies one of the major issues facing the organisation: "Volunteers are elected and set direction for those who work for the GAA." The GAA is not the only organisation where this situation prevails. In fact, the majority of sporting organisations in Irish sport are volunteer led and are responsible for evaluating professional employees' performances. The GAA is in a fortunate position where it has the potential to move to a professional board of directors, which would eliminate the situation of volunteers appraising the performances of paid individuals. Even if the organisation chooses to continue with volunteers leading the future direction of the entity, at a minimum these individuals must be trained and professionally developed to have the appropriate knowledge and expertise to review performance and set objectives and targets. Participants are correct when asserting that it remains a difficult area; however, by training and developing volunteers the organisation will benefit from that increased knowledge, and the volunteers will also benefit from the same.

One participant claims individual performance management is "new over the last few years but is becoming standard practice where paid officials are concerned". Another participant claims that although "senior managers are very aware" of the various elements and objectives of the strategic plan, in general "volunteers pay little attention to the strategic plan". Other participants agree this is a difficult area to approach as adding to the workload and commitment of volunteers may cause them to withdraw their services within the Association. One participant states that "we just try to make them better equipped; more barriers in place would make it hard for the GAA to attract volunteers". However, almost hinting at a 360-degree feedback approach, they do go on to state that "a self-appraisal system" may be an appropriate resolution to the situation. Another participant claims that the GAA is trying to "up skill people" in order to facilitate a situation where volunteer performance may be appraised: "We would like to do this, but we are a long way away still." This participant also refers to the relationship between employees and volunteers as an issue: "there is always tension between full-time people and volunteers; it is there all the time. For full-time people to set goals for volunteers would be very difficult."

Interviewees did suggest moving in the direction of establishing self-evaluation processes and making volunteers "better equipped", and perhaps this is the best way for the organisation moving forward, as the adoption of individual performance management practices is crucial to the success of the GAA's objectives given its heavy reliance on volunteers within this area. A 360-degree feedback approach is clearly applicable in this situation, where volunteers and employees can be subject to similar performance feedback, and areas of development can be easily identified.

Governance

The issue of governance in NPSOs is often a very complex one, with various facets and layers involved in this concept. When appropriate governance systems are in place, the activities of an organisation can be scrutinised to ensure the delivery of benefits to the organisation and its stakeholders (Hoye, 2006; Mason *et al.*, 2006). The GAA has a unique structure of governance within Irish sport, and indeed internationally, with a number of layers and committees and groups at various levels of its governance system. This has sometimes led to confusion relating to roles and responsibilities within the organisation and calls for a re-evaluation of the structure of governance from many critics – including those within the organisation itself – to create a more streamlined entity (Hassan, 2010). At the top of this complex network of governance within the GAA is its annual Congress which "meets once a year and determines GAA rules and policy". There are roughly 330 delegates who form the Congress to "formulate policy" and include "representatives of all units of the GAA both at home and abroad". To have a decision-making body made up of such a vast number of individuals is clearly challenging in terms of good corporate governance and remains very outdated in relation to international best practice. For instance, Yeh and Taylor (2008) suggest that decision-making bodies within NPSOs should consist of between 8–10 individuals.

Directly below Congress there is a Central Council which is made up of 40 elected delegates from each county unit (in Ireland and overseas) and meets approximately six times per year. "Between Annual Congresses, responsibility for the on-going operation and development of the GAA is vested in the Central Council" (Quinn, 2002, p. 243). One participant states that "the Central Council has a range of sub-committees to develop GAA policy and oversee initiatives. The Chairperson, secretary and members of each sub-committee are appointed by the President, subject to ratification by the Central Council." The composition of such a large group again constitutes an outdated approach to corporate governance in sport, where inefficiency, communication issues and accountability in the decision-making process remain potentially challenging problems facing this group. Furthermore, the calibre (Hoye & Doherty, 2011) and expertise of individuals within this body must be brought into question as they are responsible for major decisions relating to on-going development within the organisation, yet there is no guarantee that anybody within this body has the appropriate knowledge or expertise to execute this task effectively.

Below the Central Council is the GAA's Management Committee (board), consisting of 15 people who have a mandate from Central Council to manage the day-to-day operations of the GAA. Yeh and Taylor (2008, p. 34) state that "in a governance system, the board is a critical mechanism because its main responsibility is to make certain that the activities of the organisation are carried out in the best interests of the organisation, its members and society". In the GAA, the Management Committee essentially holds the same responsibilities as 'the board' within other NPSOs and is made up of 13 representatives from GAA membership with two independent committee members. In terms of best practice in modern sport management, it is becoming widely accepted that boards in NPSOs such as the GAA should consist of largely independent members (Hood, 1995) who have the appropriate knowledge and expertise of both the sport and traditional business acumen to develop the entity to its full potential. One participant suggests that the appointment of "two external [independent] members brings a level of expertise that we wouldn't have ourselves". They go on to claim that all external members of the committee have brought something very valuable to the Association in the past and that the Association could possibly avail itself of a greater balance of GAA and external membership within the committee. This participant is clearly supporting the suggestion that sport boards could avail themselves of more independent members who can bring knowledge of traditional management practices, such as performance management techniques, to the organisation. Supporting this, Fama and Jensen (1983) and Hoye and Doherty (2011) suggest that the incorporation of independent board members within oversight committees is widely considered to be an appropriate govern-ance mechanism designed to improve the overall capabilities of the board.

The same participant also makes the suggestion that, as a result of the GAA's 'reach' within Irish society, the organisation can seek external advice without adding further external membership to the management committee. This scen-ario would ultimately cause confusion and possible resentment amongst existing committee members who have been elected to carry out these very roles. Sup-porting Papadimitriou and Taylor's (2000) and Papadimitriou's (2007) research, another participant suggests that groups such as the Management Committee should have more representation of "people from a traditional business back-ground". They state that "people with business acumen must be on committees to support better policy making".

The majority of the GAA's national Management Committee is made up of representatives of the provincial bodies, the chairman of the British unit and members of Central Council. One participant suggests that "the GAA is at the whim of democracy, and committees within the Association can have a range of backgrounds". Another supports this synopsis, claiming that the traditional busi-ness background and expertise of the Management Committee can vary depend-ing upon board composition and "some years it may be stronger than others". They go on to claim that as "committee members change with different elec-tions, it is never guaranteed" that members will have the appropriate knowledge and experience required. The Management Committee, which may not always have strong business acumen and expertise, proposes major decisions for the daily operations of the organisation that must be ratified by Central Council before they can be acted upon. From an operational standpoint, the Central Exec-utive Committee within the organisation is the senior management team made up of a number of managers who are responsible for delivering the on-going strategic agenda within the Association. These are paid employees whose duties relate to the areas of finance, games development, marketing and commercial-ism, communications, stadium management and management of the four provin-cial unions.

Yeh and Taylor (2008) describe the complexities of the governance issue as a constant challenge for many NPSOs. This is evident in the GAA, with particip-ants claiming the GAA is a complex organisation with approximately 20,000 teams, 2,500 clubs, various county boards, provincial unions, and even retaining an overseas component. With such a complex organisation, an appropriate and effective governance structure is required to establish a much "more streamlined organisation" (Hassan, 2010, p. 420). One of the major problems with the current governance structure within the GAA, according to a participant, is that often "decision making cannot be done easily as it must be filtered through the Man-agement Committee, Central Council and then ultimately Congress who only meet once per year". A further pressure that exists within the GAA as a result of such a complex governance structure is the communication process. One parti-cipant suggests that there is often "a lack of a joined-up message" within the Association because of its size, where decisions and strategic direction set out at various levels of governance are occasionally inadequately relayed and misunderstood by elements and sections of the Association. Notwithstanding these potential shortcomings, the same participant claims that "governance is the key to success within the GAA". Therefore, the GAA must analyse its current practices and governance model in relation to the Association's "unique bottom-up approach", the size, efficiency and power of the Annual Congress, the composition of the Management Committee, the complexities of the varied components of the Association (club, county, province, overseas), and finally the issues surrounding communication with its stakeholders, complicated by the unique structure of governance currently operating within the Association.

It is clear that the entire system of governance in the GAA is complex and potentially not suitably responsive to the demands the organisation now faces (Hassan, 2010) with calls for increased transparency, professionalism, and the growth of complexities around financial management within the organisation. A tiered system of decision-making bodies, consisting of individuals who may not possess the required knowledge and expertise to govern such an entity, could be limiting the GAA's capability and is indeed causing concern with members within its own ranks (Hassan, 2010). A move to include the appointment of an independent professional board of directors would allow for a more streamlined organisation and would remove the need to constantly seek external advice, as identified by participants previously. In order for the GAA to remain relevant to its membership within Irish society (Hassan, 2010), and when there are now more opportunities to participate in other sports and entertainment than ever before, the organisation could adopt a system of governance that is appropriate to its current needs with a board of directors who hold the right mix of expertise and knowledge of the issues facing the organisation and how these might best be addressed. A successful performance management approach within an NPSO must ensure that the governance system is appropriate and ideally that the board consists of independent professional appointees. Furthermore, aside from ensuring appropriate governance structures, a performance management approach which can only be adopted when the correct expertise is present on the board will be imperative for the future success of the organisation, as it now has to respond to more performance dimensions and increased expectations of stakeholders than at any time in its history.

Finance

The major source of funding for the GAA is through gate receipts, particularly during the All-Ireland Championship campaign. In addition to the All-Ireland Championship, the GAA has benefited financially in the past by agreeing to host international association football and rugby fixtures. In fact, in 2008 gate receipts from association football and rugby fixtures accounted for 34 per cent of total revenue at Croke Park (the GAA's national stadium), as opposed to just 20 per cent from GAA fixtures (Keys, 2009). However, this revenue stream is no longer in place within the GAA as association football and rugby now host their respective fixtures at the newly renovated Aviva stadium (formerly Lansdowne Road). Gate receipts account for 41 per cent of overall GAA income, with commercial activities (Amis *et al.*, 1999) and Croke Park rental income accounting for 26 per cent and 27 per cent respectively (Keys, 2009). There has been a decline in gate receipts in recent years (Keys, 2009) and, as individuals continue to have less 'discretionary spending', it may be difficult to reverse the trend going forward. In order to combat the situation, one participant suggests that the GAA needs to improve its communications by conveying to spectators and the GAA membership that almost all income from gate receipts (78 per cent according to Keys, 2009) is "re-invested at grassroots level". However, although this may be the case, aside from merely 're-investing' at grassroots level, it can be argued that the GAA must meaningfully engage with its membership as the values of community and inclusion are some of the foundations upon which the organisation has been built. As the organisation has evolved to become an ever-more bureaucratic entity, it could be viewed that these core values have been placed to one side to focus on a more centralised approach to management. Although, it is clearly evident that the GAA must develop a professional 'ethos' to its operations and management, this must be balanced with the needs of the organisation's membership to ensure the GAA remains relevant to this integral group of stakeholders.

The Association receives approximately €3m annually from the ISC and has an overall budget of between €40–50m per year. One participant states that the Association also receives funding from various departments within the Irish government, such as the Department of Transport, Tourism and Sport, the Department of Foreign Affairs, the Department of Health and even the Department of Education and Skills, which accounts for approximately 10 per cent of GAA income. Doherty and Murray (2007) suggest that an NPSO's qualities and values can increase its potential to attract commercial sponsorship. Within the GAA, sponsorship and commercial activity generates significant income, and the Association employs a multi-sponsor approach with different companies sponsoring football and hurling within the GAA. This is a crucial revenue stream for the Association and an area which must be evaluated on a continual basis to ensure the GAA is best placed to attract potential sponsors and that companies view the GAA as a viable investment opportunity. In line with Doherty and Murray's (2007) claims, the GAA should do all it can to convey the core values of the Association as the qualities that would attract the investment from potential sponsors.

It has long been argued that non-profit organisations that deliver all types of service including sport should seek to increase the proportion of funding that they generate from non-government sources (Berrett & Slack, 2001). Almost 30 years ago, MacMillan (1983, p. 61) argued:

> At a time when long-run demands for agencies' services are likely to increase, and at a time of reduced government support, not-for-profit organisations are coming under increasing pressure to deliver more and more services with less and less resources, supplied with more and more strings attached.

In addition to government funding and gate receipts, an important and "growing revenue stream" for the GAA is the negotiation of media rights with various public and privately owned broadcasting companies. In the past, RTE (Radió Telefís Éireann, the national free-to-view broadcaster) had a monopoly on the broadcasting rights for GAA fixtures. Increased competition in the market has benefited the Association as it is now in a stronger position to negotiate better deals for increased income generation. TV3 and TG4 are "now very interested in covering GAA fixtures" and the Association has already signed contracts with these broadcasters to cover some GAA fixtures. Setanta Sports (a pay-per-view broadcaster) is also now broadcasting GAA national league fixtures. One participant states that with the emergence of "four significant players", this new "competitive element has boosted income" within the Association. However, with the organisation choosing to go down the route of 'pay-per-view' it is risking the growth of resentment amongst its broad membership base and is moving away from some of the core beliefs of the organisation.

The "income mix" (Cordery & Baskerville, 2009) within the Provincial Councils consists of funding from GAA headquarters, funding from other public departments and gate receipts. Ulster GAA for example, receives large amounts of funding from various government departments within the Republic of Ireland and Northern Ireland in relation to particular initiatives that align with government policy. One participant states it is a priority for the provincial councils to "source and secure funding, both public and sponsorship". The Provincial Councils operate in an autonomous nature to a large degree and have the ability to seek funding from various sources within the public and private sector. Although Berrett and Slack (2001) argue that NPSOs should be attempting to increase the proportion of funding they receive from non-government sources, for the Ulster GAA it would appear that it is almost exclusively funded from the public purse. In Northern Ireland alone, Ulster GAA receives funding from the Department of Culture Arts and Leisure, Sport NI, the Department of Social Development, the Department of Foreign Affairs, the Department of Education, and the Department of Environment. Provincial Councils in turn provide funding to various County Boards and clubs within their jurisdiction. Some of the Provincial Councils will assess clubs on areas such as coaching development, achievement of objectives and structures of governance before deciding the level of funding to be allocated.

The GAA has also previously availed itself of government funding in relation to the creation of new sporting infrastructure within Ireland. Previous projects saw the government and the GAA combining to provide new facilities for communities and the GAA membership at large. In the current economic climate there is almost a complete lack of capital investment in sport, with one participant claiming support for GAA infrastructure "has completely disappeared; going from €15–20m per year to zero". This will be one of the major challenges facing the Association in relation to finance and the provision of GAA sporting infrastructure moving forward. As government funding in sport is clearly becoming less available, it is now urgent for organisations such as the GAA to diversify their various revenue streams. The GAA could explore all possible options for increasing or maintaining the level of funding it and its members have become accustomed to. Areas such as gaining interest on retained earnings, applications for philanthropic grants and additional commercial activity could develop into relevant revenue streams for the organisation. If the organisation is indeed successful in diversifying its income streams, performance management practices will have to be in place to monitor and manage the various needs and demands of stakeholders associated with these various sources of income.

Participation and other performance concerns

Thibault *et al.* (1991) directly refer to a tension that exists between professional staff and volunteers within NPSOs. A major cause of concern for the GAA appears to be this emerging 'tension' between paid employees of the Association and the relationship that exists with the volunteer participant base: "Volunteer recruitment and the mixing of volunteers and employees is a major challenge for the Association." One participant claims that the number of volunteers within the Association is decreasing because of social pressures, such as people simply having less free time, and suggests the GAA "must be strategic" with its plans to recruit and retain additional volunteers. Furthermore, the GAA runs a number of participation interventions to stimulate increases in player, coach, volunteer and official numbers but does not appear to have assessment procedures in place to measure the effectiveness of these interventions.

This participant goes on to state that "the professional outlook and remit of the Association is causing problems with the amateur ethos of the organisation". All players, managers, coaches and officials (apart from the full-time coaching staff and administrators) are volunteers, and the continued increase in coaching resources and techniques has at times encouraged a professional standard of training and high performance with county-level players. An indirect result of this has been the establishment of a Gaelic Players Association (GPA), formed in 1999. This group focuses on the needs of elite players, and suggests that the 1,800 county players should receive preferential treatment and funding over club-level players and grassroots GAA members. While it claims not to seek a change from the GAA's amateur status in the direction of professionalism, its motives thus far have clearly indicated that a professional GAA at county level is its ultimate goal. One participant suggests that "the vast majority of GAA members are content with the current volunteer ethos of the GAA, and GPA's aims are seen by many as directly conflicting with the aims and values of the Association".

A further area of performance which the GAA must address is that of coach education. High levels of youth participation in GAA activities and the increasing role of amateur coaches in youth development have resulted in a need for coach education programmes. Gilbert and Trudel (1999) claim a well-designed training programme for coaches can result in improvements in various areas of coaching. These include "improved time management resulting in increased motor engagement time, positive changes in specific coaching behaviours and personality development in athletes" (Gilbert & Trudel, 1999, p. 235). One participant states that "underage coaches do not have the required philosophy or expertise" at the level at which the Association desires. They go on to suggest that "more effective coaches make more effective players" and claims the GAA is trying to implement new coaching qualifications and requirements, even exploring the possibility of establishing a diploma-level certificate through the tertiary education system. Individual performance management can play a large role in the GAA's ambitions to improve coach education; many international NPSOs have implemented successful coach education approaches and use management practices, such as individual Balanced Scorecards, to manage and measure coach performance. The GAA could become more accustomed to these practices and learn from international best practice relating to the education and evaluation of coaches in sport.

Basketball Ireland

Performance management practices

All Basketball Ireland participants were asked about the various forms of performance management systems, practices and processes that currently operate within the organisation and all provided similar responses. "Unfortunately no performance management systems and processes are utilised that I am aware of"; "There is no performance management process being used within the organisation; not because Basketball Ireland does not think it is suitable but because we have not got to that stage yet." Other participants also could not refer to any form of performance management practices operating within the organisation.

One participant, a senior figure within the organisation, claims that there was a 17-month period during which the organisation was functioning on "auto-pilot" without a CEO and is just now attempting to establish appropriate protocols and procedures. They acknowledge that Basketball Ireland is in 'Category 1' of the 64 NGBs within the country, which essentially means it is in the top six sports in terms of participation. They go on to suggest that the financial structure of Basketball Ireland and stakeholders are different to other NGBs and that a unique performance management model with specific measurements is required. Although this may be the case, the implementation of a generic performance management tool/approach in the interim could provide real benefits for the organisation by simply allowing the organisation to focus on crucial areas of performance or even align employee roles with strategic objectives, which appeared to be absent within the organisation. This participant agrees that general principles still apply across the organisation and that if a performance management system had been in operation over the previous decade it would "have prevented the build-up of such a big financial loss". The same participant goes on to claim that there were huge flaws in the governance, administration, accountability and authority of the organisation under the previous regime, which an adequate performance management system could have potentially exposed. They claim they would like to see the establishment of a performance management culture within Basketball Ireland where all employees feel they have a responsibility to the organisation and could carry out their roles with pride. They feel it should be a privilege to work for an NGB and this should be reflected in the actions and operations of each employee, department and indeed the organisation as a whole.

It appears that there are a number of obstacles to the successful implementation of an adequate performance management approach within Basketball Ireland. With any new initiative introduced to an organisation, 'change management' will always have a role to play and management must be patient and provide regular feedback to staff in relation to the adoption of a new performance management approach. Skinner, Stewart and Edwards (1999, p. 180) concluded that "organisational change is a complex phenomenon that filters through the organisation with differing ramifications at different levels". In Basketball Ireland, opportunities could be sought in all aspects of the organisation and, although it ultimately damages the capability of the NGB, a reduction in staff numbers from 27 to 12 allows for greater control, alignment with strategy (Kennerly & Neely, 2003; McNamara & Mong, 2005) and potential for more robust review of individual employee performances (Applebaum, Roy & Gilliland, 2011). One participant believes that the "current economic situation and financial difficulties" are the main obstacles the organisation faces but does not see any major obstacles in order to facilitate the implementation of a new performance management system within Basketball Ireland. As the organisation is essentially "starting from scratch", employees may be more receptive to new ideas and initiatives as opposed to those being implemented under the former regime, which ultimately proved to be ineffective.

Individual performance management

The individual is a crucial component to the overall performance within any organisation (Van Emmerik, 2008). DeNisi and Pritchard (2006) claim that appropriate appraisal, feedback and management of individual employees can facilitate a high level of individual performance, thus leading to a higher level of overall organisational performance. A senior figure within Basketball Ireland suggests that "each CEO has their own style" when it comes to the issue of assessing and appraising individual staff performance. They go on to state that "a clear job description" is the crucial starting point for the appraisal and review of any individual employee.

According to the Piggot-Irvine (2003) model, the most important elements to conducting an effective performance appraisal are respect, openness and trust. These key features should not only be present during the appraisal but they should be practiced between management and employees on an on-going basis. Applebaum *et al.* (2011) suggest that a way to foster this relationship is for management to provide feedback to their employees on a continual basis. Currently,

Basketball Ireland staff members are only assessed annually to measure agreed goals and objectives. It is abundantly clear, however, that 360-degree feedback, as argued by this book to be best practice, is currently absent from the organisation.

Research relating to the issue of performance appraisals (Shraeder *et al.*, 2007; Applebaum *et al.*, 2011; Boice & Kleiner, 1997; Piggot-Irvine, 2003) acknowledges the important role of professional development in the appraisal process. In accordance with this, an important aspect of individual assessment which a participant refers to is the on-going professional development of staff: "How has the CEO helped the staff improve their own abilities?" This has also been non-existent in the past within the organisation but is something that the participant feels is important both for the organisation and the individual, and they would like to see this area of individual performance management developed further.

Each employee within the organisation is encouraged to provide feedback to management, the board and the Council relating to any aspect of the organisation's performance that they feel could be enhanced. One participant claims that not all ideas have to come from the CEO and all staff can have a significant impact on the operations and direction of the organisation: "In forming the strategic plan, both the board and staff put forward ideas. The staff wanted ownership of the plan rather than the board just handing it out to them." This statement is supported by other interviewees: "Each staff member is encouraged to attend strategic planning meetings and provide input into the process. The staff members are invited along with the National Council to review and improve current policies." Another commented:

> Basketball Ireland holds regular staff meetings where all staff are updated on any plans. Each member of staff provides an update on their area and enlists help if required. This enables staff members to focus their efforts on specific areas where development or action is needed.

One of the most important aspects of individual performance management, as shown in the literature review conducted earlier in this book, is the requirement for employee roles to be directly linked with specific or, at a minimum, broad strategic objectives (Kennerly & Neely, 2003; Senior & Swailes, 2004; McNamara & Mong, 2005). A senior figure claims that Basketball Ireland is "just now trying to link employee job descriptions and roles to the strategic objectives". They claim that they want the strategic plan to be a "living document" and that all individual employee activities would be linked to the plan, but currently this situation does not exist within the organisation. The lack of alignment between employee roles and strategic objectives could lead to further inefficiencies and a reduction in productivity, limiting the ability of the organisation to achieve its key strategic objectives.

As highlighted by this same participant, a further area of individual performance management associated with the organisation which requires attention is the standard of coaching at all levels within basketball in Ireland. They suggest performance management not only has a place in the organisational setting put should also be applied to coaches. They claim that coaches should be evaluated on their past record, performances and achievements, and their ability, experience and knowledge of coaching should also be analysed, particularly at senior levels of the game (Mallett & Cote, 2006). The participant would like to see this approach being implemented within the game in the coming seasons and has sought the feedback of various internal and external stakeholders of the organisation in relation to the adoption of such an initiative.

Governance

Hoye and Doherty (2011, p. 272) state "the importance of [NGBs] having effective governance systems and structures in place is increasingly recognized by national government sport agencies, which have highlighted the negative impacts that poor governance structures and practices can have on organisational performance". The issue of 'poor' governance within Basketball Ireland appeared to be central to the financial turmoil the organisation faced following a number of mismanagement issues and alleged malpractice instances within the organisation. The organisation had been operating without a CEO for almost two years and in 2011 all board members stepped down from their positions and new board members were elected at an Annual General Meeting. Papadimitriou and Taylor (2000), Papadimitriou (2007) and Hoye and Doherty (2011) concluded that an important indicator of NPSO effectiveness is the calibre of the board, including its ability to liaise with external groups and state/provincial-level organisations. The impact that voluntary board members can have on organisational effectiveness was also highlighted by Bayle and Robinson (2007, p. 258) who argued that "the system of governance, most notably the permanence and position of the main executives (voluntary leaders), are one of the keys to an NGB's success". Within Basketball Ireland, the introduction of a new CEO and board was imperative for the organisation as a "significant debt was run up by the previous regime that were made up of volunteers and whose skillsets may have been suitable to running clubs but not a national organisation". Half of the board have been elected in a similar fashion to previous BI boards, with the only difference being a co-optation of four further board members. Best practices in sport governance suggests that the adoption of independent non-executive boards that are appointed following a national recruitment campaign, shortlisting and an interview process allows for the most-qualified directors to be present within sport boardrooms.

The new structure of governance within Basketball Ireland operates on the basis of a board interacting with a National Council. The board is responsible for the "business of Basketball Ireland" while the National Council:

> ...acts as the sport policy formation and activation centre of the sport. Presently the board make the financial decisions regarding the smooth and

effective management financially of the company whilst the National Council [made up of a representative from every committee in Basketball Ireland] ratifies any other decisions required for basketball Ireland members.

The need for a National Council must be brought into question as they are being charged with developing policy within the organisation yet there are no mechanisms in place to guarantee they have the knowledge or expertise to carry out this role effectively. As it stands, for the creation of a new board, four representatives were elected from within the Basketball Ireland membership and were given the authority to co-opt a further four individuals to establish an eight-person board which is joined by the Basketball Ireland CEO. Traditionally in any organisation, a CEO reports to the board and is not a board member. A board that includes the CEO may not adequately evaluate the performance of the CEO, and an independent board (of which the CEO is not a member) is potentially far greater at monitoring CEO performance.

One participant claims that the current problems of the organisation were caused by the weaknesses of an inexperienced board to whom "being a board member was just a hobby. Board members who are directors or professionals in other entities have a far greater understanding of the consequences of not doing their jobs correctly." Although the new board is not independent, its calibre appears to be far greater than the previous board and participants anticipate the new board can repair the organisation's damaged reputation and image.

The relationship between all three entities within the organisation (the board, the National Council and the staff of Basketball Ireland) is imperative for the overall success of the organisation. As highlighted by Thibault *et al.* (1991) and acknowledged by participants, "if tension builds up between the board and the Council it may damage the sport in the medium to long term". Participants suggested that the relationship between these three entities is in fact a positive one: "the working relationship between the staff members and committees is great"; "there is a good working relationship between the board and staff of Basketball Ireland". In order for this relationship to remain positive, participants claim that lines of communication must be kept open between the different entities to minimise misunderstanding, and that clearly defined roles are important to ensure accountability and transparency in all facets of the organisation: "Already there have been misunderstanding and communication issues over roles and responsibilities of the board and National Council." One participant claims this is a 'change management' issue and that these problems should resolve themselves as individuals and groups within the organisation become more familiar with the new structure of governance.

Finance

Currently the organisation has three elements to its "income mix" (Cordery & Baskerville, 2009), outlined by participants as follows: "The Irish Sports Council core grant, membership fees and corporate activity"; "The main source of funding is the Irish Sports Council. This funding affects decisions in relation to programmes that can be run";

> The "Women in Sport" funding the organisation received in 2011 was offered to all clubs across the island of Ireland. Various area boards were awarded funds to run referee courses, table official courses, coaching courses, and the Women's Premier League teams were awarded funds to run a pre-season tournament.

Over the previous number of years, the organisation has essentially been operating under two revenue streams: the ISC grant and membership subscriptions. The third component, corporate activity, "has been non-existent over the previous years due to the financial collapse of the organisation" and, according to one participant, "within three years we [the organisation] would like to see a greater balance between the three revenue streams". Berrett and Slack (2001) suggest that one reason why NPSOs have been unable to rely more heavily on corporate sponsorship in the past has been the lack of sophistication in their approaches to seeking such funding. In line with this, one participant states:

> Basketball Ireland is yet to target a major sponsor, for example, naming rights of the National Basketball Arena, but is currently very pro-active on this front. We have targeted local businesses and built up many healthy relationships that continue to improve the level of Basketball in Ireland.

A participant correctly points out that the organisation will find it difficult to attract adequate levels of corporate sponsorship until it repairs its reputation as an accountable and professional organisation and can convey to potential sponsors the benefits and rewards of becoming involved with the sport. In 2012 it was announced that national broadcaster RTE would be withdrawing its coverage of the Basketball Ireland National Cup Finals, which further damaged the organisation's ability to attract suitable sponsors. However, the organisation successfully arranged a new deal with a pay-per-view sport broadcaster (Setanta Sports) and subsequently TG4 (another broadcaster) to air the Cup Finals along with a magazine-type show aired monthly during the season.

Participation

Basketball Ireland has traditionally enjoyed high participation at the secondary schools level, but a major fall-off in numbers at post-secondary schools level is always present. The organisation "aims to provide an avenue of participation for all" but it does not appear that the organisation employs any specific interventions (or therefore evaluation of effectiveness) to stimulate participation in the sport.

Furthermore, a participant states that "low morale due to the financial trauma, the lack of Irish role models, the high cost of individual participation and hall hire, and the lack of media attention" are constant threats to initiatives and policies aimed at increasing levels of participation at all levels. They go on to claim that "the lack of achievement at the international level has not helped the growth of basketball" and "young people have a wide variety of leisure choices in today's society. The continued lack of appeal of Basketball Ireland's marquee playing divisions to the wider sporting community needs to be addressed." Although this may be the case, the lack of participation interventions, let alone an analysis of their effectiveness, are clearly absent within the operations of Basketball Ireland. This is a performance area the organisation could address without the need for large financial investment.

Irish case study summary

From analysis of the three organisations within the Irish case study it becomes abundantly clear that none of the case study organisations have adopted any traditional form of organisational performance management practices or systems – an alarming revelation given the significant amount of public finance invested within these entities. Furthermore, the practices of these organisations in relation to individual performance management are in their infancy and are not aligned with current best practice as seen within the traditional business environment and more professionalised sporting organisations. This includes a lack of evaluation of board member performances, job descriptions that are not linked to strategic imperatives, and an apparent absence of any form of 360-degree feedback, which this book has argued is the most effective way of managing and evaluating individual employee and volunteer performances.

The diversification of the 'income mix' within the ISC and Basketball Ireland is not yet strongly established. Both organisations are heavily reliant on government support, with the ISC receiving 100 per cent of its funding from government and Basketball Ireland in turn receiving the majority of their funding from the ISC. As a contrast, the GAA has successfully diversified its income streams to encompass both commercial and state support, which has created a sound financial base for the organisation to operate from. Clearly the appeal and popularity of the GAA as a national sport of significance has a substantial impact on the organisation's ability to attract commercial sponsorship and income from broadcasting rights.

The success of participation interventions within the selected NPSOs is largely unknown due to the conspicuous absence of evaluations of such interventions within these organisations. Alarmingly, this appears even to apply to the ISC, the organisation responsible for developing participation in sport and physical activity within Ireland. The ISC could act as the leader of best practice within Irish sport, improve its control function over NGBs, and be held more accountable by government for their own performance and for that of the NGBs that it funds with public finance.

Through the analysis of the data collected within the Irish case study, it has become clear that the performance dimension of 'sport governance' is a salient characteristic in determining the performance of these organisations as a whole. Unfortunately, within the three Irish case study organisations, the governance structures and practices appear outdated, with each organisation facing various challenges in this respect. Of critical importance, the election/appointment process and therefore the calibre of board members within the Irish case study organisations could be addressed, as currently these processes could be limiting the capacity of these entities to perform at optimum levels.

8 New Zealand case study

Introduction

As described previously, this book conducts a qualitative comparative analysis between NPSOs in Ireland and New Zealand as primary case study organisations. New Zealand was chosen as a nation to be compared with Ireland due to its similar demographic profile, sporting culture, and close similarities in the way sport is organised and delivered within the two nations. Although the organisation and delivery of sport within both countries are essentially identical, New Zealand continues to achieve far greater results on the world sporting stage, and management of the sport industry in New Zealand appears to be of a superior level in comparison with NPSOs within Irish sport. A relevant example of the differences in 'elite' sport performance was seen at the 2012 London Olympic Games: New Zealand finished 15th on the medal table in comparison with Ireland finishing 41st.

The following section analyses three NPSOs within New Zealand sport (Sport NZ, the New Zealand Rugby Union and New Zealand Cricket) to assess how the fundamental performance dimensions identified within this book are managed compared to the Irish case study. Sport NZ has a similar mandate to the Irish Sports Council in that it is a government agency responsible for the development of sport (both elite and community) within New Zealand and is funded directly by public finance from government. The NZRU was chosen as an NPSO to be compared with the GAA – the organisations manage the national sport of each nation. And NZC was chosen as the third case study organisation to be analysed due to cricket being a popular sport within New Zealand but not a national sport, similar to Basketball Ireland within the Irish case study.

Sport NZ

Performance management practices

The establishment of an organisational-wide performance management system is a practice that Sport NZ has yet to introduce to improve overall results and outputs and provide a more transparent and accountable workforce and organisation.

At present, a formal (on-going) performance management system does not exist within the organisation but participants believe the implementation of such a practice could provide real benefits in relation to managing performance objectives and its accountability function to government. As NPSOs become more professional in their approach, one participant believes the industry should move to a situation in which NPSOs are "appraised as a commercial entity". Another participant states that "using sustainable systems and processes … is critical and has to be led by a capable CEO and wise chairman of the board". The board within Sport NZ has been "hand-picked" by the NZ government minister to ensure that the organisation has a high calibre of expertise running the organisation, yet an on-going performance management practice (apart from the 'Organisational Development Tool' or ODT, described in the next section) has not, as yet, been implemented. A further participant claims it is "important to have a formalised system as a number of teams have to be aligned and there is a strong accountability function to government". Currently, performance management within Sport NZ is limited to quarterly reporting against financial and business plan objectives, and evaluation of the Statement of Intent (internal) and Letter of Expectation (external) provided by the Minister at the beginning of each year. One interviewee claims that a performance management culture, as described by Winand *et al.* (2010), does not currently exist within the organisation and concedes that it is a crucial "area for improvement". They provide a possible reason as to why such a practice does not currently operate in the organisation: "performance management can be seen as a frustrating time waster that takes people away from their main roles and responsibilities". It is the role of the board, CEO and senior management to stress the importance of such a practice and convey that performance management can ultimately help the organisation operate and achieve objectives far more efficiently than if there were no such practice in place. Pulakos (2009) describes how some organisations find it difficult to fully engage with suitable performance management approaches and suggests an individualised system must be adopted to suit the organisation. A performance management system that is seen to be a "time waster" by staff is clearly of little benefit to the organisation and such a system should be re-evaluated and examined to ensure it serves a real purpose within the organisation (Pulakos, 2009). It may take some time and on-going adjustment to establish a system that truly meets the needs of an organisation such as Sport NZ, which has multiple objectives operating within variable timeframes. Supporting Pulakos' (2009) research, one participant correctly states: "there is a wide range of size and capability within sport organisations; not one model suits all".

The modern NPSO is a multi-faceted entity (Chappelet & Bayle, 2005) with often-complex governance structures and various internal stakeholders who can make it difficult to implement an effective performance management approach (Pulakos, 2009). One participant suggests that one of the major functions of Sport NZ is to have the ability to measure its own performance but also to measure the performance of its partner organisations (NGBs and RSTs): "Sport NZ wants to create an environment for sport organisations to flourish." Partner

NPSOs are currently "required to submit strategic plans and must report against those plans" as a condition of funding, but more should be done to ensure a good return on investment of public finances (Berrett & Slack, 2001). Much as Sport NZ must convey to its own staff that the implementation of an appropriate performance management practice is not a "time waster" (Pulakos, 2009), it must do the same for its partner organisations and perhaps make this a condition of funding. However, as a participant points out, the organisation "must not be seen to be a bureaucracy but be highly flexible and be relevant to the sector".

The overall success of Sport NZ objectives is largely dependent on the capability and willingness of its partner organisations to align their resources and strategic direction with those of Sport NZ: "Sport NZ delivers its objectives through NGBs and RSTs." Alarmingly, one participant makes the statement: "ultimately NGBs will create direction for themselves. Hopefully it will be in line with our direction." Ideally, partner organisations could be held more accountable for the funding they receive and a common, robust performance management process could be implemented within Sport NZ and all partner organisations to ensure key alignment of objectives, resources and efforts. This situation would also address the prevalent issue of Sport NZ's inability to obtain reliable information (data) relating to various issues from its partner organisations, as described by participants. Supporting Li's (2009) research detailing how NPSOs must become more familiar with traditional business practices, a participant states: "commercial sport organisations with a product to sell are good at gathering and using information; other sport organisations need to do the same". They add that the organisation is "starting to hold individuals to account and partner organisations to account". Another participant concedes that in order to do this the organisation must "communicate expectations" in a clear, accurate and transparent manner as "improving their [partner organisations'] ability to perform is crucial". They acknowledge that "the sector is not good at monitoring and evaluating performance" but claims that Sport NZ has "invested heavily in this area", and the impending implementation of robust "performance management practices will provide better investment". Further supporting Li's (2009) research, another participant provides an appropriate case for full adoption of and engagement with performance management practices in sport: "the closer New Zealand sport gets to adopting commercial and professional approaches the more change in the culture will take place".

The Organisational Development Tool

The Organisational Development Tool (ODT) is a software application unique to Sport NZ which has been developed based on Malcolm Baldrige's (Malcolm Baldrige National Quality Award, 2005) performance management criteria – see Figure 8.1. This tool is a comprehensive 'one-off' application as opposed to an on-going performance management process to measure overall organisational effectiveness, and analyses areas as diverse as culture, values, strategy, finances and human resources. Specifically the ODT examines various aspects of the organisation related to six different areas: leadership, planning, customer focus, sport delivery, people management and sport management (Sport NZ, 2012b). It is a self-assessment tool which Sport NZ facilitates at no charge that has the ability to generate recommendations and can be applied to NGBs, RSTs and clubs. Starting in 2010, Sport NZ applied the tool to its own operations and plans to continue this practice every two years. The ODT can give a good indication of overall organisational effectiveness but it is not without limitations. The imperative aspect of individual employee performance is not assessed within its scope and it requires substantial investment of both time and cost to conduct the review. One participant, a senior figure in the organisation, claims Sport NZ has invested heavily in its implementation and is planning on "taking all the regional sports bodies through it". Although not a sufficient replacement for an on-going robust performance management process and lacking the identification of crucial performance dimensions, the creation of such a tool by Sport NZ is a positive indication that NPSOs are beginning to understand the importance of combining the various facets of their operations to create a transparent, accountable and ultimately high-performing organisation.

Figure 8.1 The Sport NZ Organisational Development Tool (ODT).

Individual performance management

Schraeder *et al.* (2007) claim that performance appraisals are the foundation for development within an organisation. Applebaum *et al.* (2011) also point out that effective performance appraisal processes provide accurate feedback to management on employee performance, satisfaction and role-alignment with strategy. Within Sport NZ there are established mechanisms in place for the assessment and appraisal of individual employees within the organisation. The organisation attempts to establish 'line of sight' between the strategic plan, the business plan and the individual staff member so that each employee can appreciate how their own performance directly relates to the broader goals and objectives of the organisation. The linking of individual employee roles to broader strategic objectives such as this has been identified as constituting best practice within the literature concerning performance appraisals and 360-degree feedback. One participant claims that "staff are very aware of objectives, both in high performance and community sport. Jobs are well aligned to the strategic plan." They go on to state that because of the organisation's relatively small size (80 employees) in comparison with some traditional business organisations, it should be easy to ensure all staff members remain aware of the broader strategic imperatives, a point that has also been made in the literature by Applebaum *et al.* (2011). Theoretically, with smaller numbers it should also be easier for the assessment and appraisal of employee performance to be carried out more robustly. Another participant claims that "each employee has a one-page document on their desk on the key strategic vision and objectives of the organisation". They add that there is "constant referral" to this document from general managers on a daily basis.

A board member within the organisation suggests that "there are a lot of private sector disciplines applicable to sport" and that modern NPSOs need to adopt the principles of individual performance management, which operate in the traditional business environment, relating to the clarity, focus and monitoring of targets that are established for employees. Li (2009) claims that human resource practices, such as performance appraisals, are 100 per cent transferable to NPSOs and are beginning to be utilised within the industry as it 'catches up' with traditional business practices. Another participant claims that in 2006 Sport NZ re-evaluated the manner in which it monitored and appraised individual performances. A further participant states that each staff member has a "performance agreement" which is designed in collaboration with their line manager and relates directly to both the business and the strategic plans of the organisation. This performance agreement forms the basis on which employee performance appraisals are conducted. Within Sport NZ, employees are appraised six monthly through an informal meeting with their line manager, which includes "an element of self-assessment" and performance feedback, followed by a formal appraisal at year end measuring success against individual KPIs. Participants also state that there is a remuneration committee within the board that looks at individual performance for the CEO and senior managers: performance-based pay only operates within the organisation for these individuals.

Governance

Sport NZ functions in a similar manner as the Irish Sports Council in that it is a government agency established to fund and influence the public sport sector within New Zealand. The governance structure within the organisation is also extremely similar to those that operate within its equivalent agency within Ireland. Ong and Wan (2008, p. 325) stated that "understanding the nature of effective board role performance is among the most important areas in management research". Within Sport NZ there are nine individuals who are appointed by the Minister for Sport and Recreation who make up the board and meet monthly to deliver its "statutory requirement of managing the funding delivered by government". One participant suggests that although the board are ministerial appointees, "they have complete autonomy in how resources from the Crown are utilised".

Papadimitriou and Taylor (2000) and Papadimitriou (2007) suggest that the 'calibre' of individual board members and the expertise they bring with them can be a determining factor of organisational performance and success. The Sport NZ board comprises a balance of individuals with business acumen who do not have previous experience within the sport sector, and individuals with business acumen who do have previous experience within the sport sector. Parochialism (Niemann *et al.*, 2011) is not an issue as there is no representation of NGBs on the board, nor individuals whose experience lies solely within the sport sector. One participant believes the latter is not an issue: "they do not need to have knowledge of sport … just like in industry, people move from sector to sector; you just have to be a quick learner". Supporting Papadimitriou and Taylor's (2000) and Papadimitriou's (2007) claims, they go on to state that some boards "have a passion for the sport but lack the industry knowledge; that's when things go wrong". Individuals with appropriate business acumen and industry experience results in a board that is capable of developing strategic direction (Ferkins & Shilbury, 2010) without any form of parochialism (Niemann *et al.*, 2011) or lack of adequate expertise in their decision making. Another participant supports this synopsis: "successful sport organisations have a strong board focused on more business-like commercial aspects". A further interviewee supports this claim: "board members must be leaders of thought and have a strong corporate background". The chairman of the board, in conjunction with the CEO, is responsible for fostering a positive working relationship with the Minister in order to receive as much support (both tangible and intangible) from government as possible.

The role of the CEO within Sport NZ is to "service the board with right information so they can critique and make decisions, and run the organisation against the strategic plan and annual business plans". Schoenberg and Shilbury (2011) outline the requirement for the CEO to be matched with the organisation by analysing their particular skills and abilities. A member of the board who was interviewed believes the current CEO is "confident and capable", and coming out of the private sector combined with his previous experience within elite-level sport makes him an ideal leader for the organisation. Other participants support this claim, suggesting that the organisation has the right CEO in place given his background in both elite sport and the corporate environment. They also suggest that the skills, knowledge and expertise of the CEO should be matched with the current situation and operating environment in which the organisation finds itself (Schoenberg & Shilbury, 2011), and claim that Sport NZ must always have a CEO who has a strong previous track record within the sports sector. In fact, they claim "all staff are employed because they are passionate about sport".

A major restructure of the governance and management systems within the organisation took place in 2009. This was carried out in order to align the strategic objectives with the structure of governance and it allowed for better alignment of teams and modification on reporting lines internally within the organisation.

Finance

Sport NZ receives almost all of its income from government sources. As outlined previously, Berrett and Slack (2001) argue that organisations should attempt to increase the proportion of funding they receive from non-government sources. Sport NZ does not appear to have any other additional revenue streams aside from government support. The organisation's budget is approximately NZ$100m which is made up of two major government sources: Crown funding (64 per cent) and the New Zealand Lotteries Grants Board (36 per cent). The New Zealand government have placed an emphasis on increasing the funding for high-performance sport within the country and the budget for high performance alone is approximately NZ$60m. One participant states that "under the current environment funding is solid", with increases in high-performance funding and no associated decreases in funding for community sport. Sport NZ is the major funder of high-performance sport in New Zealand, with the only exceptions being the NZRU and NZC. However, although the organisation invests almost half of its budget in community sport, it is a relatively small player in this field (NZ$35–40m), with gaming and community trusts (NZ$160m) and local authorities (NZ$800m–1bn) investing far greater amounts within this sector. Sport NZ's role in community sport is to be the "leaders in influence, trying to coordinate the efforts of sport investors", but as it is only a minor investor in this sector it is a major challenge for the organisation to establish control and influence over the other funding bodies. Others support this claim: "for community sport we provide leadership and influence rather than direct funding". Although one participant claims that "sector partners are doing [a] great job with money they have", another concedes that "demand for financial resources is far greater than we will ever have supply … I'm most interested in the effectiveness of what we do and being as efficient as we can". The organisation has aimed to "drive internal costs down to increase money going out the door". The risk associated with this practice is that internal processes within the organisation itself may suffer, which does not benefit the organisation and ultimately the sport sector in general.

The organisation has little commercial activity and has not targeted investment from the private sector to establish any new forms of revenue. With such an excessive demand for financial investment both within community and high-performance sport, state agencies such as Sport NZ could be assessing every possible form of increased funding and financial support. The opportunity for a potential sponsor to be associated with virtually all aspects of sport in New Zealand through private sponsorship of Sport NZ would be an exciting opportunity for many. The organisation could take advantage of the high profile that sport has in New Zealand and use that as the catalyst to attract additional finance into the organisation, ultimately improving New Zealand sport at the community and high-performance levels. One participant states they would be "very comfortable with sport moving to a business-type environment where it is not just funded but has a commercial arm" as well.

Participation

Although Sport NZ runs a number of general sport participation interventions and facilitates interventions organised by RSTs and NGBs, none of these interventions are evaluated in robust detail to determine their overall effectiveness. Furthermore, an area of participation that Sport NZ must focus on is the recreational aspect of New Zealand sport, to attempt to capture its relevance and impact within the New Zealand sporting landscape. One participant claims that "the recreational sector is going ahead without Sport NZ having a massive impact on it". Large numbers of New Zealanders partake in recreational running, swimming, walking and tramping (hiking), amongst other recreational activities. Part of the organisation's remit is to govern and manage this area of physical activity but Sport NZ is yet to fully engage with the sector. They suggest this is the case as Sport NZ does not directly fund any aspects related to the recreational sector and refers to the complexities of capturing participation numbers within this field. They suggest that the organisation should attempt to link national recreational organisations with local and regional authorities to establish better management and governance structures within the sector, and acknowledge this could play a significant role in increasing overall participation numbers in physical activity within the country.

New Zealand Rugby Union

Performance management practices

Organisational performance management forms a large part of the daily and annual operations of the NZRU. From the strategic plan, specific targets are set and broken down into annual priorities through the implementation of the organisation's business plan. Each year those priorities form the basis of a scoreboard, a Balanced Scorecard (Kaplan & Norton, 1992) which captures the essence for the organisation's existence and its various strategic imperatives. The scoreboard is directly related to bonus remuneration for all NZRU staff, with each priority given a specific percentage depending on its particular relevance within the annual business plan. A participant commented: "The overall score is related to bonus pay within the organisation and is further broken down into individual performance."

This form of Balanced Scorecard (Kaplan & Norton, 1992) was originally designed by consultants and is a well-established practice within the organisation. One participant claims that all NZRU employees are fully aware of the scoreboard and the various priorities contained within it in any given year. Another participant describes the scoreboard as an essential tool within the NZRU and attests to the transparent nature of the scoreboard which details clear targets to be achieved: "if the organisation achieves the targets, they get the percentage bonus allocation; if we do not achieve any targets, we get zero per cent". Specific performance targets, as described by Walsh (2000), are prepared by NZRU management each year and then put forward to the board for approval. Much like Kaplan and Norton's (1992) first-generation Balanced Scorecards; these targets are then placed within four quadrants within the scoreboard (see Figure 8.2): game development, representative teams, competitions, and governance and financial. Financial reporting within the organisation is also based around these four quadrants which are issued from NZRU headquarters to all of the provincial unions.

Hoye and Doherty (2011) suggest that few attempts are made to evaluate the performance of the board within NPSOs; however, one participant claims the scoreboard is also used to assess the performance of the CEO and the board, and gives a clear indication of both parties' progress towards realising the strategic vision of the organisation. They suggest that this is the most appropriate manner

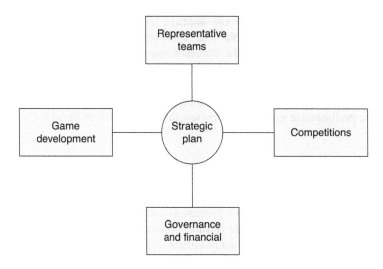

Figure 8.2 The NZRU's Balanced Scorecard performance dimensions.

to assess board performance (Hoye & Doherty, 2011), in particular as they "have been on other boards where there is disconnect between the assessment and organisational goals". Another participant also alludes to the importance of a performance management approach within sport management and how this has contributed to the growth and success of the NZRU:

> a lot of organisations are very good at saying what they would like to do, but they are poor at measuring what they have achieved towards it, and understand why they have not achieved; some organisations do achieve but do not understand how they did.

One of the major challenges in relation to performance management and the Balanced Scorecard in particular within the NZRU is the successful obtainment of data and reliable information to accurately report against priorities and targets (Walsh, 2000). The collection, analysing and reporting of this data can be perceived as a time-consuming task that does not produce any real outcomes. This theme is also evident within the Sport NZ case study and, as in that case, it is important for the NZRU to convey the importance and significance of obtaining reliable and accurate data to be reported within the scoreboard. One participant suggests there is a performance management "culture" within the organisation but claims the NZRU wants to turn this into a "high-performance culture". They add that the Kaplan and Norton (1992) scoreboard is an important part of the organisation achieving that goal.

NZRU interviewees were asked about the use of the Sport NZ's ODT and whether or not it has been adopted by any facet within the organisation. One participant claims that the NZRU does not use this tool due to the establishment of their own performance management practices within the organisation. However, they add that some provincial unions and clubs have implemented the ODT as a resource to learn how they can improve their various performance areas. Another participant makes the point that "sport organisations do not easily grasp how to copy success". Given the apparent success of the performance management scoreboard that operates within NZRU headquarters, the organisation should arguably be advising provincial unions and clubs as to how they could adopt a similar on-going practice, as opposed to merely implementing a one-off generic performance management review through the use of Sport NZ's ODT.

Individual performance management

Fletcher (2001) claims that employee performance management operating within traditional businesses has evolved into a process of continual feedback, including performance appraisals, appropriate reward structures and continuous performance reviews. In accordance with many initiatives and processes within the traditional business sector, the sport industry has been slow to develop and implement similar programmes. For instance, the individual performance of employees within the NZRU is still only appraised biannually and it would appear that little continual feedback is offered from management. However, the NZRU is unique in sport management terms in that every employee within the organisation qualifies for performance-based remuneration, which is largely based on the biannual performance appraisal process: "The information and feedback from these performance appraisals are used as inputs in a management system which determines how much of the bonus people are entitled to." Bayle and Robinson (2007) suggest that the board of an NPSO is an important aspect of driving overall organisation performance, but there have been few attempts to measure the performance of boards in these organisations. The NZRU is again an exception to this rule as the board, along with all other employees, is assessed (as a group and as individuals) against the organisation's success in achieving its targets. One participant suggests that the annual appraisal of the CEO and the board is the best they have seen even in traditional business. NZRU board members also receive remuneration for their roles and as such make a perform-ance appraisal process extremely relevant. The assessment of the board is linked directly to organisational goals in the same manner as the CEO's performance is assessed based on the organisation's progress towards various strategic object-ives. Another participant claims that individual performance appraisals are an on-going process within the organisation and that at present the NZRU is "looking at even more individualised performance plans" for both employees and board members.

One of the objectives of an effective performance management system is to ensure that employee roles are intrinsically linked to strategic objectives (Fletcher, 2001; Applebaum *et al.*, 2011). One participant suggests that all employees are very much aware of the strategic plan and the organisation's various objectives. They claim this is "well publicised" within the organisation and "everyone would have a copy of the vision, priorities and the scoreboard, either on their desk or accessible via intranet". They add that they felt confident that all staff would be able to convey what the vision and annual priorities are for the NZRU. Another participant describes how the organisation holds annual "offsite days spent talking about priorities and how individual work is directly related to the bigger picture". However, they also acknowledge that it is a chal-lenge to have all individuals directly contributing to the strategic objectives on a daily basis. They state "that 60 per cent of the performance bonus is determined by how everyone does against the annual objectives that are a direct link to strategy. Individual outcomes make up the remaining 40 per cent which are still related to strategic imperatives". They go onto suggest that "high levels of per-formance are a prominent part of individual employee lives [and that] it is all part of a commitment to be the best". A further participant also suggests that high levels of individual performance are an important aspect for individual employees. They attribute this to the fact that employees have a true passion for their role within the organisation: "people want to come and work here because it is tied to the national game and you are helping the game flourish; there is a real sense of pride within the NZRU". Others further support this view by claiming that the activities of the NZRU are "an important part of how New Zealand sells itself offshore". They also attest to the high level of morale of individual employees, stating that "the NZRU constantly scores very high in one of the best places to work".

Mallet and Cote (2006) acknowledge the importance of evaluating the performances of coaches and other members of NPSOs, and it is apparent that the NZRU also does. The NZRU not only implements individual performance management practices for its organisational employees but also for its players, coaches and officials. One participant claims that players', coaches' and officials' performances are reviewed and discussed regularly by the NZRU, and performance-based remuneration is also in place for some of these types of NZRU employees. They claim that elite-level coaches are receiving training relating to new IT software that can measure a player's on-field performances. They believe it is "important to invest in leading-edge professionalism such as this in everything the NZRU does". They go on to suggest that these practices should be introduced at the provincial level to provide the best opportunity for the sustainable future success of the All Blacks. Another participant claims that the performance reviews of players occur on a regular basis, and the appraisal of coaches' and officials' performances and development takes place biannually in line with NZRU organisational employees.

Governance

The governance structure within the NZRU follows a traditional approach in that the majority of board members are elected from the various (26) provincial unions which are divided into three zones: North, Central and South. Two members from each zone are elected and are joined by one Māori representative and two independents to form a nine-person board. The NZRU is essentially owned by the 26 provincial unions and they are allocated votes based on the number of rugby teams they have. "The NZRU board is charged with setting strategy, direction and policy for the NZRU, and is ultimately responsible for the decisions and actions of NZRU management and staff" (New Zealand Rugby Union, 2015). Board members are elected for three-year terms and can serve a maximum of three consecutive terms. There are two major sub-committees under the board, which are the Business and Finance Committee, which deals with issues related to player negotiations, expenditure and income generation, and the Rugby Committee, which is solely focused on the development and performance of players and teams at all levels of the game, both professional and amateur. For any large decisions which will ultimately have a significant impact on the stakeholders of NZRU, the board will work in collaboration with the provincial unions to ensure a democratic approach has been adopted and minimise any confusion. In line with literature related to governance in NPSOs (Hoye & Doherty, 2011; Bayle & Robinson, 2007; Auld, 1997), the CEO is responsible for "ensuring the strategic intentions of the board".

Ferkins and Shilbury (2010) suggest that being a member of a board within an NPSO requires that person to have an appropriate skillset and ideally prior business experience. The "calibre" of the board in the NZRU is strong in comparison with other NGBs examined within this study. Of the six zone representatives on the board, all have been heavily involved or are still currently involved with the sport at certain points during their careers, and only one zone representative does not have previous experience within traditional business (New Zealand Rugby Union, 2012). This provides an appropriate balance of rugby and business acumen which enables the board to make effective decisions.

One participant claims the relationship with the provincial unions is not always good: "They have occasionally provided false information about salary caps and have gotten into financial difficulties. The board cannot bail out provincial unions." Yeh and Taylor (2008) refer to the independence of the board as being a major issue in determining a board's overall effectiveness. Within the NZRU, a number of the zone representatives hold prominent positions within clubs and provincial unions, undermining the ability of the board to make truly unbiased and independent decisions. The two independent board members are vastly experienced within the traditional business sector but also have been involved at the elite level in the game previously. This is the ideal board member in any NPSO as they bring the required knowledge and experience of both the sport and traditional business, but are unbiased in their decision making towards the allocation of resources and formation of a strategic direction. The current Māori representative on the board also adds experience from the traditional business sector but has been the Chairman of a provincial union and director of a Super 15 franchise in the past, so cannot be considered an independent board member in the truest sense of the word. Participants acknowledge that even though zone representatives have combined rugby and business acumen, the "independent board members [are needed to] balance out the skill deficiencies of the elected board", even adding that "board capability is a challenge for the organisation". Ferkins and Shilbury (2010) concluded that the board must have the appropriate expertise and knowledge to develop imperative aspects of the organisation, such as strategic development. Participants' concerns over the capability of the board raise questions about the composition of the board and its 'calibre' as outlined by Papadimitriou and Taylor (2000) and Papadimitriou (2007). One participant states that "it is important to run the NZRU as a business and deliver outcomes like any other business". They add that "organisations should continue to review their governance to ensure best practice". The incorporation of more independent members within the NZRU board and less influence from zone representatives could be argued to be best practice in terms of the NZRU's governance structure:

> Financial disciplines and accountabilities that are brought over [from independent board members] are very useful; they are the most important foundation of how the NZRU has been able to grow its performance. Without it the NZRU would not have had a chance of winning the hosting rights for the Rugby World Cup 2011.

With the evolution of the professional game, the NZRU "debated whether professional and community rugby should be separated but decided it would be better being under one umbrella" to ensure an appropriate balance in terms of supplied resources. This development also "forced the introduction of a CEO with a commercial background, as opposed to a rugby background". This appointment supports Schoenberg and Shilbury's (2011) research describing how the CEO's abilities and expertise should be matched with the current situation of the organisation.

In terms of professional rugby, the NZRU has a unique structure in that professional players are essentially employees of the organisation, although individual contracts and negotiations for Super 15 players are carried out within the franchises themselves. One participant claims there is a "secondment model in place: NZRU is the player's legal employer but negotiations are between player and franchise for individual remuneration"; "Franchises have set budgets and are able to contract players up to a certain amount; after that requires NZRU approval." Centralised contracting is a point of strength for the organisation as this approach to governance removes the issue of "club versus country" and provides assurance that the All Blacks can remain successful, which is such a crucial aspect for the organisation's overall success.

Finance

The NZRU is an NPSO that is not solely reliant on funding from government sources. Cordery and Baskerville (2009) confirm the need for NPSOs to have diverse sources of income, and perhaps the NZRU is a prime example of the range of income sources an organisation could potentially attract were it to prove sufficiently astute in doing so. Commercial activity forms the majority of total income for the NZRU (NZ$72m out of NZ$93m) through broadcasting rights and sponsorship agreements. The NZRU negotiates broadcasting revenue for Super 15 fixtures in collaboration with their partners in Australia and South Africa. The broadcasting of All Blacks international test matches also provides significant income generation for the organisation, with the remainder of commercial activity consisting of sponsorship from various sporting and non-sporting companies. The All Blacks are such a viable sponsorship entity that the NZRU has gained the ability to attract sponsorship not just within New Zealand but also abroad, particularly in Asia. The organisation is fully aware that commercial revenue is the driving force behind its success and has even introduced a split within the Business and Finance Committee to focus on attracting new sponsors and developing the organisation's commercial appeal.

A further non-state-funded revenue stream within the NZRU is income generated from gate receipts at Super 15 and international test matches. One participant suggests that, in order to protect this significant income stream, the organisation must address on-going challenges in attracting supporters to games and helping franchises build a sustainable fan base. From a financial management perspective the organisation has also been able to capitalise on gains from foreign exchanges and earn interest on savings of approximately NZ$6m and NZ$500,000 respectively per annum in the 2011/2012 financial year.

A final portion of the organisation's income is generated through funding from Sport NZ. This funding is allocated for community rugby and growing the base of volunteers, coaches and officials. The funding is essentially insignificant, making up less than 2 per cent of the organisation's overall income. Although Sport NZ's influence on the NZRU is limited due to this "insignificant funding", one participant claims there is a positive, open and transparent relationship with Sport NZ and hopes that this relationship will grow as rugby sevens becomes an Olympic sport in 2016. Steinberg's (2007) research suggested that many organisations use a levy/subscription charge as an additional form of revenue; however, unlike many NPSOs, the NZRU does not charge a levy on it members at any level of participation due to its ability to generate significant income from other, more relevant sources. Ideally, this should be the goal for many NPSOs, and their ability to remove levies on members would be directly related to financial viability as an organisation.

Although the organisation would appear to be in a healthy financial situation, there are a number of challenges facing the NZRU in relation to its financial sustainability: "Ultimately the organisation has to generate more income [and] every decision must be cost effective." Furthermore, "The financial performance of the provincial unions is not good" and, supporting Cordery and Baskerville's (2009) claims, one participant adds that the NZRU cannot afford to be their sole source of income generation. Another participant, echoing findings within Steinberg's (2007) research, states that "generating sustainable new revenue [and ensuring] the financial stability and health of franchises and provincial unions are on-going issues" that the organisation must continually review and evaluate.

Participation

As per any NGB, growing the numbers of participation in rugby is a major challenge for the NZRU. One participant alludes to an alarming "drop-off rate of teenagers in high schools" and the need to "grow the female game" in all parts of the country. In line with research relating to participation in sport (Brunton *et al.*, 2003; Armstrong *et al.*, 2000), another participant describes how the trends of "more people watching sport then participating and changing lifestyles" are having an effect on participation. They suggest there needs to be better coordination between the NZRU, RSTs and local councils to ensure participation levels remain stable. A further interviewee claims that numbers participating in rugby have increased in most years but, due to New Zealand's small population, it is a constant challenge for the organisation to retain a high participation rate. Payne *et al.* (2003) suggest participation drives as an effective intervention to increase numbers of players, coaches and officials within sports. In line with this, the NZRU has an annual 'registration drive' within its community rugby division where it attempts to recruit new individuals into the game from a playing, coaching and officiating standpoint. However, participants do not suggest that an evaluation of these interventions takes place, which has been highlighted as an important aspect of participation interventions in the literature. Participants also describe how approximately 600 players leave New Zealand each year to play overseas. This demographic is largely made up of young males who use this opportunity as their 'overseas experience', a popular occurrence amongst young New Zealanders.

New Zealand Cricket

Performance management practices

Organisational performance management is slowly beginning to play a major role within NZC and in fact a cultural change is currently taking hold. The organisation has adopted a form of Balanced Scorecard (Kaplan & Norton, 1992) to measure end-of-year performance and uses a 'traffic light' system to assess on-going performance issues. These practices have been driven by the board downwards, providing evidence for the positive influence that corporate knowledge as described by Hoye and Doherty (2011) can provide for an NPSO. One participant states: "all [traditional business] processes are 100 per cent transferable to the sport organisation; there are no barriers to it". Another participant claims that the adoption of the Kaplan and Norton (1992) Balanced Scorecard "allows all initiatives to be interlinked to deliver on strategic objectives". Others suggest that through a combination of these tools the organisation can gain "a clear illustration of how the business has gone over various components".

The Kaplan and Norton (1992) Balanced Scorecard adopted by the organisation is not the traditional four-quadrant model as NZC have grouped targets and objectives together under five performance dimensions of the organisation (see Figure 8.3). 'High-performing teams' relates to the success of the national teams

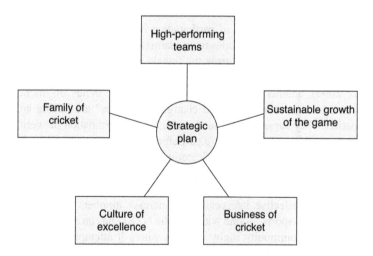

Figure 8.3 New Zealand Cricket's Balanced Scorecard performance dimensions.

at international competitions and test matches. The performance of national teams is a strategic priority within NZC and their success is the driver for other elements of the organisation's activities: "Significant resources are invested in developing and supporting our elite teams, including specialised high-performance programmes, expert coaching at national and major association levels, comprehensive support systems and a focus on maintaining world-class playing grounds" (New Zealand Cricket, 2011). 'Family of cricket' is the organisation's way of detailing the relationship it has with some vital stakeholders. Such stakeholders include the ICC, major associations and the New Zealand Cricket Players Association. Stakeholder management is an important aspect within NZC as it must attempt to satisfy these various groups without losing focus on core strategic imperatives. One participant suggests that "support and buy-in of stakeholders can be hard; it takes over communication; it's a constant challenge, we can never communicate well enough with stakeholders". 'Sustainable growth of the game' relates to the organisation's policies to stimulate participation of players, coaches, officials and volunteers. Like many NPSOs, NZC relies heavily on the willingness of volunteers to carry out a number of functions related to strategic objectives (Thibault *et al.*, 1991): "Volunteers are essential to the effective running of the game of cricket and every year hundreds of people give up their time to help grow the game at grassroots level" (New Zealand Cricket, 2011). A 'culture of excellence' relates to a number of internal processes and structures and external initiatives with various stakeholders to optimise the performance of the organisation. The processes of attracting high-calibre personnel to the management side of the organisation falls under this performance dimension, along with training and development of current staff and fostering the strategic capability of the board (Ferkins & Shilbury, 2010). The external initiatives involved in this area relate to the use of consultants to analyse current remuneration practices and risk management issues within the organisation. Finally, the so-called 'business of cricket' is solely focused on the financial performance of the organisation in relation to income generation and expenditure (Cordery & Baskerville, 2009). This section of the scorecard incorporates elements of commercial sponsorship, information on ICC distributions, and income from gate receipts and other revenue streams. It also details where certain expenditure has been budgeted for directly related to objectives contained within the strategy (NZC, 2010).

One participant suggests that the implementation of the Kaplan and Norton (1992) Balanced Scorecard is testament to the organisation's commitment to "always be looking to go forward and keep pace with best practice". Another participant believes the adoption of the Balanced Scorecard is important for NZC and claims there is a good balance of cricket measures, business measures and internal staff measures within the tool. They add that the tool is similar to Balanced Scorecards used within the corporate environment but concedes, as with individual performance appraisals, that "people are not used to it within NZC". They also state that the Balanced Scorecard "takes effort to set up and implement" but that the benefits for the organisation outweigh these issues in terms of managing on-going performance areas and aligning all organisational activities with the strategic plan. A further participant attests to the transparency of the tool, stating that "everyone can see what all the priorities are", and claims that the organisation revisits these priorities every quarter using the traffic light system. Although participants believe the organisation is moving in the right direction with performance management practices, they also claim that further improvement is necessary:

> In time the performance management system will progress substantially; the expectations of stakeholders, the board and business partners are at such a high level that NZC needs to be managing and measuring all KPIs a lot better; there have been improvements in previous years but it is still in its infancy.

Aside from the use of the Kaplan and Norton (1992) Balanced Scorecard and the traffic light system to manage on-going organisational performance, NZC has also engaged with the ODT developed by Sport NZ. The ODT can be used as a one-off analysis of all aspects of an organisation's activities but is not suitable as an on-going performance management practice. NZC has implemented this tool within its 22 districts and six major associations but is yet to adopt it at NZC headquarters. One participant claims that NZC wants to create a performance management culture throughout all of its operations but concedes that as an organisation and governing body it is "not there" yet.

Individual performance management

Although it is widely accepted that the performance of individual employees is integral to the overall success of an organisation, individual performance management practices were only introduced within NZC in 2008. One participant suggests there was a complete re-evaluation of how individual employee roles would be assessed and adds: "up to two years ago there were many roles in the organisation that did not have position descriptions and a HR manager was absent from the workforce". They suggest that this provides an insight into how "core business processes are yet to be fully implemented within the organisation". As recommended by Schoenberg and Shilbury (2011), the organisation introduced a new CEO with a traditional business background who implemented employee appraisals, with agreement over KPIs and a minimum six-monthly review relating to performance issues. Participants claim this practice has been "adopted from the corporate background and works well within NZC". They also refer to the implementation of a new approach to assessing employee performance. They claim this process did not exist prior to its implementation of a CEO with corporate experience (Schoenberg & Shilbury, 2011). They add that each employee creates a personal development plan with input from their line manager, which incorporates "clear outcomes to be achieved during the year". They state that this document is reviewed three or four times during the year and progress towards agreed-upon objectives is assessed.

One participant supports another interviewee's claims relating to individual performance management practices but suggests that the use of these practices remains quite immature. In line with Mallett and Cote's (2006) research, they state that there are "better processes in place to evaluate performance of players and coaches compared to employees within the organisation". They add that "compared to the corporate environment it is in its infancy" and the process is not established "within the culture of what people in NZC are used to, who have been there for a while". This participant also provides a reason as to why individual performance management practices have not been completely successful within NZC: "in a small organisation, managers are also 'doers', so they have less time to spend one-on-one with staff". However, they also concede that this is not sufficient reason for the failings of a successful individual performance management practice within the organisation.

Applebaum *et al.*, (2011) allude to the importance of individual performances being directly related to strategic imperatives. Within NZC, a participant states that "all individual roles are directly related to strategic objectives". This is further supported by other participants who claim the "strategic plan should be important to each employee" due to the relevance their own role has in its delivery, and there is a clear linkage between the strategic plan, the business plan and individual performance plans for each employee. Another participant goes onto state that: "we deal with four to eight annual objectives so it is very important people understand how they contribute to what the organisation is trying to achieve". A further interviewee claims that individual employees are involved in the development of the plan and are therefore very aware of how their own role within the organisation contributes to certain outcomes.

A senior figure within the organisation summarises the organisation's experiences with individual performance management practices to date: "I'd like to think we are getting there; but we are not there completely; treating NZC as a business is starting to be appreciated, there is currently a culture change taking place."

Governance

The structure of governance within NZC is unique within world cricket and New Zealand sport in that they are the first national governing body to adopt the implementation of a completely independent board of directors. The six major associations nominate directors who are then interviewed by a panel, including the board chairman, to assess their suitability for joining the NZC board. This approach was adopted following the Hood Report (Hood, 1995) which recommended NZC must implement an independent board of non-executive directors to remove issues of self-interest, and appoint individuals who can lead the organisation in challenging times for sporting entities. Following the Hood Report, the size of the board in NZC was also reduced from 13 to eight. One participant states that "independent boards have been adopted by all provincial [major] associations". In total, eight directors sit on the board for four-year terms and can also be re-elected to their positions following the end of those terms. Another participant states that "the independent board was a fantastic option" and claims that revenue doubled within three to four years following the implementation of an independent board and a CEO with business experience (Schoenberg & Shilbury, 2011). A further interviewee adds that "the intent is to elect board members to act in best interest of NZC without regional bias".

Papadimitriou and Taylor's (2000) and Papadimitriou's (2007) claims of the need for high-calibre board members is also apparent within the independent board in NZC. One participant states that "NZC looks for people with a corporate knowledge; it has moved on from just people who have a love and passion for the game to demanding high-calibre individuals with business acumen". They add that the independent board members emerge from "a variety of business backgrounds" but there is still also sufficient knowledge of how cricket and sport in general operates within the board make up. This participant supports this by adding that "the board is made up of business people and leaders" but there are also currently two ex-internationals on the board who are involved within the traditional business sector. Another participant suggests this aspect of the board is important as it is imperative "to understand the culture and ethos of an NPSO combined with professional expertise".

It has been suggested that NZC leads the sporting world in terms of sport governance and that other NPSOs, including the ICC, are also seeking advice on the implementation of an independent board. However, stakeholder management appears to be a major issue with the implementation of an independent board. One participant states that "it is not a perfect model and the previous model made it easier to connect with stakeholders through regional representation on the board". They add that stakeholder management is a key issue for the organisation under the new model to ensure all entities are communicated with pro-actively in the absence of regional representatives. Participants also allude to issues with the appointment process of independent board members: one interviewee states that NZC "is dependent on members nominating suitable candidates; putting forward high-calibre people; this does not always happen". Another participant suggests "applications for board members should be a completely open process by advertising for positions in the general media". They add that "nominations from the associations put a filter into the process which is not required". Although NZC claim to have a completely independent board, the reality is that major associations still must nominate candidates to sit on the board. Participants' suggestion of advertising positions within the general media would be the necessary move to facilitate the implementation of a 'truly' independent board. A further issue with the composition of the board is the fact that the CEO is considered a board member within the organisation. This is not regarded as being best practice within elite-level sport governance and this policy should arguably be reviewed to ensure the capability of the board is not undermined in terms of assessing management performance and forming strategic direction. Participants suggest that "80 per cent of board discussions are at the governance level but occasionally the board gets involved with management functions".

From a management perspective, participants claim that "the organisation has gone for more functional expertise" and, much like the board, "there is not a lot of cricket expertise within management either". They claim the organisation functions well but also suggest that a "three-way split of expertise relating to: the commercial end of business; people with high-performance understanding; and people who understand grassroots cricket" may be the best way forward for management.

Finance

NZC generates approximately NZ$45m in revenue per annum. Commercial revenue forms a large portion of the 'income mix' within the organisation. Some 40 per cent of total revenue is generated from the sale of broadcasting rights on both a domestic and international level. One participant suggests NZC "sees themselves as an export business" due to the volume of funding they receive from selling broadcasting rights into the Asian countries and India in particular. NZC also receives funding from broadcasting rights for local cricket through its domestic competitions, but in comparison to the sale of international rights it is not as significant.

NZC receives approximately 40 per cent of further funding from their association with the ICC. The ICC organises a 'world event' every year, so organisations such as NZC receive a steady income stream from the ICC on an annual basis.

The remaining 20 per cent of the 'income mix' within NZC comes through sponsorship of national teams and competitions and income from gate receipts at international Test matches. The organisation also receives Sport NZ funding which is estimated to be between 3–5 per cent of overall income. This funding is separated between grassroots cricket (38 per cent) and high-performance cricket (62 per cent). One participant states that "other cricket NGBs are far better funded" and "NZC has to be smarter to compete". In line with Cordery and Baskerville's (2009) research, another participant suggests that "it is challenging times for NZC" in relation to funding, and it is important for the organisation to investigate new revenue streams and create mechanisms for sustaining current income levels. One such method of generating a new revenue stream is the relationship NZC has formed with USA cricket, which allows the organisation to establish a presence in the American market by sending players over to participate in American cricket leagues.

Participation

In line with research relating to participation interventions in NPSOs (Brunton *et al.*, 2003; Eime *et al.*, 2008), increasing the numbers is also a constant challenge for NZC. One participant states that there has been "a 40 per cent growth at junior level over the last decade but there are serious problems when it comes to retaining players as they move through school". One of the major reasons he gives for this is that a conflict exists with the cricket season and the academic calendar, with the sport being played predominantly during the summer months. This situation results in little coaching and participation at the school level and clubs are left with the sole responsibility of developing potential talent at the grassroots levels. Participants suggest the organisation is currently analysing ways of addressing this issue. They also allude to the impact that "consistently winning national teams" can have on participation at the junior level. They claim that these teams are the "shop window" for the sport and the organisation and their success is paramount to the growth of the game at grassroots level. Consistent with all case study organisations within this research, there is no suggestion from participants that the various participation interventions NZC employs are assessed in any formal manner for their effectiveness.

New Zealand case study summary

Following analysis of the data collected within the New Zealand case study, it is abundantly clear that there are a number of stark contrasts between the professional management of sport within New Zealand and Ireland. One of the major foci in this book was to report on the use of traditional performance management practices, tools and systems operating within NPSOs. Within the Irish case study, none of the three selected NPSOs had engaged with these practices to a meaningful degree. In direct contrast, all three NPSOs within the New Zealand case study have adopted various tools and systems relating to overall organisational performance management in their organisations. The NZRU and NZC have adapted the Balanced Scorecard to suit the specific needs of their organisations and these systems are an integral component of managing overall organisational performance. Sport NZ has developed a unique performance management tool (ODT) which it has encouraged all NGBs within New Zealand to engage with. Individual performance management is also far more developed within the New Zealand case study, with all organisations linking job descriptions directly to strategic imperatives. There are also elements of 360-degree feedback in operation within Sport NZ and the NZRU through self-assessment of employee performance appraisals. In addition, the NZRU have evaluation procedures for members of the board within the organisation.

Sport NZ, much like the Irish Sports Council, is solely reliant on government investment and has not been proactive in seeking commercial sponsorship to subsidise that funding, although a number of interviewees suggested this may be in the future financial plans for the organisation. The NZRU and NZC have been successful in diversifying their 'income mix' to create financially viable organisations. However, participation interventions are not evaluated for their effectiveness within any of the NZ case study organisations.

The most obvious contrast between the two case study countries is within the performance dimension of 'sport governance'. Sport NZ has appointed a board with a skillset that is appropriate to governing such an organisation and has no representation of NGBs within that board. Likewise, the NZRU have a board that also possess strong business acumen. The independent board operating within NZC is acknowledged as being best practice within sport governance and the organisation can ensure that a defined skillset of appropriate knowledge and expertise is constantly present within the boardroom.

It is clear within the New Zealand case study organisations that there is a direct relationship between a board of high calibre, the implementation of performance management practices and a financially viable organisation. Through the adoption of independent board members it can be ensured that the required skillset to successfully govern an NPSO is consistently present within the organisation.

9 International case study

Introduction

In order to increase the ability for generalisation of the reported results in this book, secondary case study organisations were also analysed for their management of the fundamental performance dimensions explored within this text. The purpose of this international case study was not to directly compare similar organisations, as was the case between the Irish and New Zealand NPSOs. Rather, the objective of this case study was to ensure that all issues related to the identified performance dimensions were uncovered in the primary case study data through a comparison of major themes that emerged from these secondary case study organisations.

However, in choosing organisations to be examined within the international case study, it was imperative to select countries and entities that shared somewhat similar characteristics as the primary case study organisations, either through sport culture, demographic profile, service or other comparable qualities. This was necessary to ensure that each performance dimension could be readily analysed and compared against the findings of the primary data.

UK Athletics (UKA) was chosen as the first organisation due to the UK's similar culture, organisation and delivery system of sport compared with Ireland and New Zealand. Likewise, the Australian Football League (AFL) was chosen due its similar culture, organisation and delivery systems of sport (to both Ireland and New Zealand), and the fact that AFL is a national sport (comparable to the GAA and the NZRU). The final organisation chosen as part of the international case study was the National Olympic Committee and Sports Confederation of Denmark (DIF). This organisation carries out similar roles to that of the Irish Sports Council and Sport NZ. Denmark also shares much common ground with Ireland and New Zealand demographically and has similar sport and physical activity participation figures (European Commission, 2010) and GDP (Hansen & Emsden, 2012) to that of the primary case study countries.

The following analysis describes the similarities and contrasts in the ways the identified fundamental performance dimensions are managed within the three secondary case study organisations listed above.

Performance management practices

Participants within this case study claimed that UKA is in the process of forming a performance management tool to measure and report on organisational performance. They add that the extent of performance management within UKA has previously been at the individual level where the organisation has adopted a robust performance management practice labelled the Performance Development Review System (PDRS). Although PDRS represents an adequate work practice for monitoring the performance of individuals, it does not capture how the organisation is performing as a whole in relation to the achievement of objectives contained within and measured against its overall strategy. One participant acknowledges this and adds that, due to the relatively recent adoption of the PDRS (following the implementation of non-executives on the board), it has a number of "teething" problems and is not suitable as an organisation-wide performance management tool. They state this is the reason for UKA seeking to implement performance management practices or tools such as the Kaplan and Norton (1992) Balanced Scorecard, which they believe will "be a good thing for UKA", and stress that "the Balanced Scorecard is something that UKA is now considering".

The AFL is another NPSO that has begun to engage with the practice of organisational-wide performance management practices. Like UKA, the AFL had previously limited performance management to individual employees but was lacking a similar practice to monitor and report against on-going strategic objectives. One participant acknowledges the importance of such a practice and states that the AFL is currently adopting a form of the Kaplan and Norton (1992) Balanced Scorecard for organisational activities. Furthermore, in line with Mallett and Cote's (2006) research, another participant suggests that the organisation employs a form of Balanced Scorecard to evaluate the performance of coaches within the AFL. They add that this practice was introduced by a private consultancy firm and has been in operation for approximately five years. Participants suggest that this practice is also to be adopted within the organisational activities of the AFL.

One participant claims that DIF "is not using any performance management systems or processes at the moment ... although there is a discussion at senior management level if the organisation should use a moderated version of the Balanced Scorecard for future reviews of performance management". They add that there is no culture of performance management operating within the organisation. They go on to suggest that the adoption of an organisational-wide performance management practice "would improve results and goal achievement". They also refer to some of the pitfalls commonly associated with performance management practices:

> the introduction of a performance management system ... must not grow into a bureaucratic paper-producing control mechanism, which is not creating a better performance and securing a steady development but results in a lot of paperwork ... at no use.

Another participant also confirms that no performance management practices are used within DIF and that a performance management culture does not exist. They do not provide a reason for the lack of such a practice but allude to the benefits that it would have for the organisation: "we could be better at setting goals for the whole organisation and evaluating performance according to the goals. We could also make an effort to measure management performance". A further interviewee supports these statements relating to the lack of any performance management practices in DIF. They claim that they are familiar with tools such as the Kaplan and Norton (1992) Balanced Scorecard and suggest that lack of management expertise is the reason why DIF has failed to adopt such a practice or another system of measuring, monitoring and reporting against organisational performance. They add that there is no culture of performance management within DIF and suggest that the establishment of such a culture "would improve results and goal achievement". One participant claims that the adoption of organisational perform-ance management practices would "give the organisation a clear mind towards what tasks and jobs … need to be focused on".

Individual performance management

Although UKA does not implement a 360-degree feedback approach, as argued to be best practice within this book, it would appear that they have the most robust and comprehensive appraisal processes in comparison with the other case study organisations and that they are intrinsically linked to organisational strategy (Kennerly & Neely, 2003; Senior & Swailes, 2004; McNamara & Mong, 2005). The PDRS involves conducting half-year informal appraisals and year-end formal appraisals for all employees within the organisation. There are two major components involved in this performance appraisal process: the first involves the delivery of objectives for the organisation and individual profes-sional development; the other involves each employee being measured against four core competencies that the organisation deems imperative to organisational harmony and effectiveness. Individual employees are allocated up to five object-ives which contain specific and measurable KPIs for each. These KPIs are assessed against progress during the biannual performance appraisals. The professional development of the employee required in order to meet these set objectives is also identified during these appraisals. "Each individual is then measured against four core competencies: teamwork; interpersonal skills; plan-ning and organising; and driving down operational costs." Both individual objectives and organisational-wide core competencies are reviewed each year to ensure they fit with current strategic imperatives. After year-end formal perform-ance appraisals, when outcomes have been decided, each employee receives a performance standard of Gold, Silver, Bronze or 'development required'. This 'rating' is used in consideration for bonus pay reward which (like the NZRU) every employee in the organisation is entitled to, but participants suggest that, more importantly still, it is imperative in determining "if the organisation is achieving its objectives". A major strength of the PDRS is the transparency of the assessment with the "same appraisal system used from the CEO down through the whole organisation". Executives on the board are also subject to the PDRS; however, non-executive directors are not formally assessed within the organisation. One participant claims that each member of the board submits a self-appraisal to judge their own performance and suggests that the organisation uses this information to assess various development requirements of directors. The performance of the Chairman is also 'informally assessed' by the board, thus ensuring that all individuals who contribute to the organisation are performance appraised.

Like UKA, the AFL has an established and comprehensive performance appraisal system in place for all employees across the entire organisation. One participant claims that most employees would be very aware of strategic objectives and relative KPIs, and another adds that the "CEO makes a real effort to ensure all employees are aware". This participant suggests there are three levels to the performance appraisal system and details how objectives and KPIs are assigned and reported against within the organisation. At the top level, senior management report on specific KPIs set by the board; at the middle level, each department must deliver and report on KPIs to senior management; and finally at the individual level ('micro-level') employees and line managers agree on specific KPIs that contribute to departmental and ultimately organisational objectives. The performance of employees in relation to these individual KPIs are assessed at mid-year and year-end formal performance appraisals. At year-end appraisals, individual KPIs for the following year are set for the employees, and training and development needs that are required for the employee to meet these KPIs are also identified. One participant claims the AFL is a "very task-orientated" organisation due to the heavy focus on KPIs, while another adds that "goal achievement" and employee "behaviours" are the key foundations of the appraisal process. The AFL requires "all casual, part-time and full-time staff (totalling 300) to complete the process". Another important feature of this performance appraisal system is that KPI achievement is directly related to performance-based bonus pay which (like the NZRU and UKA) every employee in the organisation is entitled to. Participants claim the level of bonus pay is variable depending on the contribution and responsibility of the employee in relation to organisational KPIs and seniority.

Within DIF, one participant claims an individual "employee development talk" takes place with employee's line manager once a year, and a further participant claims that "individuals are performance assessed once a year, when they are offered a development review with the head of department". One participant suggests that the "employee development talks" consist of discussing goal achievement during the previous year and objectives for the coming year. Although there is no performance-based remuneration practice operating within DIF, the same participant suggests that employees can discuss remuneration increases with management during these "employee development talks". Other than these informal discussions, "there is no formal appraisal process". Participants also suggest that development reviews consist of "evaluating previous year's performance and what skills and work areas the individual will focus on for next year", but they do not allude to any individual KPIs being established for individual employees. They add that:

> each employee is made aware of the strategic objectives … but it does not have any influence in the review of employee performance because the organisation does not have a tradition of linking strategic goals directly with how the individual employee is performing.

Participants also suggest that employees may be aware of strategic objectives within DIF but, unlike UKA and the AFL, individual performances are not measured or 'tied in' with any of these objectives.

Governance

UKA operates under a similar governance structure as that which exists within Basketball Ireland and the GAA, both of which were addressed in the Irish case study, in that it utilises a council and a board within the organisation. The council comprises all stakeholders of the organisation. One participant claims the council "is not a decision-making body but used for ratification and feed-back". The board within UKA is essentially "the directors of the company" and carries out similar responsibilities to those as presented within the previous case study organisations. Much like NZC and the recommendations of Yeh and Taylor's (2008) research, UKA operates under a partially independent board but unlike NZC utilises an open recruitment policy for selecting members to the board. In 2006, UKA began the recruitment process to replace the CEO and Chairman of the board. For recruitment of positions such as these, the organisation used 'head-hunters' to seek out the most suitable candidates. In addition, the Chairman, along with other non-executives within the organisation, "receive a small non-executive fee" for their services. Participants suggest the organisation seeks individuals for positions on the board who have the appropriate credentials (Hoye & Doherty, 2011), regardless of their previous experience or familiarity with the sporting environment.

The AFL has followed in the footsteps of NZC by selecting and implementing an independent board as the decision-making body within its organisation. One participant suggests that the Australian National Rugby League (NRL) and Cricket Australia are working in collaboration with the AFL in the pursuit of adopting similar governance structures as the AFL in order to remove issues of self-interest and a lack of adequate expertise within their current board formations. However, there are a number of apparent flaws within the adoption of the independent board within the AFL. First, much like NZC, the AFL is reliant on clubs to nominate suitable candidates to be elected to the board: "If clubs nominate a board member they must have something that will help develop the game." Although the AFL claims to implement an independent board and participants suggests that "nobody on the board represents any states or clubs", participants concede that current board members have "previously held similar positions at club level", bringing into question the true independence of the board. A further arguable flaw within the composition of the board in the AFL is that the CEO is also considered a board member within the organisation, which goes against international best practice. This arguably serves to undermine the legitimacy and capability of the board to make wholly independent decisions and affects its ability to adequately appraise the performance of the CEO, which is one of the core responsibilities of the board within any NPSO (Fama & Jensen, 1983; Dalton *et al.*, 1998). Yeh and Taylor (2009) suggest that boards are most effective with 7–10 members. The size of the board in the AFL is large in comparison with other case study organisations, with a membership of 12–14 directors in any given year. However, aside from the issues of 'true independence', the composition of the AFL board is generally very strong. One participant claims that members of the board are "visionaries and willing to push the boundaries of what is traditionally accepted for a domestic sport", such as expansion into overseas markets. They add that a number of CEOs from large, traditional business companies are members of the board, facilitating the visionary aspect for the organisation to which he refers. Other participants support this synopsis by claiming that the board has a strong business management background with a broad range of skills. They add that board members should be experienced in business and "the ideal candidate" would have also played AFL at a reasonably high level.

DIF also implements a governance structure made up of a council and an executive committee (board). The council is made up of two representatives from all sport federations within Denmark with extra seats allocated to federations with more than 50,000 members. The council then elects the nine-person executive committee and various sub-committees to function within the organisation. One participant suggests that "from a democratic perspective the governance of the organisation is appropriate" but, due to the complexities of the decision-making processes in the council, "from a management perspective the effectiveness of the organisation is weak". Another participant refers to self-interest as an issue within the council, stating that members "can obstruct goals and ambitions since they can have different interests and opinions towards the main goals of the organisation". They go on to further illustrate the extent of self-interest within DIF by claiming the council members can be "more focused on their own sport than the development and future of sport for all in Denmark". As board members are essentially elected from representatives of the council, it can be assumed that similar issues of self-interest also exist within the board. Although the board is elected from council representatives who predominantly come from sporting backgrounds, all DIF interviewees suggested that board members should have skills and expertise from the traditional business environment as pre-requisites to becoming board members. Participants claim that in order for DIF to develop "more people with political, economic and commercial skills are needed". They suggest that "certain knowledge of the world outside sports and the logic that exists is important", and finally they add that the organisation needs more board members with "in-depth knowledge of controlling finance and economics" within an organisation such as DIF.

Finance

UKA generates income totalling approximately £26.9m per annum which is derived from three major revenue streams. Thirty per cent of the 'income mix' (Cordery & Baskerville, 2009) within UKA comes from public funding through UK Sport and Sport England, which is ultimately allocated from government. The majority of this funding is for high-performance sport, with Sport England allocating a lesser amount for investment in participation. The government allocates funds via UK Sport and Sport England on a four-year cycle and, despite an economic downturn, the government has not reduced the levels of funding for UKA during the current four-year cycle. The government has suggested that the total budget for sport will be reduced by 15 per cent but participants claim that successful sports at the London 2012 Olympics were not to be cut as severely as others that were deemed to have 'underperformed'. They add that UKA must ensure they are delivering on government objectives relative to the sport to ensure future levels of funding remain consistent. A further 30 per cent of the organisation's income is derived from the hosting and broadcasting rights associated with UKA TV events held throughout the year. This portion of income generation also includes gate receipts at these events, which take place both at indoor and outdoor venues so they can be held during winter months. The majority of the organisation's income (40 per cent) is generated through commercial activities such as sponsorship of TV events and the contribution of Aviva, the organisation's main commercial partner. Participants claim that the organisation must "recruit a new or alternative high-level sponsor to ensure financial viability" once the current contract with Aviva expires. They go on to claim that without such an imperative revenue stream, UKA would not be able to support the current level of funding it provides for the "development of coaching and expenditure on sub-elite domestic competition outside of TV events".

Attracting sponsorship and other commercial activity within the 'income mix' (Cordery & Baskerville, 2009) is becoming an important aspect of financing NPSOs (Berrett & Slack, 2001). The AFL receives the majority of its income through its commercial activities. One participant claims that broadcasting and media rights are the major source of funding for the organisation, with a new deal worth AUS$1.25bn secured with three major broadcasting companies who now own the broadcasting rights to AFL matches from 2012 to 2016. They state that "this puts the organisation in a very good position for the next five-year period". The newly negotiated deal ensures AFL matches will be televised both domestically and internationally through a combination of live free-to-view and pay TV options. This participant claims that this creates good media coverage and suggests that digital media is also a major part of this deal, alluding to the new ways that individuals are consuming sport as described by Boyle and Haynes (2009). Another participant also suggests that gate receipts form a large portion of the revenue within the AFL. Attendances at AFL matches have been rising and this is largely due to the redevelopment of many stadiums to create "people-friendly environments" where it is an all-around spectator experience.

The AFL invests heavily in clubs for "start-up capability", and clubs receive large amounts of funding from AFL headquarters, but they are not solely reliant on this income stream to finance their operations. Participants claim that most AFL clubs own gaming venues which generate large levels of revenue for the club on an annual basis, creating sustainable and viable business enterprises. They suggest that the AFL as an entire entity receives little funding from government sources. They claim that the Australian Sports Commission (the equivalent of the ISC and Sport NZ) provides approximately AUS$200,000 to AUS$300,000 per year to the AFL. They add that this funding is specifically allocated for sport development in terms of participation.

DIF receive funding from the Danish government via the national lotteries board. One participant suggests that "this kind of funding affects the decisions and performance of the organisation in a negative way, because the level of funding is already agreed ... instead of being based on the performance of the organisation". They go on to suggest that management performance suffers due to a lack of performance-based funding as income will remain the same regardless of the achievement of strategic goals and objectives. They also claim that this situation results in "a less driven management team who lack motivation to formulate concrete and measurable goals, which must be set in order to develop the organisation in the right direction". In line with Lawrence's (2008) unpublished thesis relating to government intervention in sport, participants suggest that possible changes to legislation may have a profound impact on the manner in which the organisation receives funding, which is an area of concern for DIF. In contrast with Cordery and Baskerville's (2009) research which suggests organisations should obtain funding from various sources, DIF does not receive funding from any other source and has not attempted to add a commercial revenue stream to its financial base. As participants convey their concerns relating to the future of funding for the organisation, DIF could be analysing various alternative revenue streams (Chang & Tuckman, 1990) in order to ensure the sustainability of DIF if the suggested changes were to come into effect relating to the organisation's sole revenue stream.

Participation and other performance concerns

Participants suggest that a major challenge for UKA is to build on what was achieved at the 2012 London Summer Olympics. Aside from infrastructural development largely funded by government, the organisation put a lot of emphasis on coaching development and invested heavily in sport science research in the build-up to the London Games. They claim that one of the goals of the organisation is to "be leading edge in terms of athlete support systems". They also suggest that it is imperative for the organisation to deliver on key government targets in association with UK Sport to ensure future funding. These targets are largely based around increasing participation in athletics, but participants acknowledge that participation interventions and their evaluation (non-existent) for effectiveness is a major cause of concern within the organisation. The implementation of an organisational-wide performance management approach that incorporates fluctuations in participation numbers as a performance dimension is clearly warranted to assist the organisation in meeting these demands, therefore ensuring the future sustainability of UKA.

One participant alludes to the issues of recruitment and retention of participant volunteers within the AFL, a theme that has been present in a number of the case study organisations. They suggest that "without volunteers, the AFL game would cease to exist". Another participant suggests the AFL could place more emphasis on participation strategies and agrees that these strategies must be assessed for their effectiveness. This process appears to be currently absent from the AFL. They concede that the organisation is attracting large numbers of spectators, both in a physical capacity and through television and internet, but is concerned over the future generation of players and the organisation's player development strategies. A further performance issue that participants claim is prevalent within the AFL is the new digital media age. They suggest the organisation "must embrace it to deliver a good product to consumers" and view this issue as an "opportunity rather than a challenge". They refer to the development of new online content via mobile phones, tablets and other online outlets as emerging trends within sport management and something the organisation must develop to satisfy consumer demands. Finally, one participant claims the AFL must address capability issues within clubs, ensuring they have financial resources but, of equal importance, ensuring intangible "non-financial resources" are established at the club level.

From a comparison of interviewee statements within DIF, it is clear that there are various views and opinions of what the main roles and responsibilities of the organisation are, suggesting a lack of a clear strategic vision and 'purpose' for the organisation. One participant claims that "the main purpose of the organisation is to make sure that the sport federations and sport clubs have the best conditions and environment to fulfil their goals". Another participant claims the main purpose for DIF is "to get more members in our federations, show social responsibility and be more visible as the biggest 'sport for all' organisation in Denmark". A further interviewee claims that "the main purpose for the organisation is to get as many Danes active within organised sport as possible". In relation to this statement, when questioned about strategies to increase participation the participant suggests that "the organisation has until last year not really made any special initiatives to stimulate participation". They add that just recently the organisation has developed interventions with NGBs to increase participation numbers to counteract "competition from the private market, such as fitness centres". They claim that:

> A performance contract has been agreed between the organisation and the NGBs where the NGBs are committed to recruit an exact number of people as members during the project's timeframe. If the NGB is not able to fulfil the agreed goals, the financial support from the DIF will be withdrawn.

Another participant claims that these intervention strategies aim to attract 100,000 new participants into Danish sports clubs by the end of 2014. A further interviewee also refers to the intervention strategies and claims the organisation has invested "a lot of money" in order to achieve "some precise goals". They add that before these interventions were adopted in 2010, participation development was "dependent on enthusiastic federations and people". None of the participants refer to an evaluation of the effectiveness of such interventions within DIF's activities.

International case study summary

The aim of collecting data related to these secondary case study organisations within the international case study was to ensure that all major themes related to the fundamental performance dimensions identified within this book were uncovered within the primary case study comparative analysis. Conducting an international case study has also allowed for greater generalisation of the findings within the book as it becomes clear that similar issues emerged between both the primary and secondary case study organisations.

UKA and the AFL have both begun to engage with performance management practices at the organisational-wide level and already have well-established, robust performance management practices in place at the individual level. Conversely, DIF, a similar organisation as the Irish Sports Council and Sport NZ, appears to have failed to engage with any form of organisational-wide and individual performance management practices.

UKA and the AFL also have diverse revenue streams compared with DIF, which again, consistent with the Irish Sports Council and Sport NZ, is solely reliant on government investment

In line with all case study organisations in this book, none of the three international case study organisations have robust evaluation practices for the effectiveness of participation interventions.

Consistent with the Irish and New Zealand case studies, this international case study has shown that there is a direct relationship between 'good governance' and the adoption of suitable performance management practices (both at the organisational and individual levels), and also a direct relationship between 'good governance' and the diversification of income streams, therefore creating a financially viable organisation. The governance structures of both UKA and the AFL have evolved to incorporate independent directors within their boards which has resulted in the establishment of an appropriate skillset to govern these entities. In contrast DIF, which has no independent board membership, has not engaged with performance management practices and has not successfully diversified its 'income mix'.

This international case study confirmed that all the major themes related to the fundamental performance dimensions identified by this book have been uncovered within the Irish and New Zealand case studies. Little new theoretical implications emerged from analysis of this secondary data and as such it can be assumed that the issues related to performance within the Irish and New Zealand case studies can be generalised to a wider population of similar NPSOs.

10 Conclusions

Chapter introduction

Within this chapter, the theoretical concepts that have emerged from analysis of both the primary and secondary case study organisations are drawn upon to establish an integrated view of fundamental performance dimensions and their management within non-profit national-level sport management. This chapter also formulates theoretical outcomes into some specific practical implications for industry practitioners. These practical implications address how governors and management within sport may benefit from the findings of this book. The chapter concludes by outlining areas of further research that are required to continue to progress this area of research within the sport management literature.

Research summary

The book aimed to identify fundamental performance dimensions within NPSOs and how these organisations can manage those dimensions most effectively. Broadly speaking, after an in-depth review of the literature, the fundamental performance dimensions were identified as:

- The use of performance management practices such as the Balanced Scorecard or any of its derivatives.
- How NPSOs manage individual performance (including volunteer performance).
- Governance.
- Finance.
- Issues related to participation

The literature review began with an examination of current performance management practices within traditional business, which was followed by an examination of the same within NPSOs. Even at this early stage of the book, it was clear from previous research that performance management had not been fully adopted or was perhaps understood by the NPSO sector. The majority of research in the latter focused on performance measurement which is concerned with allocating scores or measures to various performance dimensions but fails to uncover causation behind any lack of performance within these dimensions.

This book is unique in that it does identify fundamental performance dimensions but also provides a much higher degree of depth in comparison with previous research through a robust analysis of these dimensions and identification of performance failures and causation within the NPSO sector. Furthermore, case study research including a comparative analysis allowed for greater exploration of the results when the findings of the Ireland, New Zealand and the international case study were examined. Moreover, there were distinct themes within the identified performance dimensions within each of these case study locations which became apparent from the beginning of the results analysis.

Theoretical outcomes

This book argues that, in theory, an NPSO can be deemed to be managing their performance effectively if:

- They are employing some form of organisational performance management practice.
- They are engaging in individual performance management, ideally through 360-degree feedback.
- They have an independent non-executive board of a high calibre.
- They attract a diverse range of revenue streams and are able to manage the financial component of an NPSO.
- They employ suitable participation interventions which are evaluated for their contribution to increase participation numbers in their sport(s).

It is clear from an analysis of the empirical research in this book that there are common themes within the selected NPSOs that perform at a high level and those that could be deemed to be underperforming. In Ireland (see Table 10.1), it appears that the ISC, the GAA and Basketball Ireland do not use any form of performance management practices and do not have robust individual performance management practices in place. In addition, all three organisations have arguably outdated governance structures in place; the ISC and Basketball Ireland are almost solely reliant on funding from central government; and none of the three organisations evaluate participation interventions in any comprehensive manner. It can therefore be concluded that all three organisations are not performing at an optimum level in fundamental performance dimensions affecting NPSOs. The GAA is clearly deemed to be performing better than the ISC and Basketball Ireland due to their ability to attract a diverse range of income streams.

In New Zealand (see Table 10.2), Sport NZ, the NZRU and NZC have all engaged with performance management to some extent with, the NZRU and NZC adopting a form of Balanced Scorecard and Sport NZ using the ODT. NZC have a similar individual performance management practice in place to the Irish

Table 10.1 Final research outcomes – Ireland

Ireland	Performance management practices	Individual performance management	Governance	Finance	Participation interventions
Irish Sports Council	• None used	• Performance appraisal in its infancy • Not linked to strategy • No board assessment • No 360-degree feedback	• Flawed • Potential self-interest • Low calibre	• Solely reliant on government	• No evaluation of participation interventions
GAA	• None used	• Performance appraisal in its infancy • Not linked to strategy • No board assessment • No 360-degree feedback	• Outdated • Complex • Flawed • Potential self-interest • Low calibre	• Diverse range of income streams	• No evaluation of participation interventions
Basketball Ireland	• None used	• Performance appraisal in its infancy • Not linked to strategy • No board assessment • No 360-degree feedback	• Flawed • Potential self-interest • Low calibre	• Solely reliant on government	• No evaluation of participation interventions

Table 10.2 Final research outcomes – New Zealand

New Zealand	Performance management practices	Individual performance management	Governance	Finance	Participation interventions
Sport NZ	• Organisational Development Tool	• Elements of 360-degree feedback • Roles linked to strategy • No board assessment	• Limited by government priorities • High calibre	• Solely reliant on government	• No evaluation of participation interventions
New Zealand Rugby Union	• Balanced Scorecard ('Scoreboard')	• Elements of 360-dgeree feedback • Roles linked to strategy • Robust board assessment	• Flawed • Potential self-interest • High calibre	• Diverse range of income streams	• No evaluation of participation interventions
New Zealand Cricket	• Balanced Scorecard	• Performance appraisal in its infancy • Roles linked to strategy • No board assessment • No 360-degree feedback	• Independent board • Best practice • High calibre	• Diverse range of income streams	• No evaluation of participation interventions

case study organisations, but Sport NZ and the NZRU use some elements of 360-degree feedback in their individual performance management practices. All three New Zealand organisations appear to have high-calibre boards, although the boards within Sport NZ and the NZRU are not completely independent. The independent nature of the board within NZC is considered best practice in modern sport governance. Sport NZ has not developed commercial revenue streams; however, both the NZRU and NZC receive a large portion of their funding through the commercial activities they are engaged in. None of the three New Zealand case study organisations evaluate participation interventions in any meaningful manner.

Therefore, although arguably still underperforming in some fundamental performance dimensions, it is argued that the New Zealand case study organisations are performing at a much higher level than their Irish counterparts, given the analysis provided above from the findings within the empirical research in this book.

Implications for practice

For the NPSOs that have failed to engage with performance management practices, there appears to be a link with the calibre of the boards operating within these organisations. In fact, all of the performance dimensions identified within this book are directly affected by the governance structures that operate within the organisations, but most notably the appointment process and composition of the board. Board members in modern NPSOs must have the required skillset to lead such an organisation and more emphasis could be placed on this aspect of the board as opposed to their background within sport. Competencies in areas such as financial management, risk management, legal issues, strategic planning and indeed performance management are some of the crucial aspects that must be present within the skillset of a board in a modern NPSO. The failings and suggested underperformance of NPSOs in the past have often been a result of a low-calibre board that may not have possessed these competencies and as such has been unable to increase the capacity of NPSOs to perform at the required levels.

In order to ensure the skillset of the board is adequate within NPSOs, an open recruitment campaign should take place to appoint a suitable board of professional non-executive directors. This way an organisation can appoint individuals with certain expertise that may not currently be present within the board. Governing areas such as overall organisational and individual performances, finance and other fundamental performance dimensions requires specific knowledge and expertise that can only be ensured to be present on the board with the appointment of professional non-executive board members who possess such competencies. A number of areas within this book where research has not previously been conducted have been identified as requiring further enquiry. Although this book clearly confirms that it is a necessity for NPSOs to adopt performance management practices, the type of system/tool/process that is most appropriate for adoption within an NPSO requires further research. The Balanced Scorecard clearly has real benefits for an NPSO, as demonstrated in the NZRU and NZC case studies, but perhaps the

Performance Prism (Neely *et al.*, 2002) may provide equal or greater benefits given an NPSO's need for stakeholder contribution and satisfaction.

In terms of individual performance management, further research is required to uncover the applicability of 360-degree feedback to employees and volunteers within NPSOs. Although this book argues that 360-degree feedback is a best practice approach for NPSOs, it must be acknowledged that this is a theoretical assumption and the hypothesis has not been proven in practice. Furthermore, it has been revealed that a number of the case study organisations use performance-based pay as a method of motivating employees to contribute high levels of performance within their organisations. Although research has previously been conducted analysing this issue within the traditional business environment (Cornett, Marcus & Tehranian, 2008), further research is required to explore its applicability within an NPSO.

Although Chang and Tuckman's (1990) research suggests there is a direct correlation between multiple revenue streams and overall financial (and organisational) health, since then little research has been carried out supporting this hypothesis. Future research should explore this relationship in more depth, especially given the increase in revenue that some NPSOs are receiving from streams such as the sale of broadcasting and media rights. Furthermore, it has been well documented that central government investment in sport provides an excellent return on investment in terms of both tax revenue and other associated intangible benefits (Irish Sports Council, 2010; Dalziel, 2011). Given this positive return on investment, further research is required to uncover central government's motivations for decreasing financial support within the sport industry.

As increasing the numbers participating in sport has been acknowledged as a fundamental performance dimension for all the case study organisations in this book, further research is required to uncover a best practice approach to implementing successful participation interventions. This book uncovered that none of the NPSOs evaluated participation interventions in any meaningful manner. As there is also no evaluation of the effectiveness or results of various participation interventions employed by NPSOs within the literature, a best practice approach cannot currently be determined. This evaluation must be carried out through an analysis of existing participation interventions within NPSOs, and it is up to research to uncover a best practice approach to this imperative performance dimension for these organisations.

Finally, although it is becoming widely agreed, both in the literature (Hood, 1995; Walters *et al.*, 2011) and in practice (NZC; AFL), that the adoption of a professional independent non-executive board of directors is considered the best approach to modern sport governance, further research is required to determine how exactly the appointment process should take place. This book argues that an open, national recruitment campaign should take place for board positions to ensure high-calibre candidates and avoid issues of self-interest, but as yet this hypothesis has also been largely untested both within research and practice. In addition, research relating to the adoption of independent boards within NPSOs in general is scarce, and as such future research should focus on uncovering issues concerning the independent board-management relationship, the independent board appraisal processes, and the ability of the independent board to communicate with stakeholders given the absence of regional representation that comes with such an approach.

Concluding statement

This book examined fundamental performance dimensions affecting NPSOs, including the use of performance management practices within these entities. A conceptual and theoretical approach for the analysis was created from various elements in the sport management-, corporate- and non-profit-related literature. The major focus of the book relating to the use of performance management practices and the identification of fundamental performance dimensions were posed and remained relevant throughout the text.

It was concluded that NPSOs within Ireland have not engaged with performance management practices and appear to be further behind their New Zealand counterparts in terms of this imperative management practice. It was also concluded that, in general, both Irish and New Zealand NPSOs are not managing individual performances in line with international best practice. The structures and systems of governance within Irish NPSOs appear to be outdated, which is arguably limiting the capability of these entities to perform. Again, New Zealand NPSOs are closer to best practice within this performance dimension, with higher calibre boards and a greater degree of independent board membership, which in turn appears to have also contributed to greater financial health within their organisations. Finally, it was concluded that NPSOs within Ireland and New Zealand do not evaluate the effectiveness of participation interventions in any formal manner, which is alarming given that the essence of these organisations' existence lies within this integral performance dimension.

In summary, one very clear consequence from this book has become apparent in terms of the management of performance within NPSOs both within an Irish and New Zealand context: the individuals charged with leading NPSOs are the single most important determining factor in facilitating high levels of performance within these entities. This became evident within the empirical research in this book where it was shown that there is a relationship between the implementation or partial implementation of a non-executive independent board and the adoption of appropriate organisational and individual performance management practices, and diversity within the organisation's income streams. As such, changes in the governance structures within NPSOs in order to facilitate increased organisational performance are now warranted. Only then will these organisations begin to perform at increased levels through the effective management of fundamental performance dimensions. It is anticipated that future work will address the issues raised above and that changes to practice will be adopted so that NPSOs may begin to perform at levels mostly unseen as of yet within this unique industry.

References

Abzug, R. (1996). The evolution of trusteeship in the United States: A roundup of finding from six cities. *Non-profit Management & Leadership, 7*, 101–111.

Ahn, H. (2001). Applying the Balanced Scorecard concept: An experience report. *Long Range Planning, 34*(4), 441–461.

Amis, J., Slack, T., & Berrett, T. (1999). Sports sponsorship as distinctive competence. *European Journal of Marketing, 33*(3/4), 250–272.

Ammons, D. N., & Rodriguez, A. (1986). Performance appraisal practices for upper management in city governments. *Public Administration Review, 46*(5), 460–467.

Applebaum, S. H., Roy, M., & Gilliland, T. (2011). Globalization of performance appraisals: Theory and applications. *Management Decision, 49*(4), 570–585.

Armstrong, T., Bauman, A., & Davies, J. (2000). *Physical activity patterns of Australian adults: Results of the 1999 national physical activity survey*. Canberra: Australian Institute of Health and Welfare.

Auld, C. J. (1997). Professionalization of Australian sport administration: The effects on organisational decision-making. *European Journal for Sport Management, 4*(2), 17–39.

Australian Sports Commission. (2005). *Governing sport: The role of the board, a good practice guide to sporting organisations*. Canberra: author.

Australian Sports Commission. (2006). *Exercise recreation, sports survey: Participation in exercise recreation and sport annual report*. Canberra: author.

Baker, D. F. (2001). The development of collective efficacy in small task groups. *Small Group Research, 32*(4), 451–474.

Basketball Ireland. (2011). *Basketball Ireland Strategic Plan 2011–2014*. Dublin: author.

Bayle, E., & Madella, A. (2002). Development of a taxonomy of performance for national sport organizations. *European Journal of Sport Science, 2*(2), 1–21.

Bayle, E., & Robinson, L. (2007). A framework for understanding the performance of national governing bodies of sport. *European Sport Management Quarterly, 7*, 240–268.

Bergsgard, N. A., Houlihan, B., Mangset, P., Nodland, S. I., & Rommetveldt, H. (2007). *Sport policy: A comparative analysis of stability and change*. London: Elsevier.

Berman, S., Wicks, A. C., Kotha, S., & Jones, M. J. T. (1999). Does stakeholder orientation matter? The relationship between stakeholder management models and firm financial performance. *Academy of Management Journal, 43*(5), 488–504.

Berrett, T., & Slack, T. (2001). A framework for the analysis of strategic approaches employed by non-profit sport organisations in seeking corporate sponsorship. *Sport Management Review, 4*, 21–45.

Bititci, U., Mendibil, K., Nudurupati, S., Turner, T., & Garengo, P. (2004). The interplay between performance measurement, organizational culture and management styles. *Measuring Business Excellence, 8*(3), 28–41.

Blair, M. M. (1995). Ownership and control: Rethinking corporate governance for the twenty-first century. In T. Clarke (ed.), *Theories of corporate governance* (pp. 174–189). New York: Routledge.

Bloom, M., Grant, M., & Watt, D. (2005). *Strengthening Canada: The socio-economic benefits of sport participation in Canada.* Ottawa: The Conference Board of Canada.

Boice, D. F., & Kleiner, B. H. (1997). Designing effective performance appraisal systems. *Work Study, 46*(6), 197–201.

Bond, T.C. (1999). The role of performance measurement in continuous improvement. *International Journal of Operations & Production Management, 19*(12), 1318–1334.

Booth, A. (2006). Counting what counts: Performance measurement and evidence-based practice. *Performance Measurement and Metrics, 7*(2), 63–74.

Booth, M., Bauman, A., & Owen, N. (2002). Perceived barriers to physical activity among older Australians. *Journal of Aging and Physical Activity, 10*(3), 271–280.

Bourne, M., Franco, M., & Wilkes, J. (2003). Corporate performance management. *Measuring Business Excellence, 7*(3), 15–21.

Boyle, R., & Haynes, R. (2009). *Power play: Sport, the media and popular culture.* Edinburgh: Edinburgh University Press, print.

Bracken, D. W. (1996). Multisource (360-degree) feedback: Surveys for individual and organizational development. In A. I. Kraut (ed.), *Organizational surveys: Tools for assessment and change* (pp. 117–143). San Francisco: Jossey-Bass.

Bradshaw, P., Murray, V., & Wolpin, J. 1996. Women on boards of non-profits: What difference do they make? *Non-Profit Management & Leadership, 6*(3), 241–254.

Broady-Preston, J., & Steel, L. (2002). Employees, customers and internal marketing strategies in LIS. *Library Management, 23*, 384–393.

Brunton, G., Harden, A., Rees, R., Kavanagh, J., Oliver, S., & Oakley, A. (2003). *Children and physical activity: A systematic review of barriers and facilitators.* EPPI Centre, Social Science Research Unit, Institute of Education, University of London. Retrieved 10 April 2012 from http://eppi.ioe.ac.uk/cms/Default.aspx?tabid=56.

Butler, A., Letza, S. R., & Neale, B. (1997). Linking the Balanced Scorecard to strategy. *Long Range Planning, 30*(2), 242–253.

Cadbury, A. (2002). *Corporate governance and chairmanship: A personal view.* Oxford: Oxford University Press.

Cairnduff, S. (2001). *Sport and recreation for indigenous youth in the Northern Territory: Scoping research priorities for health and social outcomes.* Casuarina, NT: Cooperative Research Centre for Aboriginal and Tropical Health (CRCATH).

Callen, J. L., Klein, A., & Tinkelman, D. (2003). Board composition, committees and organizational efficiency: The case of non-profits. *Non-profit and Voluntary Sector Quarterly, 32*(4), 493–520.

Camp, R. C. (1989). *Benchmarking: The search for industry best practices that lead to superior performance.* New York: Quality Resources.

Carver, J. (1997). *Boards that make a difference: A new design for leadership in nonprofit and public organizations.* San Francisco: Jossey-Bass.

Central Statistics Office. (2012). *Census 2011 Results.* Retrieved 6 March 2012 from www.cso.ie/en/census/census2011reports/census2011thisisirelandpart1/.

Chaganti, R. S., Mahajon, V., & Sharma, S. (1985). Corporate board size, composition and corporate failures in retailing industry. *Journal of Management Studies, 22*(4), 400–417.

Chait, R., Holland, T., & Taylor, B. (1996). *Improving the performance of governing boards*. Westport, CT: Oryx Press.

Chang, C. F., & Tuckman, H. P. (1990). Why do non-profit managers accumulate surpluses and how much do they accumulate? *Non-profit Management and Leadership*, *1*(2), 117–134.

Chappelet, J., & Bayle, E. (2005). *Strategic and performance management of Olympic sport organisations*. Champaign, IL: Human Kinetics.

Chauvel, D., & Despres, C. (2002). A review of survey research in knowledge management: 1997–2001. *Journal of Knowledge Management*, *6*(3), 207–223.

Chelladurai, P. (2005). *Managing organizations for sport and physical activity: A systems perspective*. (2nd ed.) Scottsdale, AZ: Holcomb Hathaway.

Clarkson, M. E. (1995). A stakeholder framework for analyzing and evaluating corporate social performance. *Academy of Management Review*, *20*(1), 92–117.

Cleveland, J. N., Murphy, K. R., & Williams, R. E. (1989). Multiple uses of performance appraisal: Prevalence and correlates. *Journal of Applied Psychology*, *74*, 130–35.

Coalter, F. (2005). *The social benefits of sport*. Report no. 98. Scotland: Sport Scotland.

Coalter, F. (2007). *A wider social role for sport: Who's keeping the score?* London: Routledge.

Cobbold, I., & Lawrie, G. (2002). *The development of the Balanced Scorecard as a strategic management tool*. Performance Measurement Association 2002 Report.

Cordery, C., & Baskerville, R. (2009). *Financing sports organisations in New Zealand: The impact of governors' choices*. Wellington: Sport NZ.

Cornett, M., Marcus, A., & Tehranian, H. (2008). Earnings management, corporate governance and financial performance. *Journal of Financial Economics*, *87*, 357–373.

Cornforth, C., & Simpson, C. (2003). The changing face of charity governance: The impact of organizational size. In C. Cornforth (ed.), *The Governance of Public and Non-profit Organizations* (pp. 187–206). New York: Routledge.

Corti, B., Brimage, G., Bull, F., & Frizzell, S. (1996). *Health-promoting sport, arts and race settings: New challenges for the health sector*. Canberra: National Health and Medical Research Council, Australian Government Publishing Service.

Council of Europe. (1993). *European sports charter*. Belgium: author.

Cuskelly, G., Hoye, R., & Auld, C. (2006). *Working with volunteers in sport: Theory and practice*. London: Routledge.

Cuskelly, G., Taylor, T., Hoye, R., & Darcy, S. (2006). Volunteer management practices and volunteer retention: A human resource management approach. *Sport Management Review*, *9*, 141–163.

Daily, C. M., Certo, S. T., & Dalton, D. R. (1999). A decade of corporate women: Some progress in the boardroom, none in the executive suite. *Strategic Management Journal*, *20*(1), 93–100.

Dalton, D. R., Daily, C. M., Ellstrand, A. E., & Johnson, J. L. (1998). Meta-analytic reviews of board composition, leadership structure and financial performance. *Strategic Management Journal*, *19*(3), 269–290.

Dalton, D. R., Daily, C. M., Johnson, J. L., & Ellstrand, A. E. (1999). Number of directors and financial performance: A meta-analysis. *Academy of Management Journal*, *42*(6), 674–686.

Dalziel, P. (2011). *The economic and social value of sport and recreation to New Zealand: An overview*. Wellington: Sport NZ.

Daniels, A. C. (2004). *Performance management: Changing behavior that drives organizational effectiveness*. Atlanta: Performance Management Publications, print.

De Jong, J. P. J., & Den Hartog, D. N. (2007). Leadership and employees' innovative behaviour. *European Journal of Innovation Management, 10*(1), 41–64.

Delaney, L., & Fahey, T. (2005). *Social and economic value of sport in Ireland.* Dublin: Economic and Social Research Institute.

Deloitte. (2006). *A review of the performance of SPARC during the 2002–2006 period.* New Zealand: Sport NZ.

Deming, W. E. (1986). *Out of the crisis.* Cambridge, MA: MIT Press.

DeNisi, A. S., & Pritchard, R. D. (2006). Performance appraisal, performance management and improving individual performance: A motivational framework. *Management and Organisation Review, 2*(2), 253–277.

Doherty, A. J. (1998). Managing our human resources: A review of organisational behaviour in sport. *Sport Management Review, 1*(1), 1–24.

Doherty, A., & Carron, A. V. (2003). Cohesion in volunteer sport executive committees. *Journal of Sport Management, 17*, 116–141.

Doherty, A., & Murray, M. (2007). The strategic sponsorship process in a non-profit sport organization. *Sport Marketing Quarterly, 16*(1), 49–59.

Donaldson, T., & Preston, L. (1995). The stakeholder theory of the corporation: Concepts, evidence and implications. *Academy of Management Review, 20*(1), 65–91.

Douglas, E., & Morris, R. (2006). Workaholic or just hard worker? *Career Development International, 11*(5), 394–417.

Driscoll, K., & Wood, L. (1999). *Sporting capital: Changes and challenges for rural communities in Victoria.* Melbourne: Centre for Applied Social Research, RMIT.

Driscoll, K., & Wood, L. (2001). *Directions for physical activity. VicHealth discussion document: Literature review.* Melbourne: Centre for Applied Social Research, RMIT.

Eagleson, G. K., & Waldersee, R. (2000). Monitoring the strategically important: Assessing and improving strategic tracking systems. *Performance Measurement Past, Present and Future – Second International Conference on Performance Measurement.* Cambridge, UK.

EFQM (European Foundation for Quality Management). (2005). *The EFQM framework for knowledge management.* European Foundation for Quality Management. Brussels: author.

Eime, R. M., Payne, W., & Harvey, J. (2008). Making sporting clubs healthy and welcoming environments: A strategy to increase participation. *Journal of Science and Medicine in Sport, 11*(2),146–154.

Emsley, D. (2003). Multiple goals and managers' job-related tension and performance. *Journal of Managerial Psychology, 18*(4), 345–356.

Epstein, M. J., & Manzoni, J. F. (1997). The Balanced Scorecard and *tableau de bord*: Translating strategy into action. *Management Accounting, 79*(2), 28–37.

Essers, J., Bohm, S., & Contu, A. (2009). Corporate Robespierres, ideologies of management and change. *Journal of Organizational Change Management, 22*(2), 129–140.

European Commission. (2010). *Sport and physical activity.* Retrieved 1 November 2012 from http://ec.europa.eu/public_opinion/archives/ebs/ebs_334_en.pdf.

Evans, M. G. (1970). The effects of supervisory behavior on the path–goal relationship. *Organizational Behavior and Human Performance, 5*, 277–298.

Fama, E. F., & Jensen, M. C. (1983). Separation of ownership and control. *Journal of Law and Economics, 26*, 301–326.

Fariborz, P. Y. (2001). An analytic model to quantify strategic service vision. *International Journal of Service Industry Management, 12*(5), 476–99.

Feeney, R. J. (2009). *Governmentality and the sports sector: An investigation into the effects of government modernisation and the application of good governance to the sports sector in Northern Ireland: Case study: Ulster Council GAA*. Queens University: Belfast.

Feigenbaum, A. V. (1991). *Total quality control*. (3rd ed.) New York: McGraw-Hill.

Ferkins, L., & Shilbury, D. (2010). Developing board strategic capability in sport organisations: The national–regional governing relationship. *Sport Management Review*, *13*(3), 235–254.

Ferkins, L., Shilbury, D., & McDonald, G. (2005). The role of the board in building strategic capability: Toward an integrated model of sport governance research. *Sport Management Review*, *8*(3), 195–225.

Fitzgerald, L. A., & Van Eijnatten, F. M. (2002). Reflections: Chaos in organisational change. *Journal of Organisational Change Management*, *15*(4), 402–411.

Fletcher, C. (2001). Performance appraisal and management: The developing research agenda. *Journal of Occupational and Organizational Psychology*, *74*, 473–487.

Folger, R., & Cropanzano, R. (1998). *Organizational justice and human resource management*. Beverly Hills, CA: Sage.

Freeman, R. E. (1984). *Strategic management: A stakeholder approach*. London: Pitman.

Fried, G., Shapiro, S., & DeSchriver, T. (2008). *Sport Finance*. Champaign, IL: Human Kinetics, print.

Fuller, C. W., & Vassie, L. H. (2002). Assessing the maturity and alignment of organisational cultures in partnership arrangements. *Employee Relations*, *24*(5), 540–555.

GAA. (2009). *Strategic vision and action plan 2009–2015*. Dublin: author.

GAA. (2010). *GAA official guide*. Dublin: author.

Gamble, J., Strickland, A., & Thompson, A. (2007). *Crafting and executing strategy*. (15th ed.). New York: McGraw-Hill.

Garavan, T., Morley, M., & Flynn, M. (1997). 360 degree feedback: Its role in employee development. *Journal of Management Development*, *16*(2), 134–147.

Garratt, B. (1996). *The fish rots from the head*. London: Harper Collins Business.

Gilbert, W., & Trudel, P. (1999). An evaluation strategy for coach education programs. *Journal of Sport Behaviour*, *22*, 234–250.

Goodstein, J., Gautam, K., & Boeker, W. (1994). The effects of board size and diversity on strategic change. *Strategic Management Journal*, *15*, 241–250.

Greasley, K., Bryman, A., Dainty, A., Price, A., Soetanto, R., & King, N. (2005). Employee perceptions of empowerment. *Employee Relations*, *27*(4), 354–368.

Green, M., & Houlihan, B. (2005). *Elite sport development: Policy learning and political priorities*. London and New York: Routledge.

Greenhaus, J. H., Callanan, G. A., & Kaplan, E. (1995). The role of goal setting in career management. *International Journal of Career Management*, *7*(5), 3–12.

Hansen, F. E., & Emsden, C. (2012). *Danish GDP drops more than expected*. Retrieved 1 November 2012 from http://online.wsj.com/article/SB10000872396390444914904577 618674218400782.html.

Hassan, D. (2010). Governance and the Gaelic Athletic Association: Time to move beyond the amateur ideal? *Soccer & Society*, *11*(4), 414–427.

Herman, E. S. (1981). *Corporate control, corporate power*. New York: Cambridge University Press.

Herman, R. D., & Renz, D. O. (2008). Advancing non-profit organizational effectiveness research and theory. *Non-profit Management and Leadership*, *18*, 399–415.

Hoffman, R. (1995). Ten reasons you should be using 360-degree feedback. *HR Magazine*, *40*, 82–85.

Hofstede, G. (2001). *Culture's consequences: Comparing values, behaviors, institutions and organizations across nations*. (2nd ed.). Thousand Oaks, California: Sage.

Hood, C. (2003). Control, bargains, and cheating: The politics of public-service reform. *Journal of Public Administration Research and Theory, 12*(3), 309–332.

Hood, J. (1995). *The Hood report: A path to superior performance*. Christchurch: New Zealand Cricket.

Houle, C. O. (1989). *Governing boards: Their nature and nurture*. San Francisco: Jossey-Bass.

Houlihan, B. (2005). Public sector sport: Policy developing a framework for analysis. *International Review for the Sociology of Sport, 2*, 163–185.

Houlihan, B. & White, A. (2002). *The politics of sports development*. London: Routledge.

Houlihan, B., Nicholson, M., & Hoye, R. (eds.). (2010). *Participation in sport: International policy perspectives*. London: Routledge.

House, R. J. (1971). A path–goal theory of leader effectiveness. *Administrative Science Quarterly, 16*, 321–339.

House, R. J. (1996). Path–goal theory of leadership: Lessons, legacy and a reformulated theory. *Leadership Quarterly, 7*(3), 323–352.

House, R. J., & Mitchell, T. R. (1974). Path–goal theory of leadership. *Journal of Contemporary Business, 3*, 1–97.

Howes, F., Doyle, J., Jackson, N., & Waters, E. (2004). Evidence-based public health: The importance of finding 'difficult to locate' public health and health promotion intervention studies for systematic reviews. *Journal of Public Health, 26*(1), 101–104.

Hoye, R. (2004). Leader-member exchanges and board performance of voluntary sport organizations. *Non-profit Management & Leadership, 15*(1), 55–70.

Hoye, R. (2006). Leadership within voluntary sport organization boards. *Non-profit Management & Leadership, 16*(3), 297–313.

Hoye, R., & Auld, C. (2001). Measuring board performance in non-profit sport organizations. *Australian Journal of Volunteering, 6*(2), 109–116.

Hoye, R., & Cuskelly, G. (2003). Board–executive relationships within voluntary sport organisations. *Sport Management Review, 6*(1), 53–74.

Hoye, R., & Cuskelly, G. (2004). Board member selection, orientation and evaluation: Implications for board performance in member-benefit voluntary sport organisations. *Third Sector Review, 10*(1), 77–100.

Hoye, R., & Cuskelly, G. (2007). *Sport governance*. Oxford: Elsevier Butterworth-Heinemann.

Hoye, R., & Doherty, A. (2011). Non-profit sport board performance: A review and directions for future research. *Journal of Sport Management, 25*(3), 272–285.

Hums, M. A., & MacLean, J. C. (2004). *Governance and policy in sport organisations*. Arizona: Holcomb Hathaway.

Huse, M. (2005). Accountability and creating accountability: A framework for exploring behavioural perspectives of corporate governance. *British Journal of Management, 16*, 65–79.

Hussain, M., & Islam, M. (2003). Different nature of non-financial performances and their measurement practices in financial services industry. *Humanomics, 19*(3), 18–35.

Hylton, K. & Bramham, P. (eds.). (2008). *Sports development: Policy, process and practice*. (2nd ed.) London: Routledge.

Inglis, S. (1997). Roles of the board in amateur sport organizations. *Journal of Sport Management, 11*, 160–176.

Irish Sports Council. (2009a). *Statement of strategy 2009–2011*. Dublin: author.

Irish Sports Council. (2009b). *Quadrennial high-performance review*. Dublin: author.

Irish Sports Council. (2009c). *The Irish sports monitor*. Dublin: author.

Irish Sports Council. (2010). *Assessment of economic impact of sport in Ireland*. Dublin: author.

Irish Sports Council. (2012). *Irish Sports Council announces funding plans for 2012*. Retrieved 25 August 2015 from www.irishsportscouncil.ie/Media/Latest_News/2012/April/Irish_Sports_Council_Announces_Funding_Plans_for_2012.html.

James, E., & Young, D. R. (2007). Fee income and commercial ventures. In D. R. Young (ed.), *Financial non-profits: Putting theory into practice* (pp. 93–119). London: Altamira Press.

Jegers, M., & Verscheuren, I. (2006). On the capital structure of non-profit organisations: An empirical study for Californian organisations. *Financial Accountability and Management, 22*(4), 309–329.

Jensen, M. C. (1993). The modern industrial revolution, exit, and the failure of internal control systems. *Journal of Finance, 48*(3), 831–880.

Kanfer, R., & Ackerman, P. L. (1989). Motivation and cognitive abilities: An integrative/aptitude-treatment interaction approach to skill acquisition. *Journal of Applied Psychology, 74*, 657–690.

Kaplan, R. (1993). 360-degree feedback PLUS: Boosting the power of co-worker ratings for executives. *Human Resource Management, 32*(2), 299–314.

Kaplan, R. S., & Bruns, W. (1987). *Accounting and management: A field study perspective*. Boston: Harvard Business School Press, print.

Kaplan, R. S., & Norton, D. P. (1992). The Balanced Scorecard: Measures that drive performance. *Harvard Business Review*, January, 71–80.

Kaplan, R. S., & Norton, D. P. (1993). Putting the Balanced Scorecard to work. *Harvard Business Review*, September, 2–16.

Kaplan, R. S., & Norton, D. P. (1996a). Using the balanced scorecard as a strategic management system. *Harvard Business Review*, January, 75–85.

Kaplan, R. S., & Norton, D. P. (1996b). *Balanced Scorecard: Translating strategy into action*. Boston: Harvard Business School Press, print.

Kaplan, R. S., & Norton, D. P. (2001). *The strategy-focused organization: How Balanced Scorecard companies thrive in the new business environment*. Boston: Harvard Business School, print.

Kaplan, R. S., & Norton, D. P. (2004). *Strategy maps: Converting intangible assets into tangible outcomes*. Boston: Harvard Business School Press, print.

Kearns, K. P. (2007). Income portfolios. In D. R. Young (ed.), *Financing non-profits: Putting theory into practice* (pp. 291–314). Lanham, MD: Altamira Press.

Kennerley, M., & Neely, A. (2002). A framework of the factors affecting the evolution of performance measurement systems. *International Journal of Operations and Production Management, 22*(11), 1222–1245.

Kennerley, M., & Neely, A. (2003). Measuring performance in a changing business environment. *International Journal of Operations & Production Management, 23*(2), 213–229.

Keys, C. (2009). *GAA coffers duffer €5m 'gate' decline*. Retrieved 15 December 2011 from www.independent.ie/sport/gaelic-football/gaa-coffers-suffer-5m-gate-decline-1684911.html.

Kikulis, L. M., Slack, T., & Hinings C. R. (1995). Does decision making make a difference? Patterns of change within Canadian national sport organizations. *Journal of Sport Management, 9*, 279–299.

Kilmister, T. (1996) Governance. In S. Leberman, C. Collins, & L. Trenberth (eds.), *Sport business management in New Zealand* (pp. 147–175). Andover, Hampshire: Cengage Learning.

Kotter, J. (1996). *Leading change*. Boston: Harvard Business School Press, print.

Kurtzman, J. (1997). *Is your company off course? Now you can find out why*. Fortune, February, 128–130.

Lam, J. (1997). Transformation from public administration to management: Success and challenges of public sector reform in Hong Kong. *Public Productivity and Management Review, 20*(4), 405–418.

Landy, F. J., & Farr, J. L. (1980). Performance rating. *Psychological Bulletin, 87*, 72–107.

Lawrence, H. D. (2008). *Government involvement in New Zealand sport: Sport policy: A cautionary tale*. Unpublished Master's thesis, University of Waikato, Waikato.

Leontief, W. W. (1986). *Input–Output Economics*. (2nd ed.) New York: Oxford University Press.

Lepsinger, R., & Lucia, A. (1997). *The art and science of 360° feedback*. San Francisco, CA: Jossey-Bass-Pfeiffer.

Li, L. (2009). *Study review of performance appraisal in sports organizations*. ISECS, International Colloquium on Computing, Communication, Control and Management. Report.

Locke, E. A. (1968). Toward a theory of task motivation and incentives. *Organizational Behavior and Human Performance*, (3)2, 157–189.

Locke, E. A., & Latham, G. P. (2002), Building a practically useful theory of goal setting and task motivation. *American Psychologist, 57*(9), 705–715.

London, M., & Beatty, R. W. (1993). 360-degree feedback as a competitive advantage. *Human Resource Management, 32*, 352–373.

Longenecker, C. (1997). Why managerial performance appraisals are ineffective: Causes and lessons. *Career Development International, 2*(5), 212–218.

Lopez, S. P., Peon, J. M., & Ordas, C. J. (2004). Managing knowledge: The link between culture and organizational learning. *Journal of Knowledge Management, 8*(6), 93–104.

Luoma, P., & Goodstein, J. (1999). Stakeholders and corporate boards: Institutional influences on board composition and structure. *Academy of Management Journal, 42*(5), 553–563.

Lynall, M. D., Golden, B. R., & Hillman, A. J. (2003). Board composition from adolescence to maturity: A multitheoretic view. *Academy of Management Review, 28*(3), 416–431.

Lyons, P. (2006). Team member involvement in team leader training and performance. *Team Performance Management, 12*(4), 102–114.

McAfee, R. B., & Champagne, P. J. (1993). Performance management: A strategy for improving employee performance and productivity. *Journal of Managerial Psychology, 8*(5), 24–32.

McBain, R. (2007). The practice of engagement. *Strategic Human Resources Review, 6*(6), 16–19.

McCárthaigh, S. (2011). Garda investigation begins into Basketball Ireland grant. Retrieved 14 November 2011 from www.irishexaminer.com/ireland/garda-investigation-begins-into-basketball-ireland-grant-173564.html.

McCarthy, A. M., & Garavan, T. N. (2001). 360° feedback process: Performance, improvement and employee career development. *Journal of European Industrial Training, 25*(1), 5–32.

McCracken, G. D. (2012). *Culturematic: How reality TV, John Cheever, a pie lab, Julia Child, Fantasy Football, Burning Man, the Ford Fiesta movement, Rube Goldberg, NFL films, Wordle,* Two and a Half Men, *a 10,000-year symphony and ROFLcon memes will help you create and execute breakthrough ideas.* Boston, MA: Harvard Business Press, print.

MacMillan, I. (1983). Competitive strategies for not-for-profit agencies. *Advances in Strategic Management, 1,* 61–82.

McNamara, C., & Mong, S. (2005). Performance measurement and management: Some insights from practice. *Australian Accounting Review, 15*(35), 14–28.

McNulty, T., & Pettigrew, A. (1999). Strategists on the board. *Organization Studies, 20*(1), 47–74.

Madella, A., Bayle, E., & Tome, J. (2005). The organisational performance of national swimming federations in Mediterranean countries: A comparative approach. *European Journal of Sport Science, 5*(4), 207–220.

Mahony, D., & Howard, D. (2001). Sport business in the next decade: A general overview of expected trends. *Journal of Sport Management, 15,* 275–296.

Malcolm Baldrige National Quality Award. (2005). *Criteria for performance excellence.* Gaithersburg, USA: National Institute of Standards and Technology.

Maleyeff, J. (2003). Benchmarking performance indices: Pitfalls and solutions. *Benchmarking: An International Journal, 10*(1), 9–28.

Malina, M.A., & Selto, F.H. (2001). Communicating and controlling strategy: An empirical study of the effectiveness of the Balanced Scorecard. *Journal of Management Accounting Research, 13,* 47–91.

Mallett, C., & Cote, J. (2006). Beyond winning and losing: Guidelines for evaluating high-performance coaches. *The Sport Psychologist, 20*(2), 213–221.

Manasa, K., & Reddy, N. (2009). Role of training in improving performance. *The IUP Journal of Soft Skills, 3,* 72–80.

Mason, D. S., Thibault, L., & Misener, L. (2006). An agency theory perspective on corruption in sport: The case of the International Olympic Committee. *Journal of Sport Management, 20,* 52–73.

Mayer, C. M., & Gavin, M. B. (2005). Trust in management and performance: Who minds the shop while the employees watch the boss? *Academy of Management Journal, 48*(5), 874–888.

Maylett, T. (2009). 360-degree feedback revisited: The transition from development to appraisal. *Compensation and Benefits Review, 41*(5), 52–59.

Michie, J. (2000). The governance and regulation of professional football. *The Political Quarterly, 71*(2), 184–191.

Michie, J., & Oughton, C. (2005). The corporate governance of professional football clubs in England. *Corporate Governance, 13*(4), 517–531.

Miller, K. L. (1997). *Sport business management.* Gaithersburg, MD: Aspen Publishers.

Miller, L. E., Weiss, R. M., & MacLeod, B. V. (1988). Boards of directors in non-profit organizations: Composition, activities and organizational outcome. *Journal of Voluntary Action Research, 17,* 81–89.

Miller-Millesen, J. L. (2003). Understanding the behavior of non-profit boards of directors: A theory-based approach. *Non-profit and Voluntary Sector Quarterly, 32*(4), 521–547.

Mintz, S. M., & Morris, R. E. (2008). *Ethical obligations and decision making in accounting: Text and cases.* Boston: McGraw-Hill.

Mitchell, R. K., Agle, B. R., & Wood, D. J. (1997). Toward a theory of stakeholder identification and salience: Defining the principle of who and what really counts. *Academy
of Management Review, 22*(4), 853–886.

Moffat, J. (2000). Representing the command and control process in simulation models of
conflict. *Journal of the Operational Research Society, 51*(4), 431–438.

Mooraj, S., Oton, D., & Hostettler, D. (1999). The Balanced Scorecard: A necessary good
or an unnecessary evil? *European Management Journal, 17*(5), 481–491.

Muczyk, J. P., & Gable, M. (1987). Managing sales performance through a comprehensive performance appraisal system. *Journal of Personal Selling and Sales Management, 7*(3), 41–52.

Neely, A. (2005). The evolution of performance measurement research: Developments in
the last decade and a research agenda for the next. *International Journal of Operations
& Production Management, 25*(12), 1264–1277.

Neely, A., Adams, C., & Crowe, P. (2001). The Performance Prism in practice: Measuring business excellence. *Emerald Performance Management, 5*(2), 6–12.

Neely, A., Adams, C., & Kennerley, M. (2002). *The Performance Prism.* Upper Saddle
River, NJ: FT Prentice Hall.

New Zealand Cricket. (2007). *NZC strategic plan 2007–2011.* Christchurch: author.

New Zealand Cricket. (2008). *NZC annual report.* Christchurch: author.

New Zealand Cricket. (2011). *NZC annual report.* Christchurch: author.

New Zealand Rugby Union. (2008). *NZRU strategic plan.* Wellington: author.

New Zealand Rugby Union. (2015). *Our board.* Retrieved 2 March 2015 from www.
nzrugby.co.nz/about-us/our-people/our-board.

New Zealand Rugby Union. (2012). *About us.* Retrieved 2 February 2012 from www.
nzru.co.nz/about_us.

Niemann, A., García, B., and Grant, W. (eds.). (2011). *The transformation of European
football: Towards the Europeanisation of the national game.* Manchester University
Press, Manchester.

Nies, M. A, Vollman, M., & Cook, T. (1998). Facilitators, barriers and strategies for exercise in European American women in the community. *Public Health Nursing, 15*(4),
263–272.

Niven, P. R. (2006). *Balanced Scorecard step-by-step: Maximizing performance and
maintaining results.* London: Wiley.

Norreklit, H. (2000). The balance on the Balanced Scorecard: A critical analysis of some
of its assumptions. *Management Accounting Research, 11*(1), 65–88.

O'Boyle, I., & Hassan, D. (2014). Performance management and measurement in national
level non-profit sport organisations. *European Sport Management Quarterly.* DOI:
http://dx.doi.org/10.1080/16184742.2014.898677.

O'Donnell, M. (1998). Creating a performance culture? Performance-based pay in the
Australian Public Service. *Australian Journal of Public Administration, 57*(3), 28–40.

Oliver P. (2006). What's the score? A survey of cultural diversity and racism in Australian sport. *Human Rights and Equal Opportunity Commission.* Retrieved 5 April 2012
from www.hreoc.gov.au/racial_discrimination/whats_the_score/index.html.

Olson, D. H. (2000). Circumplex model of marital and family systems. *Journal of Family
Therapy, 22,* 144–167.

Olve, N., Roy, J., & Wetter, M. (1999). *Performance drivers: A practical guide to using
the Balanced Scorecard.* UK: Wiley.

Ong, C., & Wan, D. (2008). Three conceptual models of board role performance. *Corporate Governance, 8*(3), 317–329.

Oster, S.M. (1995). *Strategic management for non-profit organisations: Theory and cases*. New York: Oxford University Press.

Papadimitriou, D. (2002). Amateur structures and their effect on performance: The case of Greek voluntary sports clubs. *Managing Leisure, 7*(4), 205–219.

Papadimitriou, D. (2007). Conceptualizing effectiveness in a non-profit organizational environment: An exploratory study. *International Journal of Public Sector Management, 20*, 572–587.

Papadimitriou, D., & Taylor, P. (2000). Organisational effectiveness of Hellenic national sports organisations: A multiple constituency approach. *Sport Management Review, 3*, 23–46.

Pawson, R. (2006). *Evidence based policy: A realist perspective*. London: Sage.

Payne, W., Reynolds, M., Brown, S., & Fleming, A. (2003). *Sports role models and their impact on participation in physical activity: A literature review*. Victoria, Australia: VicHealth.

Peters, T. J., & Waterman, R. H. (1982). *In search of excellence: Lessons from America's best-run companies*. New York: Warner.

Pettijohn, L., Parker, R., Pettijohn, C., & Kent, J. (2001). Performance appraisals: Usage, criteria and observations. *The Journal of Management Development, 20*, 754–771.

Pfeffer, J., & Salancik, G. R. (1978). *The external control of organizations: A resource dependence perspective*. New York: Harper & Row.

Piggot-Irvine, E. (2003). Appraisal training focussed on what really matters. *The International Journal of Educational Management, 17*(6), 254–261.

Pointer, D. D., & Orlikoff, J. E. (2002). *The high performance board: Principles of non-profit organization governance*. San Francisco: Jossey-Bass.

Priest, N., Armstrong, R., Doyle, J., & Waters, E. (2008). Interventions implemented through sporting organisations for increasing participation in sport. *The Cochrane Library*, Issue 3. Art. no.: CD004809.

Provan, K. G. (1980). Board power and organisational effectiveness among human service agencies. *Academy of Management Journal, 23*(2), 221–236.

Pulakos, E. D. (2009). *Performance management: A new approach for driving business results*. Chichester, West Sussex: Wiley-Blackwell, print.

Putnam, R. (2000). *Bowling alone: The collapse and revival of American community*. New York: Simon and Schuster.

Quinn, P. (2002). *Enhancing community identity: GAA strategic review*. Dublin: author.

Rhoades, D. L., Rechner, P L., & Sundaramurthy, C. (2000). Board composition and financial performance: A meta-analysis of the influence of outside directors. *Journal of Managerial Issues, 12*(1), 76–91.

Richter, D. L., Wilcox, S., Greaney, M. L., Henderson, K. A., & Ainsworth, B. B. (2002). Environmental, policy and cultural factors related to physical activity in African American women. *Women and Health, 36*(2), 91–109.

Rossouw, D., du Plessis, C., Prinsloo, F., & Prozesky, M. (2009). *Ethics for accountants and auditors*. South Africa: Oxford University Press, print.

Rousseau, D. M., & Wade-Benzoni, K. (1994). Linking strategy and human resource practices: How employee and customer contracts are created. *Human Resource Management, 33*(3), 463–489.

Rummler, G. A. & Brache, A. P. (1995). *Improving performance: How to manage the white space on the organization chart*. San Francisco, CA: Jossey-Bass.

Ryan, N. (2012). *The Performance Prism*. Association of Chartered Certified Accountants. Report. Retrieved 12 March 2012 from www.accaglobal.com/content/dam/acca/global/PDF-students/2012s/sa_mar12_p5_perfprism.pdf.

Rynes, S. L., Brown, K. G., & Colbert, A. E. (2002). Research findings versus practitioner beliefs: Seven common misconceptions about human resource practices. *Academy of Management Executive, 16*(3), 92–102.

Saka, A. (2003). Internal change agents' view of the management of change problem. *Journal of Organizational Change Management, 16*(5), 480–496.

Salmon, J., Owen, N., Crawford, D., Bauman, A., & Sallis, J. F. (2003). Physical activity and sedentary behaviour: A population-based study of barriers, enjoyment and preference. *Health Psychology, 22*(2), 178–188.

Schacter, M. (2002). *Not a tool kit: Practitioner's guide to measuring the performance of public programs*. Ottawa, Canada: Institute on Governance.

Schneier, C., Shaw, D., & Beatty, R. (1992). Predicting participants' performance and reactions in an experiential learning setting: An empirical investigation. *Proceedings of the Association for Business Simulation and Experiential Learning, 19th annual conference, Reno, NV*.

Schoenberg, G., & Shilbury, D. (2011). Don't put a square piece in a round hole: Match the CEO to the strategic plan. *Proceedings of the Sport Management Association of Australia and New Zealand 2011 Conference: Program and Book of Abstracts*.

Schraeder, M., Becton, J., & Portis, R. (2007). A critical examination of performance appraisals. *The Journal for Quality and Participation, 30*(1), 20–25.

Senge, P. (1994). *The fifth discipline: The art and practice of the learning organization*. New York: Doubleday Currency.

Senior, B., & Swailes, S. (2004). The dimensions of management team performance: A repertory grid study. *International Journal of Productivity and Performance Management, 53*(4), 317–333.

Shilbury, D. (2001). Examining board member roles, functions and influence: A study of Victorian sporting organisations. *International Journal of Sport Management, 2,* 253–281.

Shilbury, D., Deane, J., & Kellett, P. (2006). *Sport management in Australia: An organisational overview* (3rd ed.). Bentleigh East, Victoria, Australia: Strategic Sport Management.

Shulver, M., Lawrie, G., & Andersen, H. (2000). A process for developing strategically relevant measures of intellectual capital. *Proceedings of the Second International Conference on Performance Measurement and Management*. Cambridge, July.

Silverthorne, C. (2001). A test of the path–goal leadership theory in Taiwan. *Leadership & Organization Development Journal, 22*(4), 151–158.

Simmons, J. (2008). Employee significance within stakeholder-accountable performance management systems. *The TQM Journal, 20*(5), 463–475.

Skinner, J., Stewart, B., & Edwards, A. (1999). Amateurism to professionalism: Modelling organisational change in sport organisations. *Sport Management Review, 2,* 173–192.

Slack, T., & Parent, M. M. (2006). *Understanding sport organizations: The application of organization theory*. Champaign, IL: Human Kinetics.

Slesinger, L. H. (1991). *Self-assessment for non-profit governing boards*. Washington, DC: National Center for Non-profit Boards.

Soltani, E. (2005). Conflict between theory and practice: TQM and performance appraisal. *The International Journal of Quality and Reliability Management, 22,* 796–818.

Spinks, N., Wells, B., & Meche, M. (1999). Appraising appraisals: Computerized performance appraisal systems. *Career Development International, 4*(2), 94–100.

Sport England. (2004). *Driving up participation: The challenge for sport*. Retrieved 4 April 2012 from www.sportengland.org/research/idoc.ashx?docid=28e3555f.

Sport NZ. (2004). *Nine steps to effective governance: Building high performing organisations*. Wellington: author.

Sport NZ. (2006a). *Volunteers: The heart of sport*. Wellington: author.

Sport NZ. (2006b). *Nine steps to effective governance: Building high performing organisations*. (2nd ed.) Wellington: author.

Sport NZ. (2009a). *Strategic plan 2009–2015*. Wellington: author.

Sport NZ. (2009b). *The active New Zealand survey 2007–2008*. Wellington: author.

Sport NZ. (2011). *Sport NZ annual report*. Wellington: author.

Sport NZ. (2012a). Retrieved 23 January 2012 from www.sportnz.org.nz/en-nz/our-partners/Regional-Sports-Trusts/.

Sport NZ. (2012b). *Organisational development tool*. Retrieved 3 March 2012 from www.sportnz.org.nz/en-nz/our-partners/Developing-Capabilities/Development-and-support/SportNZ-Repository/ODT-Resource-Links/.

Sport Recreation South Africa. (2007). Knowledge base: Sport development. Retrieved 4 April 2012 from www.srsa.gov.za/KnowledgePage.asp?id=31.

Spriggs, M. T. (1994). A framework for more valid measures of channel member performance. *Journal of Retailing, 70*, 327–343.

Srivastava, R. K., Shervani, T. A., & Fahey, L. (1998). Market-based assets and shareholder value: A framework for analysis. *Journal of Marketing, 62*, 2–18.

Standing Committee on Recreation and Sport. (2006). *Participation in exercise, recreation and sport annual report 2006*. Retrieved 25 August 2015 from www.ausport.gov.au/__data/assets/pdf_file/0003/142563/ERASS_2006-Revised_June_2010.pdf

Steinberg, R. (2007). Membership income. In D. R. Young (ed.), *Financing non-profits: Putting theory into practice* (pp. 121–125). Lanham, MD: Altamira Press.

Stephenson, J., Bauman, A., Armstrong, T., Smith, B., & Bellew, B. (2000). *The costs of illness attributable to physical inactivity in Australia: A preliminary study.* Canberra: Commonwealth Department of Health and Aged Care and the Australian Sports Commission.

Steptoe, A., & Butler, N. (1996). Sports participation and emotional well-being in adolescents. *Lancet, 347*(9018), 1789–1792.

Stewart, B. (2006). *Sport funding and finance*. Oxford: Butterworth-Heinemann.

Stewart, B., Nicholson, M., Smith, A. & Westerbeek, H. (2004). *Australian sport: Better by design? The evolution of Australian sport policy*. London: Routledge.

Stone, W., & Hughes, J. (2001). *Social capital: Linking family with community*. Melbourne: Australian Institute of Family Studies.

Sudarsan, A. (2009). Performance appraisal systems: A survey of organizational views. *Journal of Organizational Behavior, 3*(1), 54–69.

Thibault, L., Slack, T., & Hinings, B. (1991). Professionalism, structures and systems: The impact of professional staff on voluntary sport organizations. *International Review for the Sociology of Sport, 26*(2), 83–99.

Tinkham, R., & Kleiner, B. (1993). New approaches to managing performance appraisals. *Work Study, 42*(7), 5–7.

Town, S. J. (2000). Performance or measurement? *Performance Measurement and Metrics, 1*(1), 43–54.

Twomey, D., & Harris, D. (2000). From strategy to corporate outcomes: Aligning human resource management systems with entrepreneurial intent. *International Journal of Commerce and Management, 10*, 43–55.

UK Department of Health. (2004). *Health survey for England 2003 – volume 2: The risk for cardiovascular disease*. London: Stationery Office.

UK Sport. (2004). *Good governance guide for national governing bodies*. London: author.

Ukoumunne, O. C., Gulliford, M. C., Chinn, S., Sterne, J. A., & Burney, P. G. (1999). Methods for evaluating area-wide and organisation-based interventions in health and health care: A systematic review. *Health Technology Assessment, 3*(5), iii–92.

United States Department of Health and Human Services. (2002). *Physical activity fundamental to preventing disease*. Retrieved 6 March 2012 from http://aspe.hhs.gov/health/reports/physicalactivity/.

Unterman, I., & Davis, R. H. (1982). The strategy gap in not-for-profits. *Harvard Business Review, 60*(3), 30–40.

Van Dooren, W., & Van De Walle, S. (2008). *Performance information in the public sector: How it is used*. England: Palgrave Macmillan, print.

Van Dyk, L., & Conradie, P. (2007). Creating business intelligence from course management systems. *Campus-Wide Information Systems, 24*(2), 120–133.

Van Emmerik, I. J. (2008). It is not only mentoring: The combined influences of individual-level and team-level support on job performance. *Career Development International, 13*(7), 575–93.

Vroom, V. H. (1964). *Work and motivation*. New York: Wiley.

Walsh, P. (2000). Targets and how to assess performance against them. *Benchmarking: An International Journal, 7*(3), 183–199.

Walters, G., Tacon, R., & Trenberth, L. (2011). *The role of the board in UK national governing bodies of sport*. London: Birkbeck Sport Business Centre Research Paper Series.

Weisbrod, B. A., & Dominguez, N. D. (1986). Demand for collective goods in private non-profit markets: Can fundraising expenditures help overcome freerider behavior? *Journal of Public Economics, 30*, 83–95.

Weldy, T. (2009). Learning organization and transfer: Strategies for improving performance. *The Learning Organization, 16*(1), 58–68.

Winand, M., Rihoux, B., Qualizza, D., & Zintz, T. (2011). Combinations of key determinants of performance in sport governing bodies. *Sport, Business and Management: An International Journal, 1*(3), 234–251.

Winand, M., Zintz, T., Bayle, E., & Robinson, L. (2010). Organizational performance of Olympic sport governing bodies: Dealing with measurement and priorities. *Managing Leisure, 15*(4), 279–307.

Wongrassamee, S., Simmons, J., & Gardiner, P. (2003). Performance measurement tools: The Balanced Scorecard and the EFQM Excellence Model. *Measuring Business Excellence, 7*(1), 14–29.

Yeh, C., & Taylor, T. L. (2008). Issues of governance in sport organisations: A question of board size, structure and roles. *World Leisure Journal, 50*(1), 33–45.

Yermack, D. (1996). Higher market valuation of companies with a small board of directors. *Journal of Financial Economics, 40*(2), 185–211.

Yetman, R. J. (2007). Borrowing and debt. In D. R. Young (ed.), *Financing non-profits: Putting theory into practice* (pp. 243–270). Lanham, MD: Altamira Press.

Zahra, S. A., & Pearce, J. A. (1989). Boards of directors and corporate financial performance: A review and integrative model. *Journal of Management, 15*(2), 291.

Further reading

O'Boyle, I. (2014). Determining best practice in performance monitoring and evaluation of sport coaches: Lessons from the traditional business environment. *International Journal of Sports Science and Coaching, 9*, 233–246.

O'Boyle, I., & Bradbury, T. (eds.). (2013). *Sport governance: International case studies*. Routledge: London.

O'Boyle, I., & Hassan, D. (2013). Organizational performance management: Examining the practical utility of the Performance Prism. *Organization Development Journal, 31*, 51–58.

O'Boyle, I., & Shilbury, D. (2015). Exploring issues of trust in collaborative sport governance. *Journal of Sport Management*. Advance online publication. http://dx.doi.org/10.1123/jsm.2015-0175

O'Boyle, I., Murray, D., & Cummins, P. (eds.). (2015). *Leadership in sport*. Routledge: London.

Shilbury, D., & Ferkins, L. (2011). Professionalisation, sport governance and strategic capability. *Managing Leisure, 16*(2), 108–127.

Slack, T. (1997). *Understanding sport organisations*. Champaign, IL: Human Kinetics.

Index